DATE DUE

MAY 1 8 1994 ILC 14-23-94		
SEP 0 6 2001		

DEMCO 38-297

FAMILIES
ON THE
FAULT LINE

FAMILIES
ON THE
FAULT LINE

AMERICA'S WORKING
CLASS SPEAKS ABOUT THE
FAMILY, THE ECONOMY,
RACE, AND ETHNICITY

LILLIAN B. RUBIN

HarperCollins*Publishers*

HarperCollins books may be purchased for educational, business, or sales promotional use. For information please call or write: Special Markets Department, HarperCollins Publishers, Inc., 10 East 53rd Street, New York, NY 10022.

FIRST EDITION

Designed by George J. McKeon

Library of Congress Cataloging-in-Publication Data

Rubin, Lillian B.
  Families on the fault line/Lillian B. Rubin.—1st ed.
    p. cm.
  Includes bibliographical references and index.
  ISBN 0-06-016741-6 (cloth)
  1. Working class families—United States. 2. United States—Social conditions—1980– . I. Title.
HQ536.R78 1994
306.85'0973—dc20   93-27900

94 95 96 97 98 ❖/HC 10 9 8 7 6 5 4 3 2 1

For Hank and Marci

CONTENTS

ACKNOWLEDGMENTS

In the background of every book stands a small army of unseen contributors. Foremost among them in this case are the people who participated in this study. Their thoughtfulness as they talked about their lives, their generosity in sharing them with me, set the stage for a profoundly enriching and moving experience. No words can repay such a gift. I can only hope that they will agree that what I have written here is true not just to the words they spoke but to the spirit that underlay them.

Then there are the friends, family, and colleagues who listened, advised, and read various drafts of the work in progress. For their part in this background drama, I want thank Troy Duster, Barry Glassner, Arlie Hochschild, Dorothy Jones, Michael Kimmel, Iona Mara-Drita, Walter Meade, Hank Rubin, Marci Rubin, and Arlene Skolnick, whose critical readings of all or part of the manuscript were enormously helpful.

Three friends were so close to this work that, it seemed to me, they were more foreground than background. Kim Chernin, Diane Ehrensaft, and Michael Rogin not only read every word of every draft of the manuscript but spent hours in fruitful discussion with me from the time the project was only an idea until I wrote the last word of the book. For this, and for the many years of friendship that have nourished and enriched both my personal and my intellectual life, I am deeply grateful.

To Courtney Goodhope, who helped with the interviews, a special thanks for a job well done.

Iona Mara-Drita also gets a nod for coming up with the idea for the title for the book over dinner one night.

Rhoda Weyr, my agent, was, as always, one of the more important background people. She not only listened to my agonizing when the writing wasn't going well but was always there to remind me that she'd "heard it before."

I'm grateful to Hugh Van Dusen, my editor, whose wise counsel and unswerving support of this project long before I put a word on paper has been important in bringing it from idea to reality.

Stephanie Gunning, too, deserves a bow for her grace and competence as she shepherded the manuscript through the publication process.

Most important of all, there is my family—my daughter, Marci, and my husband, Hank. They were always available whenever I needed them—whether it was to discuss, to read, to criticize, to listen to my anxieties, to comfort me, or to feed me chocolate. Without their steadfast love, friendship, support, and intellectual nourishment both my work and my life would be measurably impoverished. To them I dedicate this book with love and gratitude.

PROLOGUE

As I struggled to write this book in just the way I had envisioned it when it was still only an idea, I was reminded of an experience with a patient a few years ago. In the closing weeks of her pregnancy, her obstetrician told her that the baby she was carrying was lying the wrong way in her uterus. He turned the baby so that she was facing the right way, head down into the birth canal, only to find that the baby turned herself back to her original position a day or two later. He tried again; the baby stubbornly refused to be pushed around. Fearing a breech delivery and the possibility of a cesarean section, my patient anxiously sought other advice. A healer laid on hands and spoke a mantra; an herbalist prepared special potions. Nothing moved the baby, who remained stubbornly in her preferred position while her mother became progressively more distraught.

I watched the drama unfold with a combination of concern and amusement—concern, because my patient was so anxious; amusement, because I kept thinking: *This may be a good experience for the future, an early reminder that this isn't just "a baby." She's also a person with a will of her own.* After two weeks of listening quietly to my patient's distress, I spoke the words aloud. Two days later, little Susanna was born. "You were right," the new mother reported happily when she phoned with the news. "This child has a mind of her own. At the last minute, she turned herself around and came out head first, just like she was supposed to."

This book, too, has been like a willful child, often going its own way despite my anxious and earnest efforts to control it. In some ways, it should have been my easiest book, since I have been thinking and writing about families, class, race, and gender—all the issues the book addresses—for the whole of my professional life. Instead, it has been my hardest, a fact that puzzled me throughout the many long months of writing. At first, I thought the project was so difficult because I started with the fantasy that this would be my contribution to the resolution of these issues, which have concerned me for so long and which so trouble our national life. But I gave that dream up early in the process, telling myself that my aspirations were too grand, reminding myself that this was just another book. But nothing changed.

Eventually I got it: It was the subject matter itself that was making me so apprehensive. Trying to write authoritatively about family life in a historical moment when social, economic, political, and personal life are all changing so rapidly was problem enough. But to be writing about working-class families in a nation that's determined to believe that we are all middle class was even more daunting. Finally, adding race and ethnicity to the stew made the task seem virtually impossible.

How does a white professional middle-class woman talk honestly about race today? What words could I use to speak of issues that have become the red flags in our society? Some readers of an earlier work criticized my use of the word *black* instead of the recently preferred *African-American*. But preferred by whom? The people I talked to almost universally referred to themselves as "black." What obligation do I have, I kept wondering, to honor my respondents' definition of self? What responsibility to the political nuances of the day? What to my own political convictions?

It isn't that I felt impelled to be politically correct. That's too simple an explanation, as is so much of the talk about political correctness. For it looks merely at the external constraints on the expression of ideas without understanding that such restrictions can work only when they tap something inside us—some sense that we ought *not* say, do, feel those things; some fear in this polarized period of our nation's history that we might give aid and comfort to the other side.

I don't mean to suggest that the pressure to be politically correct hasn't made its mark on people of all political hues. Or that it hasn't impoverished the social and political discourse in the nation. The agony of our times, however, is not that people feel forced to be politically correct but that these pressures are felt so keenly because of the deep and seemingly unbridgeable divisions in American life today.

Except for the catchy language—"Politically Correct," or "PC" for short—there's nothing really new about any of this. Whenever ideological lines get drawn very sharply, when political discourse takes on the semblance of religious belief and gives way to a moral crusade, the PC mandate comes into action. The right has made political capital of some of the politically correct follies on the left, but as social critic Robert Hughes points out so eloquently, "The right has its own form of PC—Patriotic Correctness, if you like— equally designed to veil unwelcome truths. It has a vested interest in keeping America divided, a strategy that bodes worse for the country's polity than anything the weak, constricted American left can be blamed for."[1] And, I would add, it has its own form of CC as well—Cultural Correctness—a social and cultural agenda that permits no deviation and that has helped to turn the nation into a cultural and political battlefield.

But even in less troubled and divisive periods, writers, whether of fiction or nonfiction, have always been constrained by and responsive to the politics of the times in which they were working. Just as their social position and political convictions have colored their work, even when they don't acknowledge it. Or perhaps *especially* when they don't acknowledge it. For there's no such thing as a text that's not a product of the consciousness of the person who wrote it, as well as of the time and place in which it was conceived.

In my own case, I have spent a good part of my life concerned about class, race, and gender inequalities and about the injustices to which working-class people, women, and people of color have been subjected. The last thing I want is for anything I write to play into the hands of those who would deny that these are central problems in American life. And in a nation where the class, race, and ethnic cleavages are great and growing, where sensitivities are exquisitely acute, where the possibilities for misunderstanding are enormous, it's reasonable to worry about whether my words will be misinterpreted, my thoughts misunderstood.

Families on the Fault Line is about working-class family life in a contracting economy. It is about how the particular problems of working-class families have been increasingly ignored, making this enormous sector of our population nearly invisible. It is about how class, race, and gender affect everyday lives, hopes, dreams, and aspirations—and how these various aspects of social and personal life interact with each other. And it is about the fissures in the working class—about how people of different races and ethnicities feel about the social and economic forces that have changed the face of working-class life, about how they cope with those changes, how they have benefited from them, what they have cost.

Few people today would argue with the notion that what happens in the social, economic, and political world outside the family affects life inside. But we too often overlook the other side—that is, that people in families respond to those external forces in ways that change both the institutions and the discourse of public life. Therefore, this book also explores the connection between the increasing racial presence in our social world and the recent rise of white ethnicity.

My argument is that the economic decline of the last two decades coupled with the rising demands of our minority populations have led whites to try to establish a public identity that would enable them to stand against the claims of race. By reclaiming their ethnic past, whites can not only retell the ordeals of their immigrant ancestors, they can use those stories to document that transcendence is possible for those who are worthy. At the same time, their ethnicity becomes the vehicle through which whites can, as one of the men I interviewed said, "take their place at the multicultural table."

But before I begin, a personal comment is in order. For many years now I have been writing about those in our society whose voices are muted or silent. The subject matter has been diverse—class, race, and gender—but always the intent has been to give voice to the voiceless. Scratch the intellectual preoccupations, however, and there's almost always a personal source. So although these issues have been at the heart of my professional concerns for nearly a quarter of a century, my interest and involvement in them grows out of personal experiences long before I was old enough to think about such concepts as "the voiceless." As a child whose first language wasn't English, I didn't have to *think* about not having a voice that could be heard. I experienced it viscerally each time I stepped outside the small, dark apartment my family called home.

But I wasn't alone. The streets of the Bronx neighborhood where I grew up teemed with immigrant children trying to become Americans. Some of us were born "over there"—a village in Sicily, a shtetl in the Ukraine, a hamlet in Germany, a county in Ireland. Others were born here—*real* Americans, we called ourselves proudly, as we lorded it over those who weren't. The common tongue was English, a language we spoke imperfectly, if at all, when we first emerged from the shelter of the family to make our way in urban America.

"Greenhorn!" we shouted derisively at the new kids who entered our street world and struggled for the few words we had mastered by then. We didn't think we were being cruel. We were simply mimicking our parents, who, in their own search for acceptance on these shores, turned on those who embarrassed them with their old country ways and sneered: "Greenhorn!"

I still cringe at the sound of that word, and at the memory of the shame I felt later when I would hear my mother's accented English in public. But I didn't think about shame and self-hatred then. I just thought about finding my voice and becoming an American as fast as I could. Although what that meant in positive terms was something of a mystery. The negative side was perfectly clear: Being American meant giving up all visible signs of being Jewish. A nearly impossible task, since being Jewish was second only to being poor in coloring the experience of my youth.

As children, our American veneer was paper thin and our command of the language feeble at best. But these realities only made the newcomers on the block seem more of a threat. It was too easy to pierce the facade, too easy to lapse with them into the language of our birth, too dangerous to the new American selves we were struggling so hard to build. So easy, in fact, that in moments of stress, anger, or excitement, English was forgotten; the mother tongues took over, and the streets became a babble of Italian and Yiddish, with a sprinkling of German, the Irish brogue, and bits and pieces of broken English in the background.

Fighting was as natural as playing, as were the epithets we screamed at each other when we fought: wop, kike, mick. We didn't know exactly what those words meant, where they came from, or why they were insults. But we knew they hurt, and we used them accordingly. As we grew, so did the stereotypes. The Jews were defined as money-grubbing sneaks; the Italians, as people with broad backs and small minds; the Irish, as drunks and liars. But whatever divided us, we were also united by the knowledge that we were white. That was the one thing we had going for us: there was always someone below us, people even more reviled than we, who were foreigners.

It's one of the remarkable qualities of the American experience that it doesn't take long to infuse its European immigrants with a self-conscious reverence for their whiteness. People who, before they came to these United States, took being white for granted, cling to it like a badge of honor soon after they arrive. No matter how poor, no matter how degraded their status, they learn quickly that they're better than "them."

In my neighborhood, "them" meant the blacks and the Chinese—more likely referred to as "niggers" and "chinks." The Chinese owned the hand laundry down the street or the little restaurant around the corner. I don't know where they lived, perhaps in back of the store, as so many poor immigrants did in those days. But they were never visible on the same side of the counter as whites.

"Colored people," as we called them then, when we were being polite, were nowhere in sight in my early years. Later, as the Irish, who were the janitors in the neighborhood buildings, moved up and out of the dungeon-like basement apartments that went with the job, black families moved in. The men took care of the buildings; the women left each day to clean the houses of people who lived elsewhere—rich people, we supposed, whose lives we could hardly imagine, there being no television around then to give us a glimpse into how they lived.

The shift from white to black in the basement of the buildings changed the dynamics on the floors above, and on the street as well. Whatever divisions existed among us before then, *this* became the big one, the alien other, visible right there on our turf. Undoubtedly, the children's attitudes and behaviors were colored by what they heard in their homes, where the racial divide was clearly and cleanly drawn, grasped quickly and easily by even the most recent arrivals. We all knew the line: We were poor but white; they were niggers, permitted among us only in servile capacities. In all my years in those impoverished Bronx six-story walk-up buildings, not one person of color ever lived there as a neighbor and an equal.

When I was twelve, the first black janitor on the block moved into the basement of our building. With him came his family: Kathleen, also twelve, her mother, an older brother, and a younger sister.[2] I don't think I'd ever seen a black girl my age up close before. So I was curious. By then, too, I, who had been raised on tales of anti-Semitic atrocities, who had been hurt and humiliated by being called "kike" and "sheeny," couldn't understand why a Jew would participate in heaping similar indignities on others.

"Why do you say 'nigger,' when you hate it when someone calls you a 'kike'?" I'd ask my mother, only to be answered with an impatient shrug.

"What? Are you comparing us to *them?*" she'd ask, as if I'd committed some terrible sin.

"They're people, aren't they?" I'd demand.

"They shot your uncle, and you call them people!" she'd shout, referring to an uncle who owned a butcher store in Harlem.

"He puts his hand on the scale when he weighs out the meat. You'd want to shoot him, too!" I'd scream back.

Those conversations never ended satisfactorily. My mother shrugged off my questions, dismissing me as a willful and ignorant child. I felt hurt and angry at being treated with such disdain. But with Kathleen's arrival, I had a chance to satisfy my curiosity and, not incidentally, to show my mother that she was wrong. So I sought out my new black neighbor, and we soon became fast friends.

As we spent more and more time together, both our families

became edgy about our friendship. My mother, worried that I was isolating myself, couldn't understand why I didn't just hang out with the white kids. Even the Italians, formerly scorned as inappropriate companions, became acceptable.

Kathleen's parents, uneasy about the neighborhood reaction, were torn. On the one hand, they knew she'd be wholly alone if our friendship ended. On the other, they desperately needed the small income and the apartment that went with the job, since the prospects for replacing either in the middle of the Great Depression were singularly dismal for a black man. So they warned Kathleen to tread with care, asked her not to be seen so often with me in public, suggested that she find some other way to spend her time.

Being twelve-year-old girls, there were no secrets between us. We repeated our parents' cautionary words, even laughed at their fears. But it wasn't long before they seemed prophetic. At home, the white kids on the block began to exclude me. At school, classmates looked the other way when Kathleen and I walked by. We noticed and were frightened; but we were also determined not to be intimidated. Then one morning, when I went down into the basement to call for Kathleen, I was met by her father. "Kathleen's not going to school today," he said in a voice that was choking back tears.

"Is she sick?" I asked.

"No," he replied. "She just won't be going today." Then he swallowed hard and said quietly but firmly, "Please don't come call for her again."

Kathleen and I talked briefly and stiffly two days later when she returned to school. Some of the neighbors complained to the landlord, she explained, and her father was warned to keep his children in their place if he wanted to stay on the job.

That was the last conversation we ever had.

PART 1

THE INVISIBLE AMERICANS

1

INTRODUCTION

The Bardolinos

The scene is a northern California morning in late June. I'm irritated and impatient as I maneuver my car through the San Francisco traffic and ease my way onto the Bay Bridge, where headway often is measured in yards, not miles. Finally off the bridge, I turn onto the freeway and head north, past Berkeley and some of the smaller communities beyond that college town. A few miles farther along, I come to the turnoff that will take me to my destination—Antioch, a small, semirural, working-class city about forty-five miles from San Francisco.

I'm on my way to interview Marianne and Tony Bardolino—part of my new research on working-class families. I don't know much about the Bardolinos, only that she's thirty-two and works nights at the telephone company; that he's thirty-four and has been unemployed for some months; and that they must have been married young, since they have two children, ages twelve and fourteen. But I've already interviewed about sixty families of different ethnic and racial groups in various cities around the country, so I have some idea about what to expect. As I drive along, therefore, my mind is humming—sorting out what I know from what I still need to understand, trying to anticipate what I'll find when I arrive at the Bardolino home.

As I have made my way from place to place and from family to family during these recent months, I keep comparing the lives of the people I meet today with those I interviewed two decades ago. In some ways, twenty years is a long time; in others, it seems too short to have been the incubator for the changes in family and social life that have taken place in these years.

When I turn onto the road that traverses the hills to Antioch, the heavily residential areas that line the main highway are quickly left behind, exchanged for rolling hillsides with their scrub oaks clustered in every gully and ravine—trees so gnarled by age, wind, and lack of water that they seem darkly, mysteriously beautiful in their deformity. I'm only minutes away from the noise and crowds of city life, yet there's little to disturb the tranquil scene here—no people in sight, only an occasional car passing in the opposite direction. In this setting the world seems too beautiful, too peaceful to be real, and the buzzing in my head abates as I relax into the quiet around me.

Since it's the dry season, the hillsides have turned an almost indescribably subtle, honey-colored brown, the insignia of summer throughout the state. With every bend in the road, the color changes; sun, clouds, and wind all create different shadings, from golden honey to deep taupe. Each new hue has its own claim to beauty; all take on a soft, velvety cast that makes the hands itch to touch.

"Antioch NEXT RIGHT," the sign says, jarring me back to my mission. I exit the highway and check the directions Tony Bardolino gave me. Looking around for signs that will point the way, I'm struck by the changed scene. On this street, crowded with all the detritus of exurban life, the pastoral beauty of the drive fades quickly.

It seems to me this could be Anytown, U.S.A. The same shabby shops along a main street that probably never saw better days; the same small houses that long ago gave up trying to put on a show. But here, after several years of drought, there are only dry, brown patches where lawns once thrived. Here, too, I see the signs of neglect that go with hard times—a rickety fence; a rutted driveway; a pick-up, once painted a proud, bright red, now dented and bruised, almost colorless; a child's tricycle lying forlornly on its side, its handlebar pitted with rust, a rear wheel askew.

Five miles and a few twists and turns later I pull up in front of the Bardolino house. It's a small house, old, somewhat ramshackle—a house whose sagging parts announce that it hasn't aged well despite the cosmetic efforts of its owners. The front porch, which shows signs of a recent application of paint, provides an incongruous accent to the peeling exterior elsewhere. A sign, faded by sun, wind, and rain, proclaims that the Bardolino family lives here.

As I look around, I'm reminded about how different hard times look on the East and West Coasts. The first time I saw the poor districts of Los Angeles and San Francisco, I wondered why people thought they were slums. To my eastern eye, they looked like more pleasant places than the densely populated working-class neighborhood in the Bronx where I was raised. And compared to Harlem, Watts, with its single-family houses, looked downright inviting. It took years of living in the West before I could look at poor and working-class neighborhoods, no matter what the color of those who lived there, and not think, *No matter how hard it is here, it's nothing compared to surviving in the East.* And even now, perhaps because I've spent so much time living and working in New York City in recent years, the contrast strikes me again.

With these thoughts spinning around in my head, I ring the bell and wait. No answer. I try again. Still no response. *Damn, did I drive all the way out here only to have them forget?* I think irritably. It happens sometimes, one of the aggravations of doing the kind of research where you have to depend on others to be in a certain place at a specified time. I long ago learned to call ahead to confirm the appointment before starting out. But I had set up this interview only three days earlier, and the Bardolinos had been so open to my request that I was certain there'd be no problem.

I decide to look around back. Land used to be cheap out here, so older houses like this sometimes stand on large lots. *Maybe they can't hear the front doorbell ring back there*, I tell myself reassuringly. As I round the corner, I see them. Tony is driving a fence post into the ground; Marianne is trying valiantly to keep her vegetable garden alive and producing under drought conditions. I call out; they stop their work, wave, and come to greet me.

We introduce ourselves, make some chitchat about the weather, the drive from San Francisco, the drought. Finally, we get around to the subject of my visit. "Who goes first?" I ask.

"I thought we were going to do this thing together," Tony says, looking a little puzzled.

"No," I reply. "I'm sorry if I wasn't clear enough when we spoke, but I like to interview people separately."

They look at each other, waiting for a signal. Finally, Marianne laughs, "I get it; you want to see if we both say the same thing. You want to go first?" she asks her husband.

"No," he answers. "I've got plenty of work out here; you go ahead."

I smile to myself; his answer doesn't surprise me. I've been interviewing all kinds of people for nearly twenty-five years, and it almost always works this way. The woman goes first. Sometimes a man—especially a working-class man for whom this usually is a wholly alien experience—won't agree to an interview until after I've talked to his wife. Then, generally because she has found the experience interesting, perhaps even useful, she becomes an ally and helps to convince him. But even when, as is the case with the Bardolinos, they both agree in advance, he's likely to hesitate, to have some reservations, to want the reassurance of seeing her go first.

"Okay, let's go on in," says Marianne, her voice cutting through my thoughts. I follow her up the back steps and into a well-worn kitchen, the linoleum so old its pattern is faded beyond recognition, the once-white tiles on the countertops now a cracked and mottled gray.

She notices my glance and says wistfully, "Some day I'm going to have a decent kitchen. That's my dream, to have one of those really nice modern kitchens, you know, the kind that always looks all sparkly clean. I try to keep this place up, but no matter how much I scrub it never looks clean anyway. So it gets kind of discouraging sometimes."

We talk for a moment about the kitchen of her dreams while she pours out two glasses of iced tea. Realizing she hasn't asked if I want a drink, she turns to me questioningly: "You do want some, don't you? It's so hot out there; I just assumed." On hearing my reassurance, she turns and, carrying both glasses, leads the way into the small, sparsely furnished living room. She settles herself on the couch; I pull up a straight-backed chair so that my computer, on which I'll record the interview, can sit comfortably on my lap, and the work begins.

*   *   *

Two decades ago I did a study of white working-class family life that led to the publication of a book entitled *Worlds of Pain: Life in the Working-Class Family.*[1] In the intervening years, enormous social, political, and economic changes have been at work, defining and redefining family and social life, relations between women and men, between parents and children, and among the various ethnic and racial groups that make up the tapestry of American life. The time had come, therefore, to take another look at working-class family life, to compare then and now, to examine how the changes of these past years have affected life inside working-class families and, in turn, how these changes have helped to form their responses to the world outside, to the social and political issues of the day.

Twenty years ago it was reasonable to study white working-class families without reference to race or ethnicity. Given the heightened ethnic and racial strains with which we live now, it's unthinkable to leave these out. There was plenty of racial anger around then, too, of course. The rancorous conflicts about school busing all across the land made it obvious that racial tensions were an intensely felt part of our national life.[2] Nevertheless, race wasn't high on the list of issues the people I interviewed wanted to talk about then—an impression confirmed by a recent *New York Times* article that traced the results of forty-five years of Gallup polls asking people what they thought were "the most important problems facing the country."[3] Race relations, which was seen as a significant issue from the mid-1950s through the early years of the 1960s—the years when the civil rights movement was in full swing—was replaced by concerns about the cost of living toward the end of that decade. By the beginning of the 1970s, the period when I was doing the research for *Worlds of Pain*, race wasn't even mentioned. Two decades later, racial issues were prominent again. In the research for this book, race was a recurrent theme, most of the time arising spontaneously as people aired their grievances and gave vent to their wrath.

At the same time that race once again came to center stage in the public consciousness, white ethnicity emerged with a new face and ethnic identities that had lain dormant, sometimes for generations, suddenly blossomed.[4] Germans, Italians, Greeks, Poles, Irish, Croats, Lithuanians, Hungarians—white ethnics who for years had made only perfunctory bows in the direction of their ancestors—began to lay claim to their ethnic heritage. So much so that by now New York, the premier melting-pot city of the nation, routinely gives over its Sunday streets to ethnic parades as each group struts its stuff and proclaims its connection to the culture of its past.

What happened? For decades the emphasis for most Americans of European descent was on assimilation.[5] There were differences among immigrant groups, of course. Some, like the Italians, resisted Americanization; others, like the Jews, welcomed it. And here and there, usually in rural areas, small ethnic enclaves managed to remain relatively impervious to intrusion from the larger society for considerable periods of time.[6] But generally, the process of Americanization was not only inexorable but desirable.

Most families undoubtedly wanted their children to retain some connection to the language and culture of their European past. But that was largely in the private realm. In the public domain the children were expected to become Americanized, at least to the extent that they learned English—at first so that they could help their elders negotiate the alien world outside the family; later so that they could fulfill their parents' dreams and repay their sacrifices by becoming successful in that world.

As successive generations grew more distant from their immigrant roots, social, economic, and geographic mobility demolished the structural foundations on which white ethnic group solidarity and identity once rested. When people no longer live in the same neighborhood, work at the same occupation, socialize almost exclusively with members of their group, language facility falters, manners and mores undergo change, and ethnic identity wanes. Therefore, although some *subjective* sense of ethnic identity remains, recent researchers in the field insist that it has little *objective* reality. And it certainly isn't strong enough to contain the soaring rates of ethnic intermarriage, which now involve roughly three in four American-born whites. But while the structural basis for white ethnic identification has dwindled—and will continue to do so—the psychological and political foundations are in their ascendancy.[7]

Psychologically, identifying with an ethnic group allows people some sense of community, a feeling of connection with others who share a common history, therefore some elements of a common culture—a few rituals, a feast day, a saint's day. Politically, an ethnic group becomes a vehicle through which whites can take their place in the identity politics of our time and stake a claim in the competition for scarce resources.

To understand why and how this comes to pass, we must look to the social, economic, and political changes of these past decades and to their impact on the lives of the women and men who live on the pages of this book. For it is at this intersection of public and private life that we can begin to understand the social and psychological meanings of ethnicity today.

The Tomalsons

Sunday afternoon in New York City. My purse hanging from one shoulder, my portable computer from the other, I approach the turnstile in the subway station at 59th Street and Lexington Avenue, deposit a token, and head down the stairs to the station platform. New York's famous Bloomingdale's is at this station as, at the time, was Alexander's, another of the city's old-time department stores that has since gone bankrupt. So even on Sunday, the platform is a busy mix of people—young and old, working class and middle class, Puerto Rican, African-American, white, an Asian or two. You don't have to be an expert to make a good guess about their class backgrounds; the shopping bags they carry do the job. For the middle class, it's Bloomie's—upscale, pricey, its signature "Brown Bag" almost a status symbol. For the working class, it's Alexander's, whose move to this midtown location years ago did little to change its downscale image.

I'm apprehensive as I wait for the number 5 train to take me up to 138th Street in the Bronx. Friends warned me against going "up there"—which in New York's coded language means into a neighborhood that's predominantly black and poor. The idea that I might take the subway was unthinkable to them, but I have no other means of transport. When the dispatcher of the car service I use from time to time heard the address, he said flatly, "None of my cars will go up there." Four others said one version or another of the same thing. So I ride the subway.

The train roars in, and the platform empties quickly as people of all hues board. As it travels uptown, however, its internal landscape shifts. At 86th Street, many of the whites leave; at 96th, they exit en masse. By the time we're at 125th Street, I'm the only white person left in the car. *Does my uneasiness show?* I look around. An older man eyes me questioningly; a young woman holding a small child on her lap offers a tentative smile; the others are dozing, reading, or preoccupied with their own thoughts.

Suddenly, the train comes up from its underground tunnel onto an elevated track. The buildings that line its path would look dingy and decrepit on any day. But on this drizzly, gray November afternoon, they're particularly depressing. From time to time as we rush by, I catch a glimpse of a face in a window—a child, hand raised in a wave; a woman staring blankly into space. *How do people sleep with the trains rumbling by all night long?*

After several more stops during which the train gets progressively emptier, we approach the 138th Street station. I gather up my belongings and lurch toward the door. It's raining harder when I leave the train, so I walk to the exit quickly. But even with my head ducked down I'm aware of the ugliness of my surroundings. Graffiti lines the walls, almost wholly obscuring the billboards and posters; signs of age and neglect are everywhere.

Once on the street, I follow the directions Gwendolyn Tomalson gave me. Perhaps because of the rain, the street is almost empty. Two women, huddled under a single umbrella, hurry along. A young man, his jacket covering his head, his eyes downcast, lopes past. An older man, seemingly heedless of the weather, shuffles by.

I don't have far to walk before I come upon a typical New York public housing project—block after block of huge, densely packed, graffiti-covered buildings. This is my destination. I find the right building, ring for the elevator, and wait. Nothing happens. I try again. *There are two elevators here; surely both can't be broken*, I say to myself. I'm wrong. A boy, perhaps fifteen, comes out of a door marked STAIRS and says, "Don't bother to wait; they ain't been working since yesterday."

I panic. *Maybe I should just leave.* I've heard about the danger of going into the stairwell in a building like this, about the mayhem that can go on there. *Dammit, no, I'm not going to be scared off,* my inner voice says. So off I go, huffing and puffing my way up to the ninth floor.

It's not bravery that pushes me on; fear is my companion as I make my way up the stairs. I have a moment of heart-stopping terror when I meet a young black man coming down as I'm going up. But after looking me over and flashing a mischievous grin—one that seems to say he's angry at having stirred my fear and also pleased to see my discomfort—he continues on his way. So why did I do it? I'm not sure. Perhaps it is, as any psychologist would say, counterphobic behavior—that is, behavior that flies in the face of one's fears. Or perhaps I just wanted the interview that badly. Probably a little of both.

Breathless, I push the stairwell door open and stand in the hallway of the ninth floor. I'd already become accustomed to the acrid smell of urine as I climbed the stairs. Here, in the dank and airless hall, it mixes with the other odors of living to create a stench that assaults me like a blow. I choke up, trying not to breathe too deeply as I look for apartment 9E. I find it at the other end of a narrow hall lined with gray metal doors that would be more fitting for a prison than for an apartment building. I ring the bell, hear the tapping of small feet running to the door, then a child's voice calls out: "Who is it?" I tell her my name and ask to talk to her mother or father. A moment or two later, George Tomalson, a tall, slim man in his early thirties, opens the door, welcomes me in, and says with a smile, "Gwen'll be right out; she's doing whatever women do when they expect company."

Inside, the tiny kitchen is directly ahead, the living room a step to my right. As we move toward it, I see that it's nearly empty of furniture. A long, wooden table and four chairs of indiscriminate age and style stand against one wall; a small television set sits on a crate across the room. Nothing more, except some pillows lying on the floor a few feet from the TV. Perhaps George has noticed my eyes taking in the barrenness; perhaps it's self-consciousness that motivates his explanation. "Pretty empty, huh? We had a real apartment until last year, but I got put out of work and we lost it all—every damn thing we owned, even the kids' beds. They just came and took it away, didn't hardly give us a chance," he says, his voice etched in weary bitterness.

Before I can reply, three-year-old Michelle comes running across the room and hurls herself at me. I drop my things and pick her up, then turn back to her father, who continues: "I guess we can't complain. This place ain't no great shakes, but at least we're not on the street."

Eight-year-old Julia, who until then had been standing at the other end of the room eyeing the scene cautiously, edges forward, picks up my computer, and tries to lug it around on her shoulder. After a few steps, she drops it and asks, "What's in there? It's heavy." I tell her it's a computer and ask if she wants to see it. By the time their mother arrives, I'm sitting on the floor, a child on each side, showing them how the computer works.

When Gwen enters the room, Julia jumps up, grabs her hand, and pulls her over to where I'm trying to rise: "Look," she cries, "she's got a computer, and she let me write on it." Gwen smiles at the child, then turns to me: "Sorry, I see the kids took you by storm." Then to the children, "What way is that to treat a guest—on the floor? Couldn't you sit at the table?"

By now George, who had left the room a few minutes earlier, is back, wearing a dark wool jacket and Mets baseball cap, his arms piled high with the children's coats and rain gear. "C'mon kids, we're going out," he commands.

When I made the appointment, I told Gwen that we'd need a quiet, private place for the interviews. So George is taking the kids to his mother's house, which is some distance away. Gwen will call him there when we're finished, and he'll come back and take his turn.

The next few minutes are tumultuous as the children are pushed and prodded into their outdoor clothing and their parents discuss the logistics for the rest of the day. Finally, dressed and ready to go, they race out into the hall, while Gwen and George say a final word before he, too, leaves.

With their departure the apartment becomes unnaturally quiet.

Gwen sighs and brushes her hand across her brow in a gesture that seems to say she's relieved to have this brief respite from their presence. Then she turns to me with a broad smile, and says, "Okay, let's do it."

*   *   *

I started this work because I wanted to understand the lives of ordinary working-class families today—families whose voices are seldom heard in the cacophony of noise and demand that make up our public life. I wanted to listen to the issues that engage them now and compare them with the families I wrote about two decades ago. How have the roles and rules that guided working-class family life changed? What has been the impact of the shifts in the economy? For some years now, we've been hearing talk about the failure of "family values." But just what are we talking about? What has changed? What values do working-class Americans actually adhere to?

I was also interested in the resurgence of what one writer has called "ethnic fever."[8] On the surface this looks like a turning away from the idea of the melting pot—an explanation favored by many observers. But even if true, it doesn't explain why and how this has come to pass. So I asked: What is the meaning of the new emphasis on ethnicity among whites? Does it simply tap felt needs about continuity and connection to the past? Or is it also a cover for something else? What is the relationship of the mounting interest in ethnicity to the economic decline of the past decades? To our increasingly large immigrant population, most of them people of color? To the emergence of racial conflict as whites and others find themselves competing for scarce resources? Is the recent furor about multiculturalism relevant to these families and the issues in their daily lives?

In this context, I make a distinction between race and ethnicity. Both are complex phenomena that defy easy definition. Stripped to their essence, however, ethnicity is related to ancestry and culture, race to color or the perception of it.[9] Ethnicity is seen as a social phenomenon, race as a biological one. Given our preoccupation with race and the prejudices that are so deeply rooted in our social history, most white Americans have a far greater tolerance for ethnic variation than for racial diversity. My argument, therefore, is that in a nation where perceptions of racial difference form one of the most fundamental divides in social life, it obscures and confuses reality to conflate race and ethnicity—to discuss, analyze, and treat them as if they were one.

The research for this book took me into the homes of 162 working-class and lower middle-class families who live in cities across the country—92 white ethnics, 30 blacks, 20 Latinos, 20 Asians. Among the white families, there were 32 whom I had interviewed twenty years ago for *Worlds of Pain*. Some I had kept in touch with through the years, playing the role of friendly adviser, family therapist, and general facilitator when I was needed. Others I tracked down, sometimes with the help of their family and friends, sometimes simply by looking in a telephone directory. All agreed to talk with me again.

The new families came to me in a variety of ways. At the time of the study, I was living and working in both San Francisco and New York City, spending the fall semester in the East and the rest of the year on the West Coast. I had plenty of contacts in both cities, and developing a snowball sample of families was no problem at all.[10] In other cities, I started with one or two families who were referred to me by someone I knew there—a friend, a colleague, a person in an organization that had invited me to lecture in the city. Once that contact was made successfully, I asked for referrals to others in the area.

The median age of the women in this study is thirty-two; of the men, thirty-seven. Their ages range from twenty-three to fifty-five. Sixteen percent of the families are headed by a woman—three-quarters because they're divorced; the rest, except for one who is widowed, because they have never married.[11] Roughly one-third are second marriages for at least one of the partners. The husband-wife families have been married at least five years, the range is five to thirty years. Whenever possible, I interviewed wives, husbands, and teenage children, for a total of 388 separate in-depth, face-to-face, focused interviews.

Experience long ago taught me that my best chance for getting cooperation is to approach the woman in the family first. If I could convince her, she almost always became my ally in helping to persuade the other family members. So I phoned the woman, introduced myself, and explained what I was doing and why it was important for me to talk with her. Only four refused my request for an interview. Some of the women were able to secure the promise of cooperation from their husbands and, where they had any, their teenage children, even before I arrived on the scene. In other families, it had to wait until afterward, by which time I had become something of a family event, provoking the curiosity of other family members sufficiently so that they didn't need much convincing to talk to me.

Although the white ethnic families are the central actors in the drama I will present, the African-American, Asian-American, and Latino-American families provide comparison—not just about racial beliefs, attitudes, feelings, and behavior, but about values and aspirations as well. *Indeed, one of the surprising findings of this study is how much in common all these families have, how much agreement they would find among themselves—even about some of the hottest racial issues of the day—if they could put away the stereotypes and hostilities that separate them and listen to each other talk. For if we set aside race, there's far more to unite working-class families than there is to divide them.*

The Riveras

Next stop, Chicago on a Saturday afternoon in late October. From the window of my taxicab, I see that the brilliant sunshine has turned the wind-whipped lake into a sea of sparkling jewels. New York and San Francisco are home territory; I grew up in one, have lived in the other for many years. But Chicago is a city I pass through quickly, never staying more than the day or two it takes to complete the business that brought me there. This time I'm here for a week that's heavily booked with interviews. Despite so many years of doing this kind of research in cities around the country, I'm edgy in this alien environment, an uneasiness I experience every time I go to work in a strange city. *Why is it easier, I wonder, to invade people's lives and privacy in familiar territory?*

The taxi leaves the lakefront and heads across town, where I'm due to interview some members of the Rivera family. I made the appointment two weeks ago and confirmed it with Ana Rivera before I left my hotel a few minutes earlier. Even so, I'm not sure who will greet me. She'll be there, I know; and her husband, Rick, has promised to be available sometime during the afternoon. But their two teenage sons were evasive, unsure, I suspect, about whether they wanted to talk to some *gringa*. And the Riveras' daughter, who works as a desk clerk in a local hotel, was unexpectedly called in to work graveyard last night. So she'll be asleep for most of the day. I'm wondering, too, how, with so many people wandering in and out, we'll manage the privacy these interviews require.

I try to still my anxieties and settle back to watch the changing panorama in this city, where real estate values decline progressively as you move away from the shores of Lake Michigan. In just a few blocks, we've gone from the gleaming spaces of the wealthy Water Tower district, with its broad avenues, elegant shops, and sleek buildings guarded by liveried doormen, to the narrower, darker streets of the downtown Loop. The people change along with the landscape: predominantly well-dressed whites in the upscale neighborhood; largely African-American, Latino, and poorer-looking whites downtown.

As the driver turns this way and that, I lose all sense of direction. But I don't need to be familiar with the city to know that with each passing block we're moving down the socioeconomic ladder. The shops that line the thoroughfares get smaller, their wares skimpier. The signs announce Chicago's fabled ethnic diversity—here, some Arabic words; there, some with Cyrillic lettering; another in Chinese script. This potpourri of ethnic and racial groups makes this city a living laboratory for anyone interested, as I am, in ethnic working-class family life.

We turn onto a street that brings a smile of recognition to my lips. The scale is smaller than San Francisco's Mission district or New York's 14th Street, but the vibrant energy is much the same— a mix of Latin, rock, and rap music blaring from the shops whose goods are displayed on racks that line the sidewalk; people shouting to make themselves heard over the noise; families strolling along, stopping to examine a coat here, a rug there, a suitcase a little farther on; children standing enchanted before a video display, deaf to their parents, who urge them onward; a mother reaching out to catch the arm of a straggling child who cries out in indignation;

teenage girls giggling together while boys posture around them; older men out for a walk.

I sigh regretfully when we turn off the main thoroughfare and onto a side street. In a matter of seconds the buoyancy I have been witnessing is exchanged for a drab, cheerless view. The street is littered with debris—cartons from takeout food, soft-drink and beer cans, an empty wine bottle, uncollected garbage spilling out of overfilled cans. Once, I'm sure, you could see the red in the two- and three-flat brick buildings that line the streets here. Now they're mud colored, darkened by a hundred years of Midwestern soot.

Two blocks later, the taxi pulls up in front of a three-flat building. "You sure this is where you want to go?" asks the driver doubtfully.

"Yes, this is it," I say, after checking the address.

I pay him, get out of the cab, climb the few steps to the front door, and push it open. Inside, there's a small entry hall, its cracked floor tiles and dirt-streaked walls telling the story of landlord neglect that's so common in neighborhoods like this. I ring the doorbell marked "Rivera" and wait. A buzzer sounds; I push open the inside door and make my way up to the second-floor flat, where Ana Rivera beckons me in with a shy smile.

It's one of the distinguishing marks of settled working-class family life that there's not enough room in the house either for the people who live in it or the things they collect as they pursue their lives. The small, crowded Rivera apartment is no different. Non-vintage overstuffed velvet furniture, neat lace doilies decorating the arms and back of each piece, fills the living room. Every surface is covered with family photographs, knickknacks, and memorabilia that record past experience and bring it into the present. Like the other homes I've visited, the TV set is the centerpiece of the room, the object to which all others turn as if held by a magnet.

When I enter the room, eighteen-year-old Robert is lounging in one of the chairs, legs flung over its arm, watching a basketball game. He looks up for a moment, then without a word turns back to the game. Ana eyes him uncomfortably, wondering, I suspect, whether to remind him of his manners, then decides against it. "Let's go in the kitchen; maybe it'll be quiet there for a while," she says.

We go down the hall into a bright, roomy kitchen, where a Formica-topped table sits by the window. There's new linoleum on the floor, and it looks as if the Formica counters have recently been redone as well. "What a nice room," I remark.

Ana greets my comment with a pleased smile and explains, "Rick did it all; he put down the floor and made the counters. We kept asking the landlord to do something. You know, it wasn't healthy; it was so old and cracked, I couldn't keep it clean. He finally agreed to pay for the material if we did the work. I don't know why, maybe he was afraid or something; you know, sometimes those people in the city get on the landlords, so maybe he was worried about that."

We chat for a few minutes—about landlords, about Chicago, about the fact that she and her husband are native to the city, about how it compares to San Francisco, about the interview we're getting ready to begin. She's apprehensive about it but has few questions. Experience has taught me that the best way to quiet such anxiety is to get into the work, so I'm eager to start. But just as we settle ourselves at the table, Robert comes in, opens the refrigerator, and takes out a soft drink. "What're you doing?" he asks.

I tell him I'm about to interview his mother and that I'd like to talk to him afterward. He wants details. What will I ask? Why will I ask it? What will I do with his answers? I explain that I'll be writing a book about families in America and that the only way I can document their lives truthfully is by talking with them. I tell him that I'll ask questions about his life in the family, his relationships with his siblings and his parents, and also about his life outside the home—about his experience in school, in looking for a job, in being a Mexican-American in Chicago.

While I speak, he fiddles idly with my computer. When I finish, he asks, "Does this thing really work like one of those big ones?"

"Just like it," I reply. "It does everything the bigger ones do, just a little more slowly." My voice is easy, my tone casual. But inside I'm agitated. *Was he listening to my answer to his questions? Did he hear a word I said? Should I push him now or wait?* I decide on a push. "What about that interview, will you do it?"

He shrugs—a kind of typical eighteen-year-old-male gesture—

and turns away. "Gotta get back to the game." Then, as he disappears into the hall, he calls back, "Maybe."

His mother sighs and smiles helplessly. "These kids. It's so different nowadays."

*   *   *

Twenty years ago I could write that I'd interviewed 162 families and let the statement stand without explanation. Today that's no longer possible, since what constitutes a family is a matter of public debate. Are single-parent households "families"? What about gay and lesbian households? Or couples without children? Or people with children who live together without ever marrying? Who gets counted as part of the family in divorced families, remarried families, blended families, extended families?

A recent Roper Organization poll asked two thousand adults which of various types of households met their definition of family. Only a married couple living with their children met almost everyone's test. Close behind was a married couple living with children from a previous marriage. But after these two, opinions about what is a family diverged sharply. One in ten refused to grant family status to a childless married couple. Eighty-four percent thought a divorced mother living with her children deserved the title "family," but only 80 percent were willing to apply the term to a divorced father living with his children. And just about one-fourth would include a lesbian or gay couple living with children in their definition of a family.[12]

The answer to the question about what constitutes a family seems to me an obvious one: All of the above. Nevertheless, I had decisions to make. Another researcher might well have cut the pie differently and with equal validity. But these were my decisions, based on both the aims of the research and what I thought I could do effectively: I left out families who had never raised children because their lives and the issues they confront are different from those that face families with children. I included cohabiting families who had been together for five years or more and who saw themselves as living in a relationship that mirrored a marriage in all ways but the legal. I omitted gay and lesbian families because the prejudice and discrimination they live with make for unique issues that would have added another level of complication to an already difficult and complex subject.

In 1972 it was easy to find working-class families in which mother, father, and children all lived in the same household. Certainly divorce was a reality two decades ago; one-fourth of the women and one-fifth of the men I interviewed for *Worlds of Pain* were living in a second marriage. But there's a considerable difference between then and now. Then, roughly one-third of all marriages ended in divorce; now, the figure stands at about one-half.[13]

Consequently, the relatively stable cast of family characters of the past is harder and harder to find. Instead, we have single-parent families, blended families, reconstituted families, and "divorce-extended" families, each with its own particular blend of parents, stepparents, siblings, half-sibs, step-sibs, and a variety of fictive aunts, uncles, cousins, and grandparents.[14] Nearly all the remarried families in this study have some combination of his, hers, and our children living all or part of the time in the house. It was not uncommon, therefore, for the teenagers and young adults I interviewed to spend considerable time sorting out for me their relationships with various blood-, step-, and half-relatives.

One twenty-year-old, for example, spoke at length about his grandparents. "They're great, not like most grandparents. I can really talk to them, I mean about anything," he explained.

"Whose parents are they?" I asked. "Your mother's or your father's?" Laughing, he replied, "It's funny, people always ask me that, but they're not my mom's or my dad's. I don't see my real grandparents much; they don't live around here. These grandparents are. . . " He paused, looked up at the ceiling as he searched for a way to identify the relationships, then continued. "Let's see how I can explain it. It's not so complicated; it just sounds that way. They're my ex-stepmother's mother and stepfather."

The Kwans

When I say Seattle, I think rain, a kind of wet drizzle that's a semipermanent feature of the city—or so it seems to someone who's accustomed to the dry seasons of northern California. People tell me the sun shines here, but I've rarely seen it. This visit is no different; it has been nowhere in sight in the three days since I arrived. Still, this is an undeniably beautiful city—Puget Sound on its western edge, Lake Washington on the eastern side, and canals whose locks open to allow the passage of small ships from one to the other. In the background, the Cascade Mountains rise from the mists; their highest peak, snow-capped Mt. Rainier, soars over the city like a sentinel.

The Emerald City, it's called. The rainfall combined with a temperate climate means that lush, green foliage is a constant. Right now, in early May, the city also is ablaze with spring flowers. The rhododendrons and azaleas are heavy with blossoms, their reds, pinks, blues, and purples undimmed by the clouds above. The tulips, in all their brilliant colors, sit sedately in their beds, heads bowed slightly as if to protect themselves from the wind and rain. The wisteria, in full bloom, sport blossoms so dense and luxuriant they seem to weigh down the vines.

Seattle prides itself on being a "little big city," one that's still small enough to avoid some of the worst problems of modern urban life, yet cosmopolitan enough to provide a cultural smorgasbord that's sufficient to please a sophisticated palate. The total minority population in the city is about 25 percent, which is small compared to the other major West Coast cities. Not surprisingly, Asians and Pacific Islanders are the largest single group, with nearly 12 percent of the population; African-Americans are second at 10 percent; Latinos make up just over 3.5 percent; and Native Americans are close to 1.5 percent.[15]

Perhaps because the numbers are relatively small, housing patterns for groups other than blacks seem to be less highly segregated here than elsewhere in the West. There's no discernible Latino neighborhood, nor are there districts that are almost exclusively Chinese, Japanese, Korean, or Vietnamese, such as one finds in San Francisco or Los Angeles. Even in the International district, which houses a small but diverse segment of the city's Asian population and is also the site of a modest Asian business quarter, there's a visible white presence. Only in the Rainier Valley district, home to the majority of Seattle's African-American population, does the color barrier seem to hold firm.

On this late afternoon, I've crossed a good part of central Seattle as I've ridden from my downtown hotel to a section of the city near the University of Washington campus. Colleagues who have lived in the area for a long time tell me that the neighborhood has had several name changes in recent years, each one following a new round of gentrification, each designed to convey a newer and more upscale image.

I look at my watch and stir restlessly. I'm expected at 4:30 and it's almost that time now. "How much longer?" I ask the cab driver impatiently.

"Almost there," he replies, as he turns into the street we're looking for.

I see at once that the gentrification process hasn't been completed. On the corner, there's a large, relatively new, modern structure, winsomely painted in soft pastels, its trim green lawn and beautifully landscaped front yard announcing to the world that someone of substance lives inside. Two houses away, I see a small bungalow, its lawn overgrown, the woody shrubs at its foundation looking ragged and lusterless, its wood siding so faded and grayed with age that it's impossible to tell what color it once was.

As we cruise down the street, it continues to exhibit the same swift shift in tone and feel. The homes of university professors and other professionals sit cheek by jowl with those of construction workers, bus drivers, and aircraft workers at Seattle's most important employer, Boeing Aircraft—each one offering up visible clues to the class background of the family who inhabits it.

Just before the end of the block, the cab pulls up in front of a small, unassuming house much like those we passed farther up the street. But it's in much better condition than the others. Its well-kept lawn, neatly pruned shrubs, trimmed hedges, and colorful flower beds make a lovely frame for the building, with its beige paint and clean white trim.

As I leave the taxi, a woman comes down the path to greet me. I walk forward quickly, extend my hand, and introduce myself. "Hi, I'm Lillian Rubin; you must be Carol Kwan." She takes my hand and nods assent. Before she can speak, I add, "What a lovely house this is; so fresh looking, it sparkles."

She beams proudly. "Thank you. It belonged to my parents; they died two years ago and left it to me. You know, with houses costing so much, we couldn't afford to buy a home on our own, so we're really grateful to have this. My husband and I, we worked very hard to fix it up so it would look really nice."

We stand a moment, quietly admiring their handiwork, then wordlessly walk up the path and into the house. "Can I get you some coffee or tea?" she asks, as she leads me into the small, shabbily furnished living room.

"No, thank you. I'm fine."

While I get ready for the interview, she goes into the kitchen and pours herself a cup of coffee. *Clearly their energy went into the outside of the house*, I think, as I take in the threadbare furniture, the tired wallpaper, and the floors scratched and scuffed by decades of growing children and tramping feet.

"I'm really curious about what we're going to talk about," she says when she returns and settles herself in a chair opposite me.

We spend a few minutes talking about what's to come. The first time we spoke on the phone, a week or so ago, I told her something about the study and about the book I was planning to write. But she asks for clarification now, wanting to know more about me and my research, about why I want to talk to her family.

I tell her that I wrote a book about blue-collar families twenty years ago; that families like hers have always held a special interest for me, perhaps because of my own background; and that I want to compare their lives and relationships today with the way they were two decades ago. She reacts with a combination of interest and reserve.

I reassure her that I'll mask her identity in whatever I write and that her words will be held in strictest confidence. She smiles, relaxes a bit, and asks for more specifics. "Give me an idea; what are you going to ask me?"

I try to be specific enough to satisfy her and vague enough not to frighten her. I say that I'll be asking about her family history, about when they came to the United States and the difficulties they encountered. Some other questions, those about her present family life, will be quite personal, probably things she doesn't discuss much with anyone—questions about her relationship with her husband, their conflicts and how they resolve them, for example. Still others will be about her reaction to some of the social and political issues of our time. I add, too, that I hope she'll feel free to refuse to answer any questions that seem too intrusive or that make her uncomfortable in any way.

She smiles. "I don't know much about politics," she says apologetically, "but I guess I can manage the rest." Then, without prompting, she begins to talk about the many people who are out of work; about how worried she and her husband are about their future; about what's in store for their children, now seven, ten, and twelve; about how, even though she works full-time, they're still having trouble making ends meet; about how getting a paid job has changed the way she thinks about women's work and men's work.

I scurry to keep up with her words, reluctant to interrupt the flow of her thoughts, which are now coming so spontaneously. But she soon slows down, and the interview moves ahead in a more orderly fashion.

*   *   *

The interviews were more like extended conversations and included most important aspects of family and social life—from family history to sexual experience, from the details about marriage to voting behavior, from intergenerational conflicts to race relations, from religion to the division of labor in the family, from work and its meaning to ethnic identification.

As always in a study like this, the early interviews took much longer than those that came later. In the beginning, when I was still formulating some of the issues of the research, I often spent many hours talking to the people I met as I tried to understand their lives, their concerns, their attitudes, and their behaviors. Every now and then, especially in the early period, I met a family that was an uncommonly fertile source of information and understanding. I went back to those families several times, talking with each member for as many as eight or ten hours, sometimes hanging out with the whole family for all or part of a day. As the project progressed, the time each interview took became quite variable. In general, I spent two to three hours with a person; sometimes it was more, sometimes less, depending on how well the interview was going, how open and reflective the person was able or willing to be.

My concern, as in all my work, was not just to hear people's words and to give them voice but to understand the sometimes multiple meanings that lie beneath them, to apprehend what motivates the things people say and do, and to uncover the contradictions between the two. Knowing about behavior is interesting and important. But unless we understand how a person interprets the behavior, its symbolic meanings, and the way it is experienced, we know only one small part of the story.

In addition to being a sociologist, I have been a practicing psychotherapist for well over two decades. Although this work isn't directly reflected on the pages of this book, it has facilitated my research and writing in a number of ways. No skill is more central to the successful psychotherapist than the capacity to be an active, engaged listener, a quality equally crucial to research that rests on in-depth interviews. My training and experience enable me to establish quickly the same kind of nonjudgmental, encouraging environment in the research setting that's so vital to the clinical enterprise. This, in turn, makes it possible to forge the connection and rapport that allows me to probe into places hidden from view, private places that usually don't get a public airing. The years of working intensively with couples and individuals who live in families has given me an intimate, inside view of hundreds of families and is the basis of much of what I understand about the dynamics of family life.

But that's not all. Just as the clinical hour is a dialogue—a learning experience for both therapist and patient—so are these interviews. In the give-and-take of an interview, therefore, I not only got answers to my concerns but heard theirs as well. Often, then, the research seemed like a collaboration, since I learned from the people I spoke with what I had not known to ask and then incorporated it into the study, making it richer, more complex, and, I hope, more true to both the fact and the spirit of their lives.

Finally, a word about class, always a difficult problem in a society that lives with the fiction that everyone is middle class. In the research for *Worlds of Pain*, I interviewed only people who were clearly working class—that is, those who worked in blue-collar occupations and had no more than a high school education. Even then, I had questions about whether to leave out lower-middle-class white-collar families, since, as I wrote at the time, "many acute observers argue that the major division in our advanced industrial society is between the upper middle class and the combined working and lower middle class—an argument with which I concur."[16] Nevertheless, given the aims of that research, which was to specify class differences in culture and life-style, it made sense to draw the line more tightly.

It's still true, as I argued then, that a salaried white-collar worker is less susceptible to economic and seasonal fluctuations than a blue-collar worker who's paid by the hour. But it's also true that the boundary between the working class and the lower level of the middle class is even less clear today than it was twenty years ago. This time, therefore, the line is looser, and the families I write about in this book are a somewhat more varied group. Most are blue-collar, pink-collar, and service workers; some earn their keep in the menial sales and office jobs that characterize the low-level white-collar world.

None had a college degree at the time of the interview; a few had some college, usually courses taken at a two-year community college. But whatever their differences, they all have one central thing in common: They are the women and men who keep this country's wheels in motion and who—whether they work in the manufacturing or the service sector—are so little rewarded for the work they do. Although they have much to teach us about life in these United States, they are all too often the invisible ones, those whose voices rarely are heard in all their complexity, their ambivalence, and their contradictions. It's this omission, this loss, I hope to redress.

The book is divided into three parts. Part I, "The Invisible Americans," argues that the myth that we are a classless society has rendered working-class families and their problems invisible.

Part II, "The Family and the Economy," looks at the social, cultural, and economic changes of the last two decades and their impact on working-class family life. For the private arena of family living is not as separate from the public one as most Americans like to think. What happens in the world outside the family has an immediate and profound effect on life inside. The economy falters and families tremble. General Motors closes a plant and men who have supported their families for twenty years sit home and watch their wives go off to work. Or a single mother finds herself on welfare. Or a family that prided itself on its self-sufficiency suddenly is buying groceries with food stamps instead of dollars. Or a child has to leave college because parents can no longer help.

But it's not a one-way action. Frightened families also mean angry people—people who act out their anger both inside the family and outside, as they struggle desperately to avoid acknowledging their vulnerability, to escape their feelings of helplessness. Inside, substance abuse, depression, and family violence all increase. Outside, anger spills out in a dozen directions—from taxes to welfare, from politicians to homosexuals, from textbooks to rap music, from new immigrants to our home-grown racial minorities, from the homeless to the helpless.

This leads us to Part III, "Race and the Rise of Ethnicity," which argues that the social and economic realities within which working-class family life presently is lived form the backdrop against which racial and ethnic discord has escalated over the last two decades. Here I explore the ethnic revival of this period and examine the sociopolitical context within which it has taken place, along with some of the key issues that have become flash points for working-class anger.

2

THE INVISIBLE AMERICANS

Presidential electoral politics are notorious for muddling, distorting, and trivializing the issues of the day. The 1992 campaign, the election in which American politicians suddenly discovered class, was no different. With the economy stalled in its longest recession in more than half a century, both Democratic and Republican hopefuls courted what they called the "middle class" with the passion and persistence of a penitent and love-smitten suitor. They spoke soothing words about the "middle-class squeeze," offered sympathy for their plight, and promised help in a variety of ways.

But who were they wooing? The Republicans were trying to hold on to the Reagan Democrats—the white, urban, working-class and lower-middle-class voters who had defected from the Democratic Party in recent presidential elections. The Democrats were out to recapture them. Which suggests that, for some at least, "middle class" was the election-year code word for "whites." Meanwhile, both parties were ready to give the store away to the more affluent. As Gwen Ifill, writing in the *New York Times*, noted acidly: "Take the word 'needy.' It sometimes seems to have been effectively redefined to mean those who are considered to be otherwise capable of earning $50,000 or more a year."

In fact, all the talk about the middle class served to obscure class realities rather than to clarify them, since this middle class was defined so broadly that it encompassed everyone but the rich and the poor. The head of the Congressional Budget Office, for example, pronounced that any family of four with an annual income somewhere between $19,000 and $78,000 fell into the middle class—a range so wide as to be nonsensical to anyone but a politician.[1] Could a family that takes home $19,000 a year conceivably experience itself or its life choices in the same way as a family earning over four times as much?

The political director of the Democratic National Committee offered a narrower but equally flawed definition. The typical middle-class family whose vote the Democrats sought, he said, consisted of two full-time working parents who were under forty-five, lived in the suburbs with their two children, and had a combined income of $35,000.[2] Notice that in 1992 it required the full-time labor of both wife and husband to reach the $35,000 figure he cited—a major change from the past, when a single earner could still support a family of four; yet this was glossed over as if it were an insignificant detail. At the time, moreover, the Bureau of Labor Statistics reported that the median income for families with two earners—that is, where both wife and husband worked full-time in the paid labor force—was $46,777.[3]* Since income is one important determinant of class standing, at $35,000 a year the Democrats' "typical middle-class family" hardly qualifies for the label.

As the political rhetoric escalated, it became clear that the ordinary working-class families who are the subject of this book had become invisible, swallowed up in this large, amorphous, and mythic middle class. True, some candidates talked about the poor as well as the middle class. But the working class remained hidden from view. For to have acknowledged its existence would challenge the long-held American fiction that this nation has conquered the invidious distinctions of class, that the poor are an unfortunate aberration, and that, except for them, we are all middle class. All,

---

* Unless otherwise noted, all income figures in this book are in 1990 dollars.

that is, except for those we now call the "underclass"—another code word, this time for blacks.

But what difference does it make how we label people? It doesn't change their lives, does it? The answer is both yes and no. In the immediate sense, no. No matter what we call people, their daily lives remain the same. But in the larger scheme, it makes a difference. The idea of the middle class is not just a handy social category, a shorthand way of describing a segment of the population. It has broad political and policy implications as well. For the way we conceive of our people determines how we think of their needs, therefore how government policy is made. Someone benefits, someone loses each time a policy is promulgated. If the popular political language denies the very existence of a sector of the population, their needs aren't likely to be taken into account.

When, for example, the Clinton administration made public its plan to buoy the economy and reduce the deficit, the proposal promised some tax benefits to the working poor and added some burdens to the middle class and the rich. The working poor were defined as families whose annual income was less than $30,000 and the rich or near-rich as those earning over $140,000. In between was the "middle class," a vast array of people who were lumped together as if a family in which both wife and husband work at blue-, pink-, or white-collar jobs earning a combined income of $35,000 a year have any financial or social common ground with the family in which a single professional earner brings home $135,000.[4]

Psychologically, too, the labels we apply make a difference. In the short run, given the stigma attached to being working class in this country, calling themselves "middle class" makes people feel better about their social situation and, therefore, enhances their self-esteem. Over the long haul, however, the denial of their class position leads to a confused and contradictory social identity that leaves working-class people riven with status anxiety and impairs their ability to join together to act in their own behalf.

Although socially and politically working-class families are invisible, they are the single largest group of families in the country. These are the men and women, by far the largest part of the American work force, who work at the lower levels of the manufacturing and service sectors of the economy; workers whose education is limited, whose mobility options are severely restricted, and who usually work for an hourly rather than a weekly wage. They don't tap public resources; they reap no benefit from either the pitiful handouts to the poor or from huge subsidies to the rich.[5] Instead, they go to work every day to provide for their families, often at jobs they hate.

But they live on the edge. Any unexpected event—a child's illness, an accident on the job, a brief layoff—threatens to throw them into the abyss. Credit, if they're able to get it at all, is stretched to the limit. The machine spits out the plastic card that helped them deal with the steady erosion of income in recent years; the clerk hands it back to them with an embarrassed, "Sorry, the machine won't take it. Do you have another card?" They probably do, but it won't make any difference; the machine will know that one, too, is, in the words of the day, "maxed out."

No sooner do these words appear on the page than a nagging voice inside my head complains: *But middle-class families, too, are feeling the credit crunch; they, too, have had to strain their resources nearly to the breaking point to maintain their life-style.* It's certainly true that even families at the high end of middle-class incomes are feeling strapped by the cost of housing, feeding, clothing, and educating a family today. They may be unable to afford the house of their dreams, may find it a strain to pay for their children's private school, may have to go into debt to buy a new car or take a vacation. But will anyone argue that these problems are as wrenching as those of the working-class family earning $30,000 and struggling to come up with the money for the rent, the mortgage payment, a doctor bill, or a winter coat for a growing child? The subjective experience of deprivation in both instances may be real. But there's an objective difference that cannot be dismissed.

It's not just at these exalted levels that there's a difference between white-collar workers, who work for a weekly wage, and those who wear a blue collar and are paid by the hour. Hourly work isn't as steady and it doesn't pay as well. True, some of the elite workers in the building trades still may earn $20 or more an hour. But these are the rare jobs, the dream jobs of the working-class world. Most have to settle for very much less, as a comparison of the paychecks of the hourly worker with those who work for a weekly wage shows so clearly.

In recent years, the median weekly income of lower- to midlevel white-collar workers fell from $516 to $501, while the hourly pay for blue- and pink-collar service workers tumbled from $8.52 to $7.46—a $15-a-week drop for white-collar workers, over $40 for those wearing a blue or a pink collar.[6] At these figures, the service or factory worker earned $298 *if* he or she worked a full forty-hour week—a wage substantially below the $501 of the white-collar worker. For the men and women in this study, however, the blue-collar/white-collar disparity isn't nearly so great, since the white-collar workers, almost all of whom are women, usually hold the kind of low-level jobs where median income is closer to $300 than $500 a week.

For all but the top fifth of American families, the peak earning year of the last two decades was 1973. Since then, median family income has remained virtually flat—$35,474 in 1973, $35,353 in 1990.[7] But "flat" in this case doesn't mean that family fortunes were unchanged. These were the same years when women entered the labor force in increasing numbers and the single-earner family became a thing of the past for most of America. For family income to remain constant under these circumstances means that men's wages declined substantially.

Yet these income figures don't tell the whole dismal story, since they include all U.S. families—that is, families with both one and two earners, as well as the rich and the poor. If they were broken down by class, the yearly income of working-class and lower middle-class families would be substantially lower. The median annual income of the families in this study, for example, is well below the national average: $31,500, with $16,500 at the low end of the range and $42,000 at the top.

Moreover, focusing only on the national median obscures very large differences across race. In 1973 the median income for white families was (in 1990 dollars) $37,076; for Latinos, $25,654; and for African-Americans, $21,398. The comparable 1990 figures show shrunken incomes for whites and Latinos—$36,915 and $23,431, respectively—and virtually no change for blacks—$21,423.[8]

Economists offer a variety of complex explanations for the

income squeeze that has plagued American workers in these last two decades. The restructuring of American industry in response to advancing technology and the press of global competition have profoundly changed the American economy. The new technologies often mean that fewer workers are necessary to produce the required goods. The shift from a production to a service economy has been costly because, except for the most highly skilled jobs, service industry wages are substantially lower than those in manufacturing. The communication and transportation revolutions allow companies to set up shop anywhere and still have access to world markets. Many of our large corporations, therefore, have moved their production facilities to countries where wages are substantially lower than they are here, leaving fewer well-paying jobs for American workers. In 1970, the Fortune 500 companies employed 20.6 percent of the urban work force. Partly because so many of these companies left the United States, partly because they restructured, and partly because they stopped growing, by 1991 the proportion of American workers employed by these corporate giants had fallen to 10.9 percent.[9]

The decline of union power also is high on the list of reasons for the wage stagnation of American workers—a plunge that is at least in part attributable to the successful war on unions waged by the Reagan and Bush administrations. As recession followed recession, as the government participated in strike breaking while offering no protection to workers, and as unemployment rose, many workers worried more about keeping a job than about getting a raise or expanding their benefits.

Whatever the reasons, the evidence is clear: During the 1970s, the great period of economic growth that had marked the years from the end of World War II slowed dramatically. Hundreds of thousands of manufacturing jobs, which had provided the basis for whatever working-class affluence existed then, disappeared as the move from a manufacturing to a service economy accelerated sharply. Before the decade hit midpoint, the nation was mired in a recession that was felt most deeply among blue-collar workers. Men and women who lost jobs in manufacturing, construction, and other relatively high-paying occupations were forced to settle for a fraction of their former earnings in one of the service industries—that is, if they were lucky enough to find work. Those who continued to work in the same fields found that their paychecks bought less and less as wages failed to keep pace with inflation.

Then came the 1980s. The frenzied corporate spending of that decade, and the Reagan and Bush administrations' policies that lined the pockets of the rich, were of no benefit to the working-class families of the nation. Quite the opposite! While the rich were getting richer, these families—the invisible ones—were falling further and further behind.[10] In February 1992, a Census Bureau report documented what most people already knew—that is, that income inequality had grown enormously over the previous two decades.[11] During the 1980s alone, a period of high economic growth, the top 1 percent of families got 60 percent of the gains—the same 1 percent that now owns more wealth than the bottom 90 percent.[12] And the near-rich didn't do badly either. In the single decade between 1980 and 1990, the income of the top one-fifth of American families climbed steadily, rising just over 25 percent, from $73,764 to $92,663.[13] A far cry from the fate of America's working-class families.

As we entered the 1990s, the stumbling economy tripped and fell into the most serious recession in half a century. In the thirteen months between June 1990 and July 1991 alone, 804,000 jobs in manufacturing, 495,000 in construction, and 365,000 in retailing were lost. From October to December 1991, 2,600 jobs disappeared each day. And despite government pronouncements that a recovery was under way, corporate America shed over one million jobs in 1992 and another 350,000—50,000 each month—in the first half of 1993.

The American dream—a life filled with goods and comforts bought on credit; goods that in our consumption-driven society are the symbols of worth, the emblems of success—became a nightmare for vast numbers of families. The only way out for many of them was bankruptcy court. In the twelve months ending September 30, 1991, personal bankruptcy filings soared 24 percent nationwide, with parts of the Northeast spiraling up to 40 and 50 percent.[14] And these were the lucky ones. For disturbing as bankruptcy may be for those who are forced into it, it's not an option for most working-class families in America.

It takes a certain amount of knowledge, sophistication, and access to legal advice to plan for a bankruptcy—commodities often in short supply among the families who fill the pages of this book. "After the finance people came and took everything away, I found out I could have gone bankrupt," says Tom Marens, a thirty-eight-year-old white laborer, the father of three teenage children. "Maybe if I'd known about it before, we could have saved some things from those damn vultures. But I never found out about it until it was too late. I mean, I heard of people going bankrupt, but I always thought it was only businesses did that, not plain people. How would I know? Nobody tells you stuff like that, then when you find it out, it's too late, and you're stuck."

Even if he had known, however, Tom might well have discovered that he couldn't afford the luxury of having himself declared officially broke. For bankruptcy is not for the poor and the near-poor, since they rarely can afford the $1,000 or more it takes in court costs and legal fees. Instead, they lose the possessions that a bankruptcy filing would protect and remain buried under debts that the bankruptcy court would cancel. "I worked in an aluminum plant until it shut down a couple of years ago," recounts Al Brazille, a thirty-two-year-old African-American father of two children. "There was no decent, steady work around, so I was doing odd jobs wherever I could. I wasn't making much, but Emmaline was working then, waitressing in a coffee shop and making pretty good tips. So between us, we were hanging on. But then she got laid off, too, and we were really in trouble. We both kept trying to find work, but there wasn't anything around—nothing—and the bills just kept coming and coming.

"I read in the paper about people declaring bankruptcy, and I figured I had to do something or we'd drown in those goddamn bills. So I went to see this lawyer, one of them guys that advertises on TV, and he said, yeah, sure, I could go bankrupt and all my bills would be wiped out. Only problem was, it cost about $1,000. Christ, if I had $1,000 I wouldn't be bankrupt, would I? The next thing I knew, the finance people came and took just about everything we had—the car, the TV, the stereo, the sofa, everything; it's all gone. That's why the place looks like this," he explains, his hand sweeping across the nearly bare room in which we're sitting, his face a tight mask as he tries unsuccessfully to control his pain.[15]

Our denial notwithstanding, then, class inequalities not only exist in our society, they're handed down from parents to children in the same way that wealth is passed along in the upper class. True, American society has always had a less rigid and clearly defined class structure than many other nations. Poor people climb up; wealthy ones fall. These often well-publicized figures help to fuel the myth about equality of opportunity. But they're not the norm. Nor is the perpetuation of our class structure accidental. The economy, the polity, and the educational system all play their part in ensuring the continuity and stability of our social classes. Even the family does its share—sometimes intentionally, more often in unintentional ways.[16]

Take public education, for example. Myth tells us that it's the great equalizer, the one institution in our society that promises every child the same education and an equal chance at the good life. Yet everyone knows that our urban schools are in trouble today, that the same education system that once educated millions upon millions of immigrant children can't seem to teach even our native kids to read, write, and do their sums. It's no secret either that schools in poor and working-class neighborhoods have fewer resources and worse physical plants than those in wealthier ones. The best teachers, the cleanest books, the most supplies seem to find their way more often into the schools that serve white middle-class children than into those attended by the poor and working class.[17]

In his recent exposé of what he calls the "savage inequalities" of American public education, Jonathan Kozol asks: "What does money buy for children in New Jersey?" His answer: "For high school students in East Orange, where the track team has no field and therefore has to do its running in the hallway of the school, it buys a minimum of exercise but a good deal of pent-up energy and anger. In mostly upper-middle-income Montclair, on the other hand, it buys two recreation fields, four gyms, a dance room, a wrestling room, a weight room with a universal gym, tennis courts, a track, and indoor areas for fencing. It also buys 13 full-time physical education teachers for its 1,900 high-school students. East Orange High School, by comparison, has four physical education teachers for 2,000 students, 99.9 percent of whom are black."[18]

Educational researchers have known for years that the socioeconomic status of the children in a school is highly correlated with the quality of the plant as well as with the students' achievement scores. The problem is not only that schools for middle-class children are more pleasant, better equipped places than those attended by the poor and working class, although surely the environment has something to do with the way children learn. Such differences also count because they send a message about who and what this society values—a message these children hear very clearly. It may be true, as some analysts of our educational system claim, that there's no *hard* evidence that students do better in smaller classes, in more modern buildings, or with more experienced teachers.[19] But the "softer" data would tell us more.

The numbers and statistics these researchers rely on can only tell us that working-class children who have these advantages don't noticeably improve their school performance. But they can't tell us why this is so. Is their failure related to internalized notions of their own inferiority? Is it due to their conviction that however well they do in school, it won't make much difference in their life chances? Do they have to dodge crack dealers and gunshots on their way to school? Are they too hungry to learn? Too tired?

An investigation by a team of researchers at Northwestern University offers some clues. They found that when poor black single-parent families were afforded the opportunity to move out of their crime-ridden urban housing projects and into white suburbs, the mothers were more likely to become self-sufficient and the children's school performance improved dramatically.[20]

It's true that the white working-class child generally doesn't suffer the same social and psychological deprivations as the black inner-city child. But white or black, their class position makes itself felt in a hundred silent ways, from parents who are weighed down by their own sense of failure, to television images that glorify the successful professional and turn working-class men and women into doltish caricatures, to the teacher in the classroom who expects less of the working-class child than of the middle-class one. When this is the background music of a child's world, what is there to strive for?

Yet the myth that we are a classless society retains a strong grip on the imaginations of most Americans, even among those who are poor and working class. Partly, the myth is sustained by the widespread accumulation of consumer goods that somewhat erases the visible differences across class—goods that become the manifest symbol of what we now call the "middle-class life-style." If everyone owns a TV, a VCR, an answering machine, a washing machine, a dishwasher, an automobile, how much difference can there be—especially among whites? Indeed, only people of color remain visibly distinct regardless of class, life-style, or the goods they have acquired—a distinction that helps to eclipse class issues by providing what we might call a "status safety net" for whites. No matter how low they may fall, there's always someone below them, someone who serves as a reminder that they remain a step above any person of color, even a rich one.

The belief that we are a society without class distinctions, then, is a convenient fiction, one that has both psychological and political consequences. Psychologically, it frees the successful from the guilty knowledge that they had a head start, while it also fills those who don't make it with a sense of personal inadequacy. Politically, in perpetuating the myth, we ensure the *status quo*, since, when those at or near the bottom of the class hierarchy internalize the problem as one of their own making, they implicitly absolve the society from responsibility for their fate.

This is surely one reason why, even though working-class families have become increasingly vulnerable, class consciousness has not increased. In fact, if the strength of organized labor is one measure of that consciousness, then there's clearly less of it now than at any time in the last half century. Among white workers, membership in labor unions, once their hedge against exploitation, plunged from nearly 20 percent at the beginning of the 1980s to a little more than 15 percent by the end of the decade. If we separate private- and public-sector employees, the numbers are even worse. The latest estimates suggest that less than 12 percent of private-sector workers are now in unions. Only among African-Americans does the proportion of workers holding union membership remain above 20 percent, largely because so many are employed in the public sector, where, at state and local levels, joining a union is often a condition of employment.[21]

The protections that labor unions once offered have become less available at precisely the time when the fortunes of working-class families have been falling so sharply, leaving them with an acute sense of vulnerability to fates beyond their control. This would seem to be an ideal situation for the mobilization of class anger. Instead, we have seen an escalation of *racial* anger beyond anything we have known in the recent past. *In fact, the objective situation of the working class notwithstanding, at the subjective level we have been witness to the declining significance of class in favor of the increasing salience of race.*[22]

Twenty years ago David Duke, an ex-Nazi and former Grand Wizard of the Ku Klux Klan, would have been laughed off the podium. In 1991 he could run for governor in Louisiana and win 55 percent of the white vote. Two decades ago Patrick Buchanan, a wealthy, right-wing Republican newspaperman who had never held public office, would hardly have made a dent in the vote of a sitting president. In those 1992 presidential primaries in which he ran against George Bush, he was taken seriously enough to win between a quarter and a third of the vote.

It's true that economic discontent was the bedrock on which these votes were cast. But it's also true that for a considerable number of American voters this discontent found expression in the racist and xenophobic campaigns of these candidates. For despite the objective reality that working-class whites have much in common with their black counterparts, subjectively blacks provide white Americans with a safe scapegoat, an acceptable target onto whom they can displace their hostility, vent their rage, and reassure themselves of their superiority.[23]

Such defensive maneuvers, however, can provide temporary surcease at best, a momentary shelter from the tough realities of working-class lives and the long economic and psychological decline these families have suffered.[24] Two decades ago Richard Sennett and Jonathan Cobb wrote that one of the most destructive of "the hidden injuries of class" is the stigmatization of working-class status, the disrespect for the men and women who work with their hands, and the belief that it's nothing more than their own inadequacies that keep them from climbing the class ladder.[25] An analysis that's as true now as it was then.

As I reflect on these words and their meaning, I'm reminded of my childhood when my widowed mother, who worked in a coat factory, would admonish me to prepare myself for something better. "I do dirty work; you'll do clean work," was the mandate of those years. Her aspirations weren't high; "clean work" meant some kind of an office job. But it wasn't just that the factory was dirty and the office clean. The dirty–clean divide was a metaphor for something more, a way of expressing her understanding of the disdain with which she, who worked with her hands, was regarded, therefore regarded herself.

It wasn't her imagination; it was part of the daily experience of her life—the foreman who treated her and the others who worked at the machines with contempt; the women in the office who hunched their shoulders and hugged their skirts to themselves as they sidled by those who worked in the factory; even her daughter, who, in adolescence, was shamed by her mother's work and upgraded her from lining maker to designer when talking to friends. These were what "dirty work" stood for; these were what she hoped to spare me by enjoining me to prepare for clean work. Only by working with my head instead of my hands could I climb up and out of the working class; only then would I live a more self-respecting and socially respected life than she had lived.

But "climbing up" isn't a neutral phrase. It means going somewhere, getting out, moving ahead. "Upwardly mobile," we say—the words spoken almost reverently, an accolade, an acknowledgment of an accomplishment. It's an idea whose value is deeply embedded in the American culture, a powerful idea that has profound consequences both for those who move up and for those who do not. For the dictates of a culture become part of the psychology of its people. The working-class person who "makes it" by climbing the class ladder develops an enhanced sense of self. *I made it when others around me didn't.* True, the move may be a very small one and the pay no more, sometimes less, than a job in a factory—a move that doesn't change the objective conditions of life. But if it's defined as "up," it *feels* different, and, illusory or not, it has meaning in the psychological economy of the individual. For even illusions, if firmly held, make a difference.

"I used to work in an upholstery factory," Linda Polanski, a twenty-nine-year-old white word processor says with a shudder. "Yicchhh, it was so filthy; I hated it. The only thing I wanted to do when I got home was take a bath."

"What about the pay? Did you earn more then?" I asked her.

"Maybe I made a little more," she replies with a shrug that says the question doesn't mean much to her. "I don't know, it's not just the money. None of us in my family ever graduated high school. When I went and got my GED and took word processing, it was a big deal.[26] My brothers and sister thought I was loony; you know, they couldn't figure out why I needed it. I had a job. Now I think they're kind of jealous, especially my sister.

"In my job now, it's . . . ," she hesitates, her brow furrowed as she searches for the words. "I don't know, it's different. It's like they respect you more, like you're a real person. Know what I mean? If you want to stop a minute and go talk to the other girls, nobody says anything. Or you can go to the bathroom and grab a smoke, and it's no big deal. I mean, they expect you to work, but they know you can't do it every minute. If it got slow in the factory, you got laid off. But in this job, they don't just dump you if there's a couple of slow days.

"People didn't look at me the same like they do now, even my kids. Since I've been doing word processing, they're always asking me questions, like how do you spell something, things like that. My husband, too. They didn't ask me questions like that before. It's like they think I got smarter, or something."

We can't know, of course, whether people think she "got smarter" or whether she projects a different sense of herself to which others are responding. But we do know that the two are interactive, that it's all but impossible to separate one from the other. Her words tell us that in working with her head instead of her hands, in working in a clean office instead of a dirty factory, she experiences herself differently than she did before.

Never mind that the work Linda does may require no more thought than the routine in the upholstery factory. Never mind either that objectively her class position remains unchanged. It *feels* different, and, psychologically at least, that's what counts. This alone, the presentation of self that says, consciously or not, *I'm different today than I was yesterday—different and better,* is enough to engender a more validating and respectful reaction from the world around her; enough, too, to provoke the envy of her siblings.

With the move from factory worker to white-collar worker, however, the class and status divide suddenly becomes real for those on both sides of it. Linda feels different; her sister is envious. They may not articulate it in class terms, but for both of them—the one who feels as if she's climbed up and the one who believes she's been left behind—the emptiness of the myth of our classlessness stands revealed.

But it's not just stigma, the pain of feeling left behind, or the sense of indadequacy—distressing though these may be—that's so difficult for working-class families. It's also their invisibility. For while it may assuage their status anxieties to be counted among the middle class, it renders them and the particular problems that beset working-class life unnamed, therefore invisible, often even to themselves. It is, after all, hard to believe in the particularity of the class experience if there's no social category into which it fits.

Yet the social, economic, and cultural changes of the last two decades have brought with them a whole new set of difficulties for working-class families—difficulties that carom around both inside the family and in the social world outside. It's true that many of the issues of family living know no class boundaries. But what turns those issues into problems, as well as how families attend to them, is related to the resources at their disposal, which, of course, means their class position. Among those problems is the recent revolution in norms and values—cultural changes that almost invariably come down to working-class families from those above and which, when added to their economic distress, create a whole new level of pain and bewilderment, yet another aspect of life that seems to them to have ricocheted out of control.

3

"PEOPLE DON'T KNOW RIGHT FROM WRONG ANYMORE!"

"I can't believe what kids do today!" exclaims Marguerite Jenkins, a white forty-year-old divorcée whose seventeen-year-old daughter, Candy, has just had an abortion.

I last met Marguerite more than twenty years ago when I interviewed her for *Worlds of Pain*. The slim, pretty young woman who welcomed me into her home then is gone, replaced by an older, heavier version who bears the visible marks of life's difficulties. As I listen to her angry words about her daughter, the memory of our last meeting moves from the recesses of my mind into awareness. At age twenty, Marguerite already had two children under three; Candy wouldn't come into the world for another three years. Her first-born son had been conceived when she was still in high school. But abortion wasn't an option then. So a few months after she discovered she was pregnant, she left school and married Larry Jenkins, the nineteen-year-old father of the child she was carrying. By the time I met her she was a distraught and overburdened young mother, worrying because her husband had just lost yet another job, fearful that her dream of living happily ever after was crumbling.

I remember the story Marguerite told of finding out she was pregnant—her terror; her anger at her father, who wanted to throw her out of the house; her anger at her mother, who didn't protect her from her father's rage; her bitterness because they were more concerned about what others would think than about the predicament she found herself in. Hearing Marguerite now, I can understand her concern for her daughter, her fear that Candy will repeat her mistakes. But given her own experience, I wonder about her outrage, her seeming lack of compassion for Candy and for what she might be feeling. So I say, "I'm a little surprised to hear you talk so angrily, since you got pregnant when you were about her age."

She looks somewhat abashed at the reminder, shifts uncomfortably in her chair, then says, "C'mon, you know it's different now. Sure, I got caught, too, but we got married. *We had to get married; we didn't have a choice.*"

"We had to get married"—words spoken by 44 percent of the couples I interviewed two decades ago. But what does "had to" mean? These marriages weren't coerced, at least not by any obvious outside agent. There were no old-style shotgun weddings, no self-righteous fathers avenging the violation of their daughters' virtue by forcing their errant lovers into saying their vows. The compulsion was internal, part of the moral culture of the community in which they lived. It was simply what one did.

Sometimes the young couple married regretfully; often one partner, usually the man, was ambivalent. It didn't really matter; they did what was expected. If you "got caught," you got married; that was the rule, understood by all. As one of the men I interviewed then put it: "If you knocked up a girl, you married her; that was it. You just did it, that's all. End of story."

But in fact, it was only the beginning of the story. Seven years and three children after Marguerite and Larry Jenkins did what their parents and their community expected of them, he walked out. Young, unskilled, and seething at being tied down by responsibilities he was unable to meet, Larry floated from one dead-end job to another, at each one acting out his resentment until he got fired or quit. Marguerite, frightened for her children, furious with disappointment, and exhausted from their constant battles, finally gave him an ultimatum: Shape up or get out! To her surprise, he stormed out of the house and came back only to claim his belongings a few days later. "I said it, but I didn't really think he'd do it. I figured I'd finally scare him into being more responsible," she explains as she reviews those years.

With no family to help her and three small children whose father couldn't or wouldn't support them, Marguerite had no choice: She spent the next five years on the welfare rolls. "I was so ashamed to go down to the welfare office. I can't explain how bad I felt; I wasn't raised that way. My parents, they had their problems, but my father was a hard worker. He didn't make much, but we got by without charity.

"I used to think welfare people were freeloaders, you know, like they were lazy bums. Then it happened to me and I kept thinking: *I can't believe it! How did this happen to me? I'm not like that.*" She looks away, trying to contain the tears that well up as the memory of those hard times washes over her.

"Marrying Larry, that whole thing, it was a giant mistake right from the beginning. You get married with this dream that everything's going to be wonderful, but it never works out that way, does it? How could it? We were babies, and there we were trying to be grown-ups. We had two kids by the time I was nineteen and he was, I don't know, maybe not even twenty-one yet. I wasn't ready to be a wife and a mother, and he sure wasn't ready to be a decent husband and father."

The Jenkinses' story is a common one among the families I met twenty years ago. Two young people thrust into a marriage by the lack of acceptable moral or social alternatives, only to divorce a few years later. Since they married so young, sometimes even before they finished high school, the women had little opportunity to develop any marketable skills, certainly none that would enable them to support their children and pay for child care while they worked. Of the thirty-two *Worlds of Pain* families I was able to locate, eighteen (56 percent) had been divorced. All but one of the men had remarried by the time I met them again. The lone exception had separated from his wife a few months earlier and was already involved with a woman in what he took to be a serious relationship.

For the women it was different: Only eleven had remarried; the rest had been single for five years or more. All of them talked about the economic devastation divorce wrought in their families. Well over half needed some form of public assistance during the years when they were divorced. Some were on the welfare rolls; others got by with food stamp supplements alone. For the women who haven't remarried, life continues to be economically unstable at best.

If their own young marriages so often were, as Marguerite Jenkins says, "a giant mistake right from the beginning," why aren't such women more supportive of their daughters' choices? Indeed, why aren't they pleased that the young women they raised have so many more options available to them? I ask the question: "Given what's happened in your own life, I wonder why you're not glad that Candy could make other choices?"

"Don't get me wrong, I think it's okay to have an abortion; I'm—what do they call it?—oh yeah, for choice," explains Marguerite. "I mean, I don't think people should run around having abortions just like that, but nobody's got a right to tell somebody what to do about being pregnant or not. God knows, I don't want her to do what I did. It's just that . . . " She stops, searching for the right words, and after a moment or two, continues, still uncertain. "I don't know exactly how to say it. Look, I was scared to death when I found out I was pregnant, and so was Larry. These kids, they're not even bothered now."

It's this sense that their children see the world so differently that's so hard for working-class parents. For it seems to say that now, along with the economic dislocation they suffer, even their children are out of their reach, that they can no longer count on shared values to hold their families together. It doesn't help either that no matter where they look, they don't see a reflection of themselves. If they look up, they see a life-style and values they abhor, the same ones that, they believe, are corrupting their children. If they shift their gaze downward, they see the poor, the homeless, the helpless—the denizens of the dangerous underclass whose moral degeneracy has, in the working-class view, led to their fall. It's as if their beliefs and values have no place in the institutional world they inhabit, not in the schools their children attend, not on the television shows they watch, not in the films they see, not in the music they hear, not in the laws their government promulgates.

It's true that this isn't a problem only for working-class families. Middle-class parents also worry about the changing cultural norms; they also fret endlessly about "what kids do today." Indeed, generational conflict over changing values and life-styles is common to all families, with parents generally holding onto the old ways and children pulling for the new ones.[1] But it's also true that the issues that create conflict in families differ quite sharply by class.

Middle-class parents long ago accepted the norms, values, and behavior that have only recently filtered down into the working class—the open expression of premarital sex, for example, or living together without benefit of clergy. Partly, perhaps, these changes came earlier and with less upheaval in middle-class families because it was their children who initiated the struggle for change. But there are other reasons as well. High among them is the fact that middle-class parents are likely to be more educated than those in the working class. And it's widely understood that a college education tends to broaden perspectives and liberalize attitudes about the kind of life-style and value changes we have seen in the last few decades.

Since most working-class parents haven't been exposed to the array of ideas found in a college classroom, they tend to be more tradition bound. "You get used to doing things one way and then you think it's the right way," says thirty-six-year-old Jane Dawson, a white mother of two teenagers. Without the expanded horizons that higher education affords, the old way often becomes the only way. "If it was good enough for us, it's fine for my kids," proclaims her husband, Bill.

But the cultural changes that have swept the land during these past decades will not be stayed by parental nostalgia, fear, or authority. The young people in this study agree that their values about such issues as sexual behavior, marriage, and gender roles are radically different from those their parents hold. And they're pained by the family conflicts these differences stir. But they also insist that they're not the thoughtless, hedonistic lot of their parents' imaginations. "My mom thinks I think getting pregnant is no big deal, but she doesn't understand," says Candy Jenkins, her blue eyes turning stormy with anger when we talk about this a few days after my meeting with her mother. "Just because I didn't carry on like some kind of a crazy person, she thinks I didn't care. But it's not true; I did care. I was scared to death when I found out."

"I was scared to death when I found out"—the same words spoken decades apart by a mother and her daughter. Both shared the fear of their parents' response. "I thought my father would kill me," says Marguerite. "I was afraid my mother would murder me," shudders Candy. Beyond that, however, the words have entirely different meanings for each of them. For Marguerite, getting pregnant was a problem; not to have gotten married would have been a catastrophe. For her, therefore, the critical question was: *Will he marry me?* "I was terrified. What if Larry reneged and wouldn't marry me? What would I do?"

For Candy, however, the pregnancy could be taken care of; marriage loomed like a calamity. "The one thing I knew was I didn't want to get married and have a baby. I was really scared my mom would try to make me. She kept going on about how ashamed she was, and what was she going to tell grandma, and all like that. But she didn't push me about getting married. I mean, she talked about it, but she knew it was a bum idea, too. Look at what happened to her."

For Marguerite, shame was a big issue, not just the memory of her own shame, but the fact that it wasn't one of her daughter's preoccupations. "I just can't get over it," Marguerite remarks, shaking her head in bewilderment. "I wanted to die because I was so ashamed. I felt like I'd never be able to hold my head up again. Now these kids, it's like it's nothing to them; they've got no shame. I'll bet half the school knows she was pregnant. They probably compare notes about their damn abortions," she concludes with disgust.

Shame and guilt—the emotions that give evidence of the effectiveness of our social norms, that reassure us that the moral culture has been internalized, that there will be a price for its violation. If our young suffer, if they're tormented by shame, haunted by guilt, we can at least be assured that they share our values about good and evil, right and wrong. Without that, the gap between us seems disturbingly wide and the future frighteningly uncertain.

But to cast the issue in these terms—that is, either we suffer shame and guilt or we don't—misses the point. It's not true that our children don't experience these feelings. But what evokes them is not fixed in eternity. Rather, it changes with time, each historical moment delivering up its own variation of a culture's norms and values, each one defining its transgressions and eliciting shame and guilt for their violation.

For Marguerite's mother, divorce would have been unthinkable, a humiliating and guilt-ridden scandal, a painful public admission of failure and inadequacy. By the time Marguerite was divorced, it was a sad but commonplace event, certainly nothing to hide in shame about. For Marguerite, her pregnancy was a shameful confession that she had, in the language of the day, "gone all the way"—an act, once it became known, that threatened to cast her out of respectable society and to label her a "slut." For Candy, there was a mix of feelings, some of them no doubt the same as her mother felt decades earlier—regret, fear, sadness, confusion, anger at herself for taking sexual chances when she knew better. But not shame—not because she's a less moral person than her mother but because she grew up in a sexual culture that gives permission for a level of sexual freedom unknown to her mother's generation.[2]

"As long as two people love each other, there's nothing wrong with making love," declares Tory, the white sixteen-year-old daughter of the Bowen family. "I don't understand why it's only supposed to be okay if you're married. I mean, why is getting married such a big deal?"

This, perhaps, is one of the most important changes underlying the permissiveness about sex. If getting married is no longer "such a big deal," why wait for marriage to explore one's sexuality? If sexual relations outside marriage are acceptable once people have been divorced, then why not before they get married? Repeatedly, the young people I met raised these and other questions as we discussed the changing norms around marriage and sex.

The sexual revolution, which changed the rules about the expression of female sexuality; the gender revolution, with its demand for reordering traditional roles and relationships; the divorce revolution, which fractured the social contract about marriage and commitment; the shifts in the economy, which forced increasing numbers of married women into the labor force—all these have come together to create a profoundly different consciousness about marriage and its role divisions for young people today.[3]

Twenty years ago it was marriage that occupied the dreams of a working-class high-school girl. Among the *Worlds of Pain* families, the women were, on average, eighteen when they married; the men, twenty. Two decades later, none of the families I reinterviewed had a son who married at twenty or younger, and just one had a daughter who was only eighteen when she married. The others either married considerably later or are still single—some at twenty-four and twenty-five—something that almost never happened by choice twenty years ago.

The national statistics tell the same story. In 1970, the average age at which women married for the first time was 20.6 years; for men, it was 22.5. Two decades later it had jumped to 24.2 for women, 26.2 for men.[4] Today 18.8 percent of women and 29.4 percent of men are still unmarried when they reach thirty, compared to 6.2 percent and 9.4 percent, respectively, twenty years ago.[5]

Women in particular are much more ambivalent about hearing wedding bells than they were a couple of generations ago, aware that the changes they have undergone, the kind of marital partnerships they now long for, are rarely matched by the men who are their prospective mates. Therefore, they talk of wanting to explore the options available, to live life more fully and openly before taking on the responsibilities of marriage and parenthood.

But delaying the trip to the altar isn't a rejection of marriage and the commitment it entails. Rather, it's a dream deferred, part of a changing culture, which itself has developed in response to shifting social realities. For the culture of a nation, a group, or a tribe is a living thing, stretching, changing, expanding, or contracting as new needs arise and old ones die, as the exigencies of living in one era give way to new ones in the next. So, for example, now that great advances in medical technology have lengthened the life span beyond anything earlier generations ever dreamed of, the age when people marry moves upward.

When people died at fifty and large families were the norm, there was a good chance at least one parent would never live to see the children into adulthood. Therefore, it made no sense to wait until twenty-five or thirty before starting a family. Now, when, on the average, women live to nearly eighty and men to a little over seventy, we can marry and bear children very much later, safe in the knowledge that we'll be around to raise and nurture them as long they need us.[6] The forty-year-old first-time father today worries about whether he'll be able to play football with his son at twelve, not whether he'll be alive when the boy becomes a man.

I don't mean that we think consciously about the impact of our longer life. It's the kind of knowledge that generally remains out of awareness but that, nevertheless, profoundly influences our life decisions. For a social change of this magnitude, one that gives us so many more years of life, also adds stages to the life course that were unknown before. Adolescence is extended, adulthood becomes another stage in our continuing growth and development, and old age appears on the scene as a part of life that requires planning and attention—changes and additions that have social, cultural, and psychological repercussions.[7]

The same is true for the culture of marriage. When life ended at fifty, people didn't feel deprived if their relationships weren't intimate or companionable enough. They were too busy earning a living, raising their children, and hoping they'd survive long enough to see them grown. Now, when wives and husbands know they have decades of active life ahead of them after shepherding their children into adulthood, the emotional quality of the marital relationship takes on fresh importance. *What will we talk about after the children are gone?* becomes a crucial question when people expect to live thirty or forty years beyond that marker event. And marriage takes on a different and more complex character as a whole new set of needs comes to the fore.

Although class, race, and ethnicity all affect marriage patterns, only among African-Americans do the marital statistics tell a significantly different story. In 1991 just over 41 percent of black Americans were married, compared to nearly 62 percent among whites and Hispanics.[8] Thirty-five percent of blacks have never been married, while for whites the comparable figure is 20 percent. And black brides and grooms are, on the average, two years older than their white counterparts when they walk down the aisle for the first time.[9]

For as long as I can remember, I've heard these differences explained as an artifact of culture—an explanation that suggests that blacks value marriage less or that their moral code is less lofty than the one by which other Americans live. It's an easy explanation, one that allows us to look away from unpalatable social realities and their effect on the most personal decisions of our lives. If culture is the culprit, then it's the people who need fixing, not society. But, in fact, beneath these cold statistics lies a story of immeasurable human suffering and loneliness.

This is not to say that culture plays no part in the marriage patterns of African-Americans. Their history of slavery and the prejudice and discrimination they have suffered since then undoubtedly have left their mark in the shape of subcultural variations that affect beliefs and attitudes about marriage. Obviously, too, the cultural fallout from past experience can take on a life of its own and linger into the present long after the immediate provocations are gone. But in this case, it's the social and economic realities of life in the black community today, not the adversity and suffering of the past, that control the difference in marriage rates between blacks and Americans of other ethnic and racial groups.

The official unemployment rate for adult black men, for example, is roughly 15 percent, compared to 6.8 percent for white men.[10] And it's common knowledge that more than twice that number never make it to the Labor Department's unemployment statistics. At the same time, black men in the prime marriageable ages of twenty-five to thirty who are lucky enough to have jobs earn nearly one-third less than whites: $14,333 compared to $20,153.[11] With unemployment so high and underemployment virtually epidemic, it's hard to imagine how either women or men could make serious plans for marriage. A man who can barely support himself isn't likely to look forward to taking on the responsibilities of a wife and children. Nor is a woman apt to see him as a great marriage prospect. Add to these economic realities the fact that roughly one in eighty young black men is a victim of violent death[12] and that half the inmates of our state prisons are black men,[13] and we have a picture of a community with an acute shortage of marriageable men.[14]

These are the social conditions out of which the marriage patterns of the African-American community have grown. To speak of culture and its effect on the timing and sequencing of the various life stages, including when or if we marry, without knowing the particular life circumstances of a people misses the crucial connection between the emergence of cultural forms and the structure of social life. In the African-American community, eligible women far outnumber marriageable men—the major reason why fewer people are able to make the trip to the altar—and also why those who marry do so substantially later than men and women in other ethnic and racial groups.

For a black woman, then, finding a man with whom to share her life presents a far more daunting challenge than for others of the same class and age—a source of concern to both parents and daughters in the African-American families I met.[15] "I worry that my daughter's never going to find a good man," Regina Peterson, a forty-year-old black cashier says, shaking her head sadly. "It's not like when I was coming up; there were still some good men around then, like her father. He's a good man; he always took care of his family, even when it was hard. But today, whew, I don't know what these young girls will do. It's a real problem."

Regina's husband, Sherman, echoes her worries and adds angrily, "The young men today, they're nothing but bums. I don't want no daughter of mine taking up with the likes of them."

When I meet Althea, the Petersons' eighteen-year-old daughter, she talks solemnly about the difficulties the dearth of marriageable men raises for black women, then exclaims hotly: "It's crazy; it makes me so mad. The papers and the TV keep saying about how black girls are always having babies without being married and how we should wait and get married. But who are we supposed to marry, tell me, huh? It's not like there's some great guys sitting around just waiting for us. Most of the guys around here, they're hanging on the corner talking big talk, but they're never going to amount to anything. When I see those white people on the TV telling us we should get married, I just want to tell them to shut up because they don't know what they're talking about. What black girl wouldn't want to be married instead of raising her kids alone?"

I wonder, as I listen to her, what this young woman who's headed for the middle class will do when her time comes. So I ask: "What about you? Will you have children alone if you don't find someone to marry?"

She sits quietly for a moment, her chin resting on her closed fist, her brow furrowed in an expression of sober concentration, then says, "I can't say what I'll do. Right now I know I have to get educated if I want to make something of myself. When I finish college and have a good job, then I'll see. I know I want children some day; not now, but someday. And I'd like to be married like my parents; I know it's better for kids that way. But what if I can't find someone to marry? Then I don't know for sure, but I think I probably would have kids on my own. It's better than not having any, isn't it?" she concludes rhetorically.

Until recently, most white working-class women continued to believe that marriage would shelter them from the world of work. It made no difference that these women usually grew up in families where necessity forced their mothers into paid jobs outside the home. The fantasy resisted reality. Nor were the daydreams of these adolescent girls conceived in a vacuum. Partly they were responding to the gender culture of the times, a culture reinforced by media images that assured women that their salvation lay in finding the "right" man. But those images generally were bolstered in the home—by mothers who clung to the illusion that their daughters' lives could be different if only they married right; by fathers who believed that the only validation and affirmation for a woman was in the arms of a man.

"When I think about it now, it's amazing, isn't it?" reflects Roseanne Porter, a white thirty-five-year-old divorced mother of three. "Here was my mother, working her tail off, then coming home to take care of everybody. I think she used to get up about five in the morning so she could get the house cleaned up and all before she went to work. I don't know for sure, but I don't think she ever had a really good day with my father. And what do I hear from her all my life: 'All you have to do is find the right guy and you'll live happily ever after.'"

Her words jolted me, reminding me as they did of my own past and bringing sharply into focus the many such conversations I had with my mother. "You don't have to go to college; you'll get married and your husband will take care of you," she declared every time the subject of my future arose. It seemed so reasonable that neither she nor I noticed how absurd her certainty was. Absurd because her own husband, my father, died when I was five and my brother six, leaving her a twenty-six-year-old widow with two small children to support. Having emigrated to the United States from a village in eastern Europe just a few years earlier, she was virtually penniless, barely able to speak English, with neither family nor marketable skills to smooth the way. It took more than two years of bitter poverty and the humiliation of having to ask for public assistance before she finally found her way into New York's garment industry, where she was laboring as a piece worker at the very time she spoke with such certainty about my own secure future.

It wasn't that my mother was without aspirations for me. Like Roseanne Porter, I was expected to marry well, which in my family meant a middle-class man who would provide me with all my mother never could. Until that happy day arrived, I would work in an office. But so powerful was the ideology about women, men, and family life that, despite her own experience, my mother took for granted that for me work would be temporary, only until my real life as a wife and mother would begin.

But this is one of the arenas of living where race, not class, determines the hopes and dreams of a people. Few black women, even those who grew up in stable working- and middle-class homes, shared the fantasies about their role in marriage that were so common among whites twenty years ago. The black women I spoke with always knew that, married or not, they'd have to work. "I never thought about not working after I got married. I don't think I ever knew women who didn't work," says Delia Burkhard, a thirty-four-year-old married mother of two who works as an order taker for a catalog company.

Even those who might have succumbed to adolescent daydreams about being milk-and-cookie mommies whose husbands would take care of them and their children forever were quickly prodded back to reality by mothers who tried to protect their daughters from the sting of disillusion. "Black girls are brought up to know they're going to work their whole life," says twenty-nine-year-old Gloria Whittley, a legal secretary who's also a single mother. "When I was a teenager and I'd say some sappy thing about getting married and the white picket fence, my mama would remind me: 'Girl,' she'd say, 'you better put that nonsense out of your head and get down to studying so you can learn how to take care of yourself because nobody's going to do it for you.'"

With the changed economy, however, the fantasies about marriage that once separated white women from their black counterparts have faded. Like their black sisters, few white working-class girls or young women now harbor the illusion that they'll be stay-at-home moms. Since it's harder to convince themselves that they're working just to mark time until real life begins with the man of their dreams, work becomes a more central part of their life plan.

Twenty-year-old Nancy Krementz, a white clerk in a New York insurance company who lives with her family, talks about her expectations: "If I'm going to have to work after I get married anyway, I might as well wait. This way I get to do things I wouldn't be able to if I was married and had kids. This job I've got is okay, but I really want to work myself up a little. I figure if I'm going to have to work, I want to do something more interesting. So I'm taking some night courses on the computer now, and maybe I can get one of the better jobs in the company. I don't know, sometimes I even think maybe I'll go to college. I couldn't do that if I was married, could I?"

The men also have no plans to rush into marriage. "I'm not going to get married for a long time," says Nancy's nineteen-year-old brother, Michael. "It's not like it used to be when my father was growing up. People expected to get married right away out of school. But not now. I'm going to have some fun before I get married, you know, meet a lot of girls, travel around, things like that."

For the men, such dreams aren't new, even if they were rarely fulfilled. But the women's talk about work, about travel, about wanting to live on their own for a while—all options that few young working-class women dared dream of in my earlier study— represents a dramatic shift from the past. "Sure, I want to get married some day, but I'm not ready to settle down—not for a long time yet," says Claire Stansell, a white nineteen-year-old office worker. "There's too many other things I want to do, like traveling and seeing different things. You know," she says, her eyes opening wide, "the first time I was ever on an airplane was last year after I graduated high school and got a job."

The changing marriage patterns have had a profound effect on the lives of working-class families. Among the families I interviewed two decades ago, it was unthinkable for an unmarried daughter to live outside the family home. From father's house to husband's, that was the expectation, the accepted way of life for a young working-class woman then. Even sons generally were expected to live at home until they married, partly because their earnings were important to the family economy but also because it was the way of the world in which they lived. Now, both daughters and sons are eager to leave the parental roof as quickly as they can afford it.

But how does this fit with all the stories we hear about adult children who don't *want* to leave home these days because it's easier, cheaper, and more comfortable to live with their parents? Once again, class tells. Middle-class adolescents have long expected to leave home at eighteen, when they go off to college. For them, therefore, there may be some novelty in coming back into the family household as adults, essentially able to live their lives as they please.

For the grown children of working-class families, however, it isn't living at home that's new; it's the cultural changes over the last two decades that have made it possible to think about leaving. For them, this has been a liberation—a liberation the failing economy has stripped from them and about which they're unhappy and resentful.

But the culture of class isn't the whole answer. Class culture is, after all, bred in the economics of class. And it's in their different economic situations that particular attitudes about living at home are born, as this chance conversation I had with the twenty-four-year-old son of an upper middle-class white professional family shows so clearly: "I moved back into the old homestead because it's more comfortable than anything I can afford," he explained easily. "My old room's still there; the food and service is great; and it doesn't cost anything. I've got plenty of privacy; nobody pays any attention to my comings and goings. So why not? This way I get to live the life I'm used to, which I can't afford on my own. I can travel when I want and do what I want. Instead of wasting the money I make on the exorbitant rents you have to pay in this city, I put it into living a decent life. I guess it's got its down side, but the up side outweighs it by a lot so far."

He spoke so easily about freedom and privacy that I found myself wondering: *Would this be equally true for the daughters in these families? Would parents be as easy about a daughter's privacy, about her comings and goings, about where she might be spending the night, or with whom she might be sharing her bed?* Although there are no good studies to answer these questions, the significantly smaller proportion of women aged twenty-five to thirty-four who live under the parental roof (32 percent of single men, 20 percent of the women) suggests that far fewer women than men voluntarily make this choice.[16]

This digression aside, my conversation with my young friend was illuminating, since it raised so sharply the difference class makes for young adults who live at home. As Katherine Newman, an anthropologist writing about the declining fortunes of the middle class, puts it, "It is precisely among the more affluent of America's families that the drop in a young person's standard of living is most acutely apparent when they move out on their own. Hence it comes as little surprise to discover that children living in households with annual incomes above $50,000 are more likely to remain at home with their parents than those in households less well heeled."[17]

For the working-class young, living at home is a necessity, not a choice. And necessity rarely makes good bedfellows or housemates. Like the adult children of middle-class families, the young people I met also "get to live the life" they're used to. But it's not a life they covet. For there's not much of an "up side" to outweigh the down in a house that was already too small to permit privacy when they were children, a house whose walls seem even more confining in adulthood. Nor does living at home allow them the freedom to travel or the chance to do what they want—the very things that make living with Mom and Dad an attractive alternative for children of the middle class.

In working-class families, where it's a stretch to pay the bills each month, there's no free ride for adult children who live under the parental roof. Instead, a substantial portion of their income goes to paying their way. Socially, too, living at home confines their lives much more closely than if they were out of the house. For unlike the culturally liberal middle-class parents of the young man above, most working-class parents continue to try to keep a tight rein on their children and to insist on a code of moral behavior that more closely matches their own.

In *Worlds of Pain* I argued that the authoritarian child-rearing style so often found in working-class families stems in part from the fact that parents see around them so many young people whose lives are touched by the pain and delinquency that so often accompanies a life of poverty. Therefore, these parents live in fear for their children's future—fear that they'll lose control, that the children will wind up on the streets or, worse yet, in jail.

But the need for the kind of iron control working-class parents so often exhibit has another, more psychological, dimension as well. For only if their children behave properly by their standards, only if they look and act in ways that reflect honor on the family, can these parents begin to relax about their status in the world, can they be assured that they will be distinguished from those below. This is their ticket to respectability—the neat, well-dressed, well-behaved, respectful child; the child who can be worn as a badge, the public certification of the family's social position.

Since neither the internal needs nor the external conditions change when children reach adulthood, working-class parents continue to try to control their adult children's behavior so long as they live under the parental roof. "It's my house; he'll do what I say," is a favorite saying of fathers in these households. Obviously, it doesn't work that way much of the time. But this doesn't keep them from trying—an effort that makes for plenty of intergenerational conflict.

It was no surprise, therefore, that—whether male or female—every one of the working-class young adults I interviewed was itching to find a way out of the parental home. "As soon as I got a job and saved some money, me and my two friends found this apartment," explains Emily Petrousso, a white nineteen-year-old who shares a tiny one-bedroom apartment with two roommates.

"How did your parents feel about your moving out?"

She makes a face, wrinkling her nose, and says with a shrug, "My mom's okay; I think she understands. But my father, he's something else; like, he's living in another century. He still thinks it's terrible that I don't live in his house and get his permission to go out on a date. Both of them worry about the neighborhood I live in; like, they're afraid it's not safe and stuff like that. But it's okay now. It was a big deal at first, but they got used to it. And anyhow they knew they couldn't stop me."

"They knew they couldn't stop me"—a sentence her parents wouldn't have dared to speak at her age and precisely the source of parental concern. "You got no control over kids anymore!" storms Emily's father, George, a second-generation Greek-American. "What the hell's a kid like that doing out there living by herself. We got room here; nobody gets in her way. If my sister would've even *thought* about something like that, my father would've killed her. I'm just glad he's not alive to see what kids do today. It's not right; I tell my wife that all the time. But even she don't listen; she just sticks up for her."

His wife, Nicole, whose role in the family has always been to soothe and smooth the relationships between father and children, tells it this way: "He thinks I stick up for Emily; I don't know, maybe I do, but it's only because he gets so crazy sometimes, and I'm afraid if he keeps going at her like that, she'll stop coming around." She pauses, thinks for a moment, then continues with a sigh, "So I keep telling him she's a good girl, but everything's different now. You can't compare what we were like. I mean, I didn't even *think* about the things she talks about doing, like going on some kind of a trip by myself or with a girl-friend. *Who thought about things like that?* I don't know; what do you say to kids today about anything? It's so different now."

"Is it just different, or do you also think it's worse?" I ask Nicole.

She looks surprised at the question, then after a moment leans forward in her chair and lowers her voice as if to confide a guilty secret: "You know, I ask myself that question, but I don't hear any-body else wondering about it like I do. So then I think maybe there's something wrong with me. Everybody's always talking about how bad things are, you know, how the kids do such terrible things, and all that. But sometimes I sit here thinking I don't know if it's so bad; it's such a different world. I mean, some things are worse, sure, but maybe not everything. I mean, was it so good in our days?

"In a way I'm kind of glad she doesn't live here now. This way I don't have to see what she's doing all the time. I know she does things I wouldn't like; she doesn't tell me, but I know. My husband, he knows, too, I guess. It's why he's so angry at her all the time." She sighs, "Me? I worry a lot because I don't know how it'll end." She pauses as she hears her words and laughs. "That's it, you don't know the end of the story, so you worry."

"You don't know the end of the story, so you worry." This is precisely the issue. But it's not just the end of the moral story that's in question, it's the economic future that's also unknown. True, working-class parents have always worried about economic hard times for themselves and their children. But until the recent tur-moil in the economy, they could also dream about a better future. It's this new reality that has turned up the emotional register around the cultural changes. At the very moment that the economy has let them down, the moral structure on which they've built their lives has been shaken by a jolting, jarring upheaval that has shifted the ground on which they stand. If the old values are gone, what's to separate them from those below? What's to protect their chil-dren from falling into the abyss?

Is it any wonder that these families feel as if they're living on a fault line that threatens to open up and engulf them at any moment? Both economically and culturally they're caught in a whirlwind of change that leaves them feeling helplessly out of control. As they struggle with the shifting cultural norms—with the gap between the ideal statements of the culture in which they came to adulthood and the one into which their children are growing today—nothing seems to make sense anymore. Even those who inveigh most forcefully against the new morality and proclaim most angrily that "people don't know right from wrong anymore" are no longer so sure about what they really believe. Consequently, they respond to my questions about any number of the moral issues that vex them with unequivocal answers about right and wrong—only to retreat into uncertainty and ambivalence in the next sentence. They yearn for a past when, it seems to them, moral absolutes reigned, yet they're confused and uncertain about which of yesterday's moral strictures they want to impose on themselves and their children today.

It isn't that they're unaware that the absolutes didn't govern so absolutely, that what people said and what they did were often at odds. But the unambiguous rules seemed at least to promise a level of stability and a consensus that's missing now, not just in families but in the nation at large. The very clarity they seek eludes them, however, as they're forced by circumstances to make choices in their own families that fly in the face of their stated beliefs.

People who worry about the high divorce rate and insist on the sanctity of the family bond suddenly become less certain when marital misery hits home. Asked whether they would want their own child to stay in an obviously bad marriage—one where a spouse is abusive, an alcoholic, or a drug user, for example—the answer is an emphatic no, a response that's delivered especially forcefully by women who themselves have done so.

Women who say they believe mothers belong at home with their children leave to go to work every day. It's an economic necessity, they explain. But listen to them for a while and they'll soon admit that there's much about being in the world of work that they enjoy—and that they wouldn't give it up easily.

People who shudder at the idea of homosexuality take a deep breath and another look when a son or daughter comes out of the closet. They may weep bitter tears when they hear the news; they may deny the reality of what they've heard; they may rail against

God; they may blame themselves. But in most families, acceptance eventually comes. Asked how it's possible, given their earlier fears, feelings, and hostilities, they have many answers. "I see that he's happier now." "Her partner's such a nice person." "I didn't really understand about it before." "It's his choice; what can I do?" But the bottom line is: "This is my child!"

Parents who disapprove strongly of premarital sex also wish their children wouldn't marry as young as they themselves did. But they know, too, that their daughters are unlikely to remain celibate into their twenties. I say "daughters" because, despite the changing norms around female sexuality, a son's sexual activity is taken for granted, a daughter's is still a problem for most working-class parents. Asked to choose between an early marriage for a girl or premarital sex, most parents—especially mothers—opt for sex, consoling themselves with the hope that their daughters will wait until "they're old enough." What this means varies, of course, but the most common response is, "at least until they're eighteen."

People who don't approve of abortion will also tell you that they wouldn't want their sons and daughters to "have to marry." Forced to make a choice between a teenage marriage, an adoption, and an abortion, they agonize; they suffer; they equivocate. But when the last word is in, most come down on the side of abortion.[18]

This ambivalence, this simultaneous holding of two seemingly contradictory sets of beliefs, shouldn't surprise us. Changing cultures mean stormy times. The interaction between new norms and values and the people who must live them out is never tranquil and easy. The old consciousness doesn't go quietly into the night. Instead, it fusses and fumes, drags its feet, goads us with reminders of its existence, and foments an internal struggle that leaves us anxious and bewildered, wondering what we believe, how we feel.

It's not uncommon to find ourselves doing new things, even wanting to do them, while at the same time feeling uneasy about them. Many of the women who were in the forefront of the sexual revolution, for example, were surprised at the internal conflict their new behaviors stirred.[19] Observing this contest between the old and the new, some researchers concluded that the sexual constraints of the past were "natural," that women couldn't or didn't want to shed them. But those pundits misread the data. Partly they misunderstood what they saw because their vision was blurred by their deeply internalized traditional beliefs about the nature of female sexuality. But it was also because they didn't appreciate the messiness inherent in the process of cultural change, didn't understand that the internalization and integration of new cultural mores often lag well behind behavioral changes.

Indeed, the internal resistance to new ways of being generally has nothing to do with whether we can or want to change. Psychologists see this all the time—people who come into psychotherapy wanting to change, yet, when faced with the possibility, they retreat in fear. We call it "resistance," but in fact it's a normal human response. The old ways worked, perhaps imperfectly, perhaps with more pain than was necessary, but we acommodated and survived. Psychologically, therefore, it's hard to give them up even when we know there's a better way.

In our struggle to make sense of our rapidly changing world, to define rules for living that meet today's needs, old values are forced into a confrontation with the new realities of family and social life. The result is the emergence of values that are different—different and not always as firm and clear as we'd like them to be. Therefore, we become edgy and confused, wanting to reach back to the past, to a time when everything seemed more certain. But it's well to remember what historians of the family have been telling us for some time now: The golden age of the family for which we yearn with such intensity never really existed.[20] Instead, families have always been a "haven in a heartless world!" and a breeding ground for pain, sorrow, disappointment, and discontent.[21] Everyone who has ever lived in a family knows both sides. But our longing for what seems from this distance to be the simplicity and certainty of earlier times has blinded us to this complex reality of family life.

Yes, there are real problems in the family today, problems as large or larger than any we have ever known. Yes, we live in what one family scholar has called an "embattled paradise."[22] Yes, the changing cultural norms often leave parents and children without a blueprint for caring and responsible social and personal behavior. These are issues that deserve our serious attention and our considered thought. But the transformation of family life will not be reversed with endless discussions about the state of our moral culture. Instead they serve to turn our attention away from the central problems families face today—problems wrought at least in part by a government and an economy that long ago stopped working for all but the most privileged.

2

THE FAMILY AND THE ECONOMY

4

MOTHER GOES TO WORK

Has anyone ever seen a chapter in a book entitled "Father Goes to Work"? Father going to work is a fact of life, not something to write about, certainly not something to engender public concern. But when mother goes to work it's big news. Newspapers publish article after article about the numbers of married women with young children in the labor force; social scientists study the situation; politicians wring their hands in alarm and worry about the impact on the family.

Yet poor women have always held paid jobs outside the home. In fact, 58 percent of the working-class women I interviewed twenty years ago were in the labor force then, almost all of them in part-time jobs—a figure that matched the national statistics of the time. So why the flurry of public attention and concern in 1992, when there was barely a murmur in 1972?

Class plays its part. In 1972 it was poor and working-class families who needed a working wife to pay the bills. Today it's nearly everyone but the rich. When the pinch is felt by people at the lower end of the class spectrum, it's easy for politicians and the public not to notice. Or if they do, they can explain it as part of the "natural" order of things, a fact of life that the less fortunate have to endure. When it touches those who are middle class—families of relatives, friends, and neighbors who are no different from their own and who, in addition, have the social, political, and financial resources to make their discontent felt—then politicians take note and the state of the family becomes a matter of public debate and concern.

But class alone doesn't tell the whole story. Numbers, too, make a difference in bringing the issue of women, work, and family to center stage. Starting in the 1960s, the number of mothers with small children who have entered the paid work force has increased dramatically at all class levels. At the beginning of the 1960s, roughly 18 percent of married women with children under six worked outside the home; by 1970, the figure had jumped to 30 percent, an increase of 63 percent. The numbers continued to climb through the next two decades, until by 1991, 60 percent of these women were in the labor force, more than triple the 1960 figures.[1]

The older the children, the greater the number of women who work outside the home as well as inside. Over one-third of married women with children ages 6–17 were in the labor force in 1960, swelling to nearly two-thirds in 1980, and rising again to almost three-quarters by 1990.[2]

Even mothers of infants are now in the labor force in unprecedented numbers, about half of those with children under a year working at least part-time. And many, especially women at the upper and lower reaches of the work world, are back on the job full-time only weeks after the baby's birth—the professionals and executives because of the call of the work, the working-class women out of economic necessity. "I had to go back to work when my daughter was six weeks old, otherwise I would have lost my job," says Allie Wheatley, a twenty-six-year-old black clerical worker. "I cried for weeks when I had to leave that baby in day care, but what could I do? I didn't have a choice."

Add to all this the fact that women who worked part-time in 1972 are likely to be full-time workers in 1992, and it becomes obvious that these numbers are more than simple descriptive statistics. They are the driving force for change in family life. True, the modern feminist movement, which from its birth sought a fundamental reordering of the roles and relationships both inside the family and in the world outside, played an important part in the shifting nature of family life. But although feminism had independent meaning, power, and vitality, it was strengthened and reinforced by the changing economic situation of the family. Indeed, by the mid-1970s, the issues feminists had been addressing since the beginning of the movement were given urgency by the transformation in family life wrought by the declining economy. For the family and the economy are inextricably intertwined. And the interaction between them—between the economic conditions and the needs of the people who live in families—is always a significant factor in determining the quality and content of both family and social life.

It's no accident, for example, that the cult of female domesticity reached its zenith in the aftermath of World War II. A booming economy combined with families that had been torn apart by the war set the stage for the embrace of the gender roles that dominated the 1950s—the idealized mother-in-the-kitchen, father-in-the-office-or-factory family. In the 1970s, however, the economic and social situations were reversed. By then, inflation and wage stagnation were sending vast numbers of women out of the home and into the labor force at the same time that the costs of the gender role divisions of the 1950s were being counted in rising incidence of depression among women, increasing divorce rates, and a generalized sense of discontent with the quality of family life.[3]

By the 1990s, the struggle to reorder gender roles in the private realm as well as in the public one—a struggle that was once the province of the educated elite—had become part of the consciousness of women at all class levels. Twenty years ago when I asked working-class women about their response to the women's liberation movement, which was in full flower at the time, their talk was dominated largely by the negative stereotypes that were the fashion of the day. They complained that "women's libbers" held them in contempt because marriage and motherhood were at the center of their lives; they declared firmly that the issues the movement spoke to were irrelevant to them. Even when they held paid jobs outside the home, they defined themselves as wives and mothers, not as workers. Work was something they *did*, an instrumental activity that served the economic needs of the family. They may also have felt good to be out of the house for a few hours each day, to have their competence acknowledged there. But "wife" and "mother" remained at the core of their identity; these defined who they *were*. Therefore, the movement's focus on women and work seemed alien to them.[4]

Then, too, both husband and wife claimed that her income was discretionary, just so they could buy some luxury they couldn't otherwise afford—a new car, a camper, a family vacation, new furniture for the living room. Sometimes it was true. More often it was a myth constructed to protect the husband from the knowledge that he didn't earn enough to meet the family's needs. But such fictions no longer work. Now everyone agrees that a woman must work if a family is to maintain its life-style—a changed definition of the situation that has created a whole new set of expectations.

Although the women I interviewed for this book are the class and status counterparts of those I spoke with twenty years ago, they no longer think that women's issues don't have much to do with them. Quite the opposite! But the backlash against feminism in both the public world and their private one has been effective.[5] Therefore, the questions I asked about it were met with contradiction and ambivalence, depending on whether we were talking about feminism in the abstract or about specific issues feminists have engaged. Indeed, it quickly became clear to me that what women *say* about feminism and what they *do* about it—that is, how they live their lives—are strikingly different. And it's equally clear that there are some significant differences between white women and women of color.

Among the white women, I had only to mention the word *feminism* and the talk turned quickly to caricature and stereotype. Feminists, they said repeatedly, are "too hard," "too aggressive," "too pushy," "too loud," "too demanding," "not soft and feminine enough," "not like women." "I'd never be a feminist because they want women to give up being feminine and soft," explains twenty-seven-year-old Carla Kempinski, a white married mother of two daughters who works as a claims adjuster for an insurance company. "I like to be able to cry, you know, and they talk like that's being weak or something."

But when I asked about specifics—equity on the job, sexual

harassment, the glass ceiling, women in politics, or any other of the issues in the public arena where feminists have made a dent—the same women have decidedly feminist opinions, although they're rarely labeled so. "Yeah, I'm glad it [the women's movement] happened because otherwise I wouldn't have my job. My company didn't used to hire women to be adjusters before that," says Carla, who moments earlier had insisted that she'd "never be a feminist."

Women of color also often criticize feminists, but not because they're "too aggressive." They complain instead that they feel left out, that their particular needs and concerns aren't met by what they see as a white feminist movement—a criticism voiced with particular force by the African-American women I spoke with.[6] "Those feminists are all too white for my taste," says June Davis, a thirty-two-year-old black cashier, married with two children.

The complaint about the feminist movement being "too white" is a common one, whether coming from women like June or from black feminist scholars. In a critique of essentialism in feminist theory—that is, the idea that there's a unitary women's experience that's independent of race, class, or sexual orientation—Angela Harris, an African-American legal scholar, writes that "in removing issues of 'race' [feminists] have actually only managed to remove black women—meaning that white women now stand as the epitome of Woman."[7]

Certainly there are experiences that are common to all women simply by virtue of their gender. Rape, for example. But a history that for centuries made black women fair game for white men makes the *meaning* of the experience vastly different for black women than for white ones. As Harris argues: "For black women, rape is a far more complex experience, and an experience as deeply rooted in color as in gender." The rape of a black woman, for example, wasn't a crime during slavery. And even after the Civil War, when laws against rape formally included all women, black women seldom found legal protection there. "Rape, in this sense, was something that only happened to white women; what happened to black women was simply life," Harris concludes.[8]

These grievances against the feminist movement notwithstanding, even its harshest critics among women of color agree that it has been important in changing their lives. "There's lots of things I don't like about those feminists, but I know I wouldn't be where I am if those white women hadn't stood up and hollered," says Rebecca Ford, a black twenty-nine-year-old UPS driver. "They didn't get it right in lots of ways, especially about African-American women and what we want, but their hollering opened some doors for the rest of us. So I guess we owe them something, too. It wasn't black women who were making all that noise."

It's not just in the public arena that the discourse about feminism is marked by contradiction. When, for example, I asked women whether they wished for greater mutuality and equality in their relationships with men, no matter what their race or ethnic background, no matter how passionately they had disclaimed any feminist sympathies a moment earlier, they answered with a resounding yes. But rarely without the obligatory bow in the direction of tradition.

"To tell you the truth, I think they go too far. I'm a firm believer in making your man feel like a king; you know, a man's home is his castle, and all that," Maria Acosta, a white twenty-eight-year-old secretary answers airily. Then with barely a pause for breath, she adds, "But I don't mean I want to be like my mom. She waits on my father all the time, and he never does anything for her. It's like he thinks everybody's supposed to bow down to him just because he's a man, and she does. I won't do that for anybody. Why should I? I'm as equal as him." The flow of words stops; her face lights with a smile as she hears the contradiction. "That doesn't make a lot of sense, huh?"

"Well, it does sound as if maybe you want your husband to *feel* like a king, but you don't want him *acting* like one," I reply.

She laughs aloud, "I guess that's right, isn't it? That's how I was brought up, that a woman's supposed to make a man feel like a king, so I think I *should* feel that way. But why should I have to be doing for him all the time? I don't mind making him feel important; I like it sometimes. But I want him to take care of me and make me feel important, too. I think everything should be shared in a relationship."

Even the African-American women, who feel keenly the cost of the racism and discrimination that has followed black men for so long, speak with ambivalence. "Black men have had a real hard time in this country," says Melodie McGaugh, a thirty-two-year-old divorced mother of two. "When you've been knocked around the way they have, it has to threaten you as a man. So I think women have to help them that way, you know, give a little, let them feel like they're, you know, a big man, sometimes. But these brothers who think women should bow down to them, forget it; it's not going to happen.

"I look around and see all these black men who can't take care of anybody, not even themselves. It's not their fault; it's because this society doesn't give them a real chance. That makes me real mad, but it's not my fault, and I don't see how getting on my knees will help."

The yearning for change in their family relationships is powerful among virtually all the women I spoke with. But as much as they talk about it, as much as they struggle with their husbands, there's also a resigned acceptance of the limits of the possible.[9] "I guess I don't like the idea of defined roles," continues Maria Acosta. "I think people should be able to reciprocate to each other. But men, well," she sighs, "you know, they're hard to change. It makes me mad sometimes, then I think I guess I don't blame them for liking it the way it is. It's different when you're a woman; you haven't got anything to lose."

The willingness of working-class women to engage the struggle, whether around emotional reciprocity or the division of family labor—the consciousness that "it's different when you're a woman; you haven't got anything to lose"—is one of the most striking changes in recent years. It isn't that women in the past were unaware that they had less power than their husbands to define the structure of the marital relationship. But they were less willing to articulate such thoughts, often couldn't even acknowledge them to themselves. Or if they did, they were much more likely than women today to accept the difference, even to maintain that it was legitimate.

What, then, are we to make of women like Maria Acosta who dislike the traditional role definitions, long for a relationship of equality and reciprocity, yet deny any affinity with feminism and continue to wrestle with the old idea that a man ought to "feel like a king"? At the unconscious level, such words reflect the depth at which gender roles have been internalized. We may speak a new gender language, and even mean what we say, but unconsciously the old rules, battered and bruised though they may be, remain buried inside us, tripping us up when we least expect it, leaving us conflicted about issues we thought we had resolved.

Consequently, strong, independent, high-achieving women still too often want men who are bigger, better, stronger, and smarter. And men who believe in a woman's right to full independence still want women whose dependency and need will make them feel manly. Consciously, neither wants to feel this way, may even deny it to themselves. Unconsciously, the old gender rules still retain their power to make trouble for us in unexpected ways.

The phenomenon whereby people can't allow themselves to know what they know, to experience what they feel plays its part well—a situation psychotherapists confront often. Ask a question that threatens to reveal feelings or thoughts that seem dangerous, and the answer comes back filled with confusion, with anger at the questioner, or with some combination of both. It's this kind of muddling of their feelings, this kind of denial, that sets the stage for the confused and contradictory remarks women make so often. For to know how angry they are would be to jeopardize their relations with their husbands and to endanger the family they've worked so hard to maintain.

At the more conscious level, the notion that a man ought to "feel like a king" may be little more than a nod to social convention, a token bow to male authority, a way to assuage male fears. For the immediate and felt source of the expression of such thoughts is the woman's need to relieve her own apprehension, to soothe her anxiety about the future of her marriage if she asserts herself and her wishes too forcefully. "The problem is that men need to feel important," Maria confides. "So if you want to live with them . . . " Her words trail off, as if the obvious doesn't need to be spoken, perhaps is too difficult to speak aloud, too direct and overt a reminder of the distance between what her life is and what she'd like it to be.

It's no surprise, therefore, that at the same time that these women grasp eagerly at the benefits feminism has brought in the public world and wish fervently that they could put in place many of its goals in their private worlds, they also disavow any connection to feminism and shrink from applying the label to themselves. This is their sop to the scorn the word *feminist* elicits in their social world. It's their way of making a public statement that they're "real" women—soft, nurturing, caring; their way of trying to reassure themselves about their femininity, about their capacity to be good wives and mothers; and their attempt to appease the hostility of their husbands. And this, too, is their gift to their husbands—a gift to compensate for the men's pain, for the knowledge both husbands and wives carry inside about the fragility of their lives and their families; a gift that seeks to ease the men's anxiety about their manhood by allowing them to believe that they retain the power to define what a woman ought to be.

The men, hearing their wives' words, sigh with relief that the women they live with aren't "like those feminists." "These goddamn feminists and their crazy ideas, they're making women nuts today," explodes Joe Acosta, Maria's thirty-one-year-old husband of seven years. "Don't get me wrong, Maria's not one of them, no way. She knows who wears the pants, not like those, excuse me, ball-busting feminists." Words that echo on the tongues and in the hearts of about three-quarters of the working-class husbands I met.

But why focus only on working-class men? Is it impossible to imagine middle-class men speaking such words? Twenty years ago I argued that middle-class men were more facile with the language of gender equality and more ready to give verbal assent to the idea than their working-class brothers. And I also noted that the gap between word and deed was wide and deep—a gap that still exists in most middle-class families today. So while the words Joe Acosta spoke aren't likely to cross the lips of well-educated, middle-class men, the thoughts probably are not so alien to them.

In fact, it may be that over the last two decades, the greatest shifts in relations between men and women have taken place in working-class families rather than in middle-class ones. Two decades ago I found few working-class men who would even give lip service to the notion of gender equality, whether inside or outside the house. Today many of the men I interviewed are quite sensitive to the needs and wishes of their wives. It's true this sensitivity often isn't translated into action. But the very assertion of the ideology of equality by men who resisted it so thoroughly before is itself a step forward, the first perhaps in the struggle for genuine change in the family.

Why, then, do men like Joe Acosta talk about wanting to "wear the pants" and complain about "ball-busting feminists"? Such words are a way of expressing their sentiments about the changes that have been forced upon them by social and economic forces over which they have no control—their own diminished real income, their insecurity about the future, the entry of their wives into the labor force on a full-time basis, and the new demands their women are making on them. By displacing their hostility onto "those feminists," they attack women who are safe targets of their anger precisely because they're "out there."

The fears and feelings these men express are made worse by the fact that a working wife usually does mean at least some small shift in the balance of power in the marriage. "She's different since she went to work, more independent, you could say. We fight a lot more now than we used to."

Despite the stereotypic words they so often speak, however, most working-class husbands have a complicated reaction to their working wives. They appreciate the income; they feel their own burdens are better understood now; they sometimes even say their wives are more interesting since they've gone to work. "It's different; I can talk to her better now. She knows what it's like out there, so if I got a gripe, she doesn't just listen, she's got something to say back," says Doug Wright, a white thirty-year-old forklift operator, the father of two children, married eight years.

At the same time, they can't fully shake the feeling that they've failed at their primary task. They know that times are different now, that the economic pressures that sent their wives to work have nothing to do with their personal failure. But knowing these things and believing them are not always the same. "I know she doesn't mind working, but it shouldn't have to be that way," Doug says, shaking his head morosely. "A guy should be able to support his wife and kids. But that's not the way it is these days, is it? I don't know anybody who can support a family anymore, do you?" he asks rhetorically. Then, after a moment, he adds,"Well, I guess those rich guys can, but not some ordinary Joe like me."

The shared understanding that, like her husband, a wife works because she must has not only helped women to be more independent but also has freed them to own a formerly unrecognized side of themselves. Twenty years ago the women who worked outside the home almost always spoke uneasily of the gratifications they found in their jobs, as if they were betraying their families by admitting that something else could hold their interest and bring them satisfaction. Now nearly all the women I interviewed freely acknowledge that, although they may have entered the paid work force because of economic need, they enjoy the benefits they've found there and would not leave willingly.

But they also suffer plenty of guilt and anxiety about not fulfilling their maternal role in traditional ways. So the same women who talk about the rewards of work also are haunted by the ghost of the 1950s milk-and-cookies TV mom. "I like to work; it makes me feel good about myself," says Julia Rumford, a black twenty-eight-year-old mother of two children. "But I have to admit, I never feel like I'm a full mom, and that bothers me a lot. So I'm always trying to make up for it. I bake cookies; I make their Halloween costumes; I'm always volunteering for something or other, you know, like maybe I can make up for not being there all the time."

The notion that mom should be there for the children always and without fail, that her primary job is to tend and nurture them, that without her constant ministrations their future is in jeopardy, is deeply embedded in our national psyche. Therefore, no woman who is also a mother escapes guilt about not doing her job as the culture decrees it, not even the woman who has been in the forefront of the struggle to change those prescriptions. Nor does she live without anxiety about the outcome when she can't fulfill her socially ordained role. "It's hard to be away at work all day and be a good mother." "Every day I leave my kids at day care, I think to myself: *What kind of mother am I?* It's like I'm not raising my own children." "What if something happens with one of the kids? I'd never forgive myself." "When one of my kids got in trouble, even my mother said it was because I was working."

No one, not even these mothers, talk about fathers and their responsibility for how their children grow. For despite the enormous ferment in family life over these last decades, the cultural definition of the good parent has changed little. Parenting, if by that we mean the nurturing of both the body and the spirit of our children, remains woman's work. It's mother who's still held accountable for their moral development, their emotional stability, and their worldly success or failure. Father need only make a living for them to satisfy his part of the bargain. Any unanticipated ripple in the children's development is quite simply mom's failure.

Even single mothers—women who work because their children wouldn't have anything to eat if they didn't—aren't exempt from the anxiety that is every working mother's lot. "My husband walked out on me when I was pregnant with my third child. He said it was just too much; he couldn't handle it," reports Janice Wormeley, a thirty-two-year-old white secretary. "It's hard being a single mother, damn hard. Nobody gives us the credit for sticking with it and making a family for the kids. Instead of giving us some encouragement, they're talking all the time about how terrible it is for kids to grow up without a father. Yeah, well, it's terrible for me, too.

"What do they think, that I wouldn't like to have somebody to help raise and support these kids? I don't, so I do the best I can. But it gets discouraging when I keep reading that, no matter what I do, my kids are going to have trouble. I look at my kids and think they're okay. They're doing all right in school; they don't give me any trouble. But I worry anyway about it all the time. I mean, it's true: How can you be a good mother and work all day long?"

I know her question is a rhetorical one, that she doesn't expect an answer. But I wonder anyway how I would answer it. For the question of who will raise the children is surely one of the most important social issues of our time. What would our society be like if we cared enough to provide a first-rate child-care system for families with working parents? What would family life look like if fathers were expected to be real partners in caring for their children?[10]

But it's the notion of "the good mother" that engages me most deeply at the moment. What would a different conception of a good mother look like? I think about the time when I was a young child and my widowed mother left my brother and me to go to work every day. Although the streets were our home in the hours after school, no one thought she was a bad mother. She was simply doing what she had to do. Nor did anyone expect us to grow up to be delinquents or dropouts because my mother wasn't there to tend to our every need.

Why is it so different now? One answer surely lies in the realm of ideology. The ideal of the good mother that lives so powerfully inside us is a relatively new one, an ideal type that reached its zenith in the aftermath of World War II, when the economic needs of the nation came together with the psychological needs of a war-torn population. Then, the economy needed women to leave the work force and head the drive toward a greatly expanded consumer society. And people, starved for the family life they had put on hold during the war, hungry for the goods they couldn't buy before, were happy to oblige.

But the old image of mom in the kitchen with an apron tied around her middle no longer fits either the economic or psychological lives of families today. Universally, the women I interviewed work because they must. Almost as often they find a level of self-fulfillment and satisfaction on the job that they're loath to give up, even in the face of the guilt and anxiety they suffer. "I started to work because I had to. My husband got hurt on the job and the bills started piling up, so I had to do something," explains thirty-four-year-old Victoria Segunda, the assistant manager in a children's clothing store and the Latina mother of three children. "But it starts as a necessity and it becomes something else.

"I didn't imagine how much I'd enjoy going to work in the morning. I mean, I love my kids and all that, but let's face it, being mom can get pretty stale. I mean, it's wonderful, and I know it's better if I'm home when they come home from school," she hastens to add, uncomfortable about how I might interpret her enthusiasm for her work. "You know what I mean, don't you? The kids are great. But going to work, that's like, hmmmmm, that's like another reason to live. Since I went to work I'm more interested in life, and life's more interested in me."

Like so many other women, Victoria speaks of cherishing the enhanced sense of competence she has gained as a result of her work experience. "I started as a part-time salesperson and now I'm assistant manager. One day I'll be the manager," she says proudly. "Sometimes I'm amazed at what I've accomplished; I had no idea I could do all this, be responsible for a whole business like that. My husband, he keeps looking forward to when all the bills are paid and I can stay home again. But I don't ever want to stop working. Why would I?"

Her words, which had been flowing so freely, suddenly skid to a halt; her animated face turns still. She leans forward and in a voice that drops almost to a whisper, cautions me: "Don't tell him I said that. He'd feel bad if he knew. I just don't say anything when he talks about my not working. Besides I figure we'll never see the day when all the bills are paid anyway, so why should I aggravate him about it now?"

This caution put behind her, her exuberance returns as she continues to talk about her heightened self-esteem. "I feel different about myself, like sometimes I look in the mirror and say, 'Hey, Vicky, is this really you?' I mean, I deal with salespeople and customers, and I know all about inventory control, and I make out everybody's schedule—you know, all the things you have to know to manage a store like that. I'm even doing some of the buying now. It's very complicated, but I know it all," she concludes exultantly.

Repeatedly, too, women speak of being more in control of their lives. "I couldn't believe what a difference it made when I went to work," recounts Joy Siri, a thirty-nine-year-old white woman, married eighteen years and with three teenage children. "I feel like I've got my own life. I never felt like I really ruled my life before. You know, I went from my parents' house to my husband's. He's a good man, but he's bossy. Now I'm working just like him, so he can't just boss me around so much anymore. I mean, he still tries, but I don't have to let him."

For those who have never worked outside the home before, even a small income engenders a sense of financial independence in which they revel. "It's like I found out what it's really like to be grown up when I got my first paycheck. I still feel that way. Every time I go put my check in the bank, I feel proud, like, 'Wow, I earned this money; I did it,'" explains Sarah Jang, a twenty-seven-year-old Chinese cashier in a car wash, married with two children.

Feeling better about themselves, working women enter the family decision-making process in new and more forceful ways.

"Gary always made all the big decisions, and I never felt like I had a right to my say," says Phyllis Kilson, a forty-six-year-old white mother of four grown children who has been in the work force for the last four years. "I mean, I tried sometimes, but if he said no, I figured I didn't have a right to contradict him. Now I make money, too, so it's different. I go out and buy something for the grandchildren, or even for me, without asking him, and he can't say anything."

Twenty years ago most of the women I interviewed were uncertain at best about the issue of equal pay for equal work. On the one hand, they agreed that it was only fair; on the other, they believed that if a man had a family to support and a woman didn't, he *ought* to earn more than she. Now all the women, even those who greeted the idea with reservations two decades ago, endorse the principle of equal pay without equivocation. When I cited some recent statistics about the discrepancy between women's and men's earnings—for example, that median income for full-time working women in 1990 was $20,586 compared to $29,172 for men;[11] or that professional women earned on average $25,928, while men took home $47,432;[12] or that male secretaries and clerks earned $459 a week, while women doing the same jobs made $348—they were outraged.[13] "Before I went back to work I used to think that if a man was married, maybe it was okay if he made more than the woman," explains fifty-year-old Joanne Sonneman, one of the white women I spoke with two decades ago. "I figured after all, he has to support a family and the woman has a husband who supports her. But I don't think that anymore. Now it makes me really mad just to think that somebody who's doing the same work as I am is making more money.

"I mean, yeah, I've got a husband, but I'm not working for my health. We need the money, and every dollar I make helps. Anyway, when you work hard all day, you don't think about things like that; you just figure if you're doing a good job, you're entitled to the same pay as they give a man. Otherwise, it's not fair."

It's not only about pay inequities that women now cry, "It's not fair." The same women who once felt indebted to a husband who helped out—who cleared the table once in a while, who dried the dishes occasionally, who knew how to push a vacuum cleaner, who "baby sat" his children from time to time—now want their men to share more fully in the tasks of housekeeping and child rearing. "It's not fair," grumbles Josephine Kimball, a white thirty-six-year-old manicurist, married seventeen years. "Why should he get to read the paper or watch TV while I run around picking up the kids' toys and stuff, cooking supper, cleaning up afterward, and trying to give the kids some quality time? It would be different if I didn't work; then I wouldn't look for him to do any housework. But I put in my eight hours every day just like him, so I think he should do his share."

When this wish is transformed into a demand, it often becomes a wrenching source of conflict in these families.

5

THE TRANSFORMATION OF FAMILY LIFE

"I know my wife works all day, just like I do," says Gary Braunswig, a twenty-nine-year-old white drill press operator, "but it's not the same. She doesn't *have* to do it. I mean, she *has* to because we need the money, but it's different. It's not really her job to have to be working; it's mine." He stops, irritated with himself because he can't find exactly the words he wants, and asks, "Know what I mean? I'm not saying it right; I mean, it's the man who's supposed to support his family, so I've got to be responsible for that, not her. And that makes one damn big difference.

"I mean, women complain all the time about how hard they work with the house and the kids and all. I'm not saying it's not hard, but that's her responsibility, just like the finances are mine."

"But she's now sharing that burden with you, isn't she?" I remark.

"Yeah, and I do my share around the house, only she doesn't see it that way. Maybe if you add it all up, I don't do as much as she does, but then she doesn't bring in as much money as I do. And she doesn't always have to be looking for overtime to make an extra buck. I got no complaints about that, so how come she's always complaining about me? I mean, she helps me out financially, and I help her out with the kids and stuff. What's wrong with that? It seems pretty equal to me."

Cast that way, his formulation seems reasonable: They're each responsible for one part of family life; they each help out with the other. But the abstract formula doesn't square with the lived reality. For him, helping her adds relatively little to the burden of household tasks he *must* do each day. A recent study by University of Wisconsin researchers, for example, found that in families where both wife and husband work full-time, the women average over twenty-six hours a week in household labor, while the men do about ten.[1] That's because there's nothing in the family system to force him to accountability or responsibility on a daily basis. He may "help her out with the kids and stuff" one day and be too busy or preoccupied the next.

But for Gary's wife, Irene, helping him means an extra eight hours every working day. Consequently, she wants something more consistent from him than a helping hand with a particular task when he has the time, desire, or feels guilty enough. "Sure, he helps me out," she says, her words tinged with resentment. "He'll give the kids a bath or help with the dishes. But only when I ask him. He doesn't have to *ask* me to go to work every day, does he? Why should I have to ask him?"

"Why should I have to ask him?"—words that suggest a radically different consciousness from the working-class women I met twenty years ago. Then, they counted their blessings. "He's a steady worker; he doesn't drink; he doesn't hit me," they told me by way of explaining why they had "no right to complain."[2] True, these words were reminders to themselves that life could be worse, that they shouldn't take these things for granted—reminders that didn't wholly work to obscure their discontent with other aspects of the marriage. But they were nevertheless meaningful statements of value that put a brake on the kinds of demands they felt they could make of their men, whether about the unequal division of household tasks or about the emotional content of their lives together.

Now, the same women who reminded themselves to be thankful two decades ago speak openly about their dissatisfaction with the role divisions in the family. Some husbands, especially the younger ones, greet their wives' demands sympathetically. "I try to do as much as I can for Sue, and when I can't, I feel bad about it," says twenty-nine-year-old Don Dominguez, a Latino father of three children, who is a construction worker.

Others are more ambivalent. "I don't know, as long as she's got a job, too, I guess it's right that I should help out in the house. But that doesn't mean I've got to like it," says twenty-eight-year-old Joe Kempinski, a white warehouse worker with two children.

Some men are hostile, insisting that their wives' complaints are unreasonable, unjust, and oppressive. "I'm damn tired of women griping all the time; it's nothing but nags and complaints," Ralph Danesen, a thirty-six-year-old white factory worker and the father of three children, says indignantly. "It's enough! You'd think they're the only ones who've got it hard. What about me? I'm not living in a bed of roses either.

"Christ, what does a guy have to do to keep a wife quiet these days? What does she want? It's not like I don't do anything to help her out, but it's never enough."

In the past there was a clear understanding about the obligations and entitlements each partner took on when they married. He was obliged to work outside the home; she would take care of life inside. He was entitled to her ministrations, she to his financial support. But this neat division of labor with its clear-cut separation of rights and obligations no longer works. Now, women feel obliged to hold up their share of the family economy—a partnership men welcome. In return, women believe they're entitled to their husband's full participation in domestic labor. And here is the rub. For while men enjoy the fruits of their wives' paid work outside the home, they have been slow to accept the reciprocal responsibilities—that is, to become real partners in the work inside the home.

The women, exhausted from doing two days' work in one, angry at the need to assume obligations without corresponding entitlements, push their men in ways unknown before. The men, battered by economic uncertainty and by the escalating demands of their wives, feel embattled and victimized on two fronts—one outside the home, the other inside. Consequently, when their wives seem not to see the family work they do, when they don't acknowledge and credit it, when they fail to appreciate them, the men feel violated and betrayed. "You come home and you want to be appreciated a little. But it doesn't work that way, leastwise not here anymore," complains Gary Braunswig, his angry words at odds with sadness in his eyes. "There's no peace, I guess that's the real problem; there's no peace anywhere anymore."

The women often understand what motivates their husbands' sense of victimization and even speak sympathetically about it at times. But to understand and sympathize is not to condone, especially when they feel equally assaulted on both the home and the economic fronts. "I know I complain a lot, but I really don't ask for that much. I just want him to help out a little more," explains Ralph Danesen's wife, Helen, a thirty-five-year-old office worker. "It isn't like I'm asking him to cook the meals or anything like that. I know he can't do that, and I don't expect him to. But every time I try to talk to him, you know, to ask him if I couldn't get a little more help around here, there's a fight."

One of the ways the men excuse their behavior toward family work is by insisting that their responsibility as breadwinner burdens them in ways that are alien to their wives. "The plant's laying off people left and right; it could be me tomorrow. Then what'll we do? Isn't it enough I got to worry about that? I'm the one who's got all the worries; she doesn't. How come that doesn't count?" demands Bob Duckworth, a twenty-nine-year-old factory worker.

But, in fact, the women don't take second place to their men in worrying about what will happen to the family if the husband loses his job. True, the burden of finding another one that will pay the bills isn't theirs—not a trivial difference. But the other side of this truth is that women are stuck with the reality that the financial welfare of the family is out of their control, that they're helpless to do anything to prevent its economic collapse or to rectify it should it happen. "He thinks I've got it easy because it's not my job to support the family," says Bob's wife, Ruthanne. "But sometimes I think it's worse for me. I worry all the time that he's going to get laid off, just like he does. But I can't do anything about it. And if I try to talk to him about it, you know, like maybe make a plan in case it happens, he won't even listen. How does he think *that* makes me feel? It's my life, too, and I can't even talk to him about it."

Not surprisingly, there are generational differences in what fuels the conflict around the division of labor in these families. For the older couples—those who grew up in a different time, whose marriages started with another set of ground rules—the struggle is not simply around how much men do or about whether they take responsibility for the daily tasks of living without being pushed, prodded, and reminded. That's the overt manifestation of the discord, the trigger that starts the fight. But the noise of the explosion when it comes serves to conceal the more fundamental issue underlying the dissension: legitimacy. What does she have a *right* to expect? "What do I know about doing stuff around the house?" asks Frank Moreno, a forty-eight-year-old foreman in a warehouse. "I wasn't brought up like that. My pop, he never did one damn thing, and my mother never complained. It was her job; she did it and kept quiet. Besides, I work my ass off every day. Isn't that enough?"

For the younger couples, those under forty, the problem is somewhat different. The men may complain about the expectation that they'll participate more fully in the care and feeding of the family, but talk to them about it quietly and they'll usually admit that it's not really unfair, given that their wives also work outside the home. In these homes, the issue between husband and wife isn't only who does what. That's there, and it's a source of more or less conflict, depending upon what the men actually do and how forceful their wives are in their demands. But in most of these families there's at least a verbal consensus that men *ought* to participate in the tasks of daily life. Which raises the next and perhaps more difficult issue in contest between them: Who feels responsible for getting the tasks done? Who regards them as a duty, and for whom are they an option? On this, tradition rules.

Even in families where husbands now share many of the tasks, their wives still bear full responsibility for the organization of family life. A man may help cook the meal these days, but a woman is most likely to be the one who has planned it. He may take the children to child care, but she virtually always has had to arrange it. It's she also who is accountable for the emotional life of the family, for monitoring the emotional temperature of its members and making the necessary corrections. It's this need to be responsible for it all that often feels as burdensome as the tasks themselves. "It's not just doing all the stuff that needs doing," explains Maria Jankowicz, a white twenty-eight-year-old assembler in an electronics factory. "It's worrying all the time about everything and always having to arrange everything, you know what I mean. It's like I run the whole show. If I don't stay on top of it all, things fall apart because nobody else is going to do it. The kids can't and Nick, well, forget it," she concludes angrily.

If, regardless of age, life stage, or verbal consensus, women usually still carry the greatest share of the household burdens, why is it important to notice that younger men grant legitimacy to their wives' demands and older men generally do not? Because men who believe their wives have a right to expect their participation tend to suffer guilt and discomfort when they don't live up to those expectations. And no one lives comfortably with guilt. "I know I don't always help enough, and I feel bad about it, you know, guilty sometimes," explains Bob Beardsley, a thirty-year-old white machine operator, his eyes registering the discomfort he feels as he speaks.

"Does it change anything when you feel guilty?" I ask.

A small smile flits across his face, and he says, "Sometimes. I try to do a little more, but then I get busy with something and forget that she needs me to help out. My wife says I don't pay attention, that's why I forget. But I don't know. Seems like I've just got my mind on other things."

It's possible, of course, that the men who speak of guilt and rights are only trying to impress me by mouthing the politically correct words. But even if true, they display a sensitivity to the issue that's missing from the men who don't speak those words. For words are more than just words. They embody ideas; they are the symbols that give meaning to our thoughts; they shape our consciousness. New ideas come to us on the wings of words. It's words that bring those ideas to life, that allow us to see possibilities unrecognized before we gave them words. Indeed, without words, there is no conscious thought, no possibility for the kind of self-reflection that lights the path of change.[3]

True, there's often a long way between word and deed. But the man who feels guilty when he disappoints his wife's expectations has a different consciousness than the one who doesn't—a difference that usually makes for at least some small change in his behavior. Although the emergence of this changing male consciousness is visible in all the racial groups in this study, there also are differences among them that are worthy of comment.

Virtually all the men do some work inside the family—tending the children, washing dishes, running the vacuum, going to the market. And they generally also remain responsible for those tasks that have always been traditionally male—mowing the lawn, shoveling the snow, fixing the car, cleaning the garage, doing repairs around the house. Among the white families in this study, 16 percent of the men share the family work relatively equally, almost always those who live in families where they and their wives work different shifts or where the men are unemployed. "What choice do I have?" asks Don Bartlett, a thirty-year-old white handyman who works days while his wife is on the swing shift. "I'm the only one here, so I do what's got to be done."

Asian and Latino men of all ages, however, tend to operate more often on the old male model, even when they work different shifts or are unemployed, a finding that puzzled me at first. Why, I wondered, did I find only two Asian men and one Latino who are real partners in the work of the family? Aren't these men subject to the same social and personal pressures others experience?

The answer is both yes and no. The pressures are there but, depending upon where they live, there's more or less support for resisting them. The Latino and Asian men who live in ethnic neighborhoods—settings where they are embedded in an intergenerational community and where the language and culture of the home country is kept alive by a steady stream of new immigrants—find strong support for clinging to the old ways. Therefore, change comes much more slowly in those families. The men who live outside the ethnic quarter are freer from the mandates and constraints of these often tight-knit communities, therefore are more responsive to the winds of change in the larger society.

These distinctions notwithstanding, it's clear that Asian and Latino men generally participate least in the work of the household and are the least likely to believe they have much responsibility there beyond bringing home a paycheck. "Taking care of the house and kids is my wife's job, that's all," says Joe Gomez flatly.

"A Chinese man mopping a floor? I've never seen it yet," says

Amy Lee angrily. Her husband, Dennis, trying to make a joke of the conflict with his wife, says with a smile, "In Chinese families men don't do floors and windows. I help with the dishes sometimes if she needs me to or," he laughs, "if she screams loud enough. The rest, well, it's pretty much her job."

The commonly held stereotype about black men abandoning women and children, however, doesn't square with the families in this study. In fact, black men are the most likely to be real participants in the daily life of the family and are more intimately involved in raising their children than any of the others. True, the men's family work load doesn't always match their wives', and the women are articulate in their complaints about this. Nevertheless, compared to their white, Asian, or Latino counterparts, the black families look like models of egalitarianism.

Nearly three-quarters of the men in the African-American families in this study do a substantial amount of the cooking, cleaning, and child care, sometimes even more than their wives. All explain it by saying one version or another of: "I just figure it's my job, too." Which simply says what is, without explaining how it came to be that way.

To understand that, we have to look at family histories that tell the story of generations of African-American women who could find work and men who could not, and to the family culture that grew from this difficult and painful reality. "My mother worked six days a week cleaning other people's houses, and my father was an ordinary laborer, when he could find work, which wasn't very often," explains thirty-two-year-old Troy Payne, a black waiter and father of two children. "So he was home a lot more than she was, and he'd do what he had to do around the house. The kids all had to do their share, too. It seemed only fair, I guess."

Difficult as the conflict around the division of labor is, it's only one of the many issues that have become flash points in family life since mother went to work. Most important, perhaps, is the question: Who will care for the children? For the lack of decent, affordable facilities for the care of the children creates unbearable problems and tensions for these working-class families.

It's hardly news that child care is an enormous headache and expense for all two-job families. In many professional middle-class families, where the child-care bill can be $1,500–2,000 a month, it competes with the mortgage payment as the biggest single monthly expenditure. Problematic as this may be, however, these families are the lucky ones when compared to working-class families, many of whom don't earn much more than the cost of child care in these upper middle-class families. Even the families in this study at the highest end of the earnings scale, those who earn $42,000 a year, can't dream of such costly arrangements.

For most working-class families, therefore, child care often is patched together in ways that leave parents anxious and children in jeopardy. "Care for the little ones, that's a real big problem," says Beverly Waldov, a thirty-year-old white mother of three children, the youngest two, products of a second marriage, under three years old. "My oldest girl is nine, so she's not such a problem. I hate the idea of her being a latchkey kid, but what can I do? We don't even have the money to put the little ones in one of those good day-care places, so I don't have any choice with her. She's just *got* to be able to take care of herself after school," she says, her words a contest between anxiety and hope.

"We have a kind of complicated arrangement for the little kids. Two days a week, my mom takes care of them. We pay her, but at least I don't have to worry when they're with her; I know it's fine. But she works the rest of the time, so the other days we take them to this woman's house. It's the best we can afford, but it's not great because she keeps too many kids, and I know they don't get good attention. Especially the little one; she's just a baby, you know." She pauses and looks away, anguished. "She's so clingy when I bring her home; she can't let go of me, like nobody's paid her any mind all day. But it's not like I have a choice. We barely make it now; if I stop working, we'd be in real trouble."

Even such makeshift solutions don't work for many families. Some speak of being unable to afford day care at all. "We couldn't pay our bills if we had to pay for somebody to take care of the kids."

Some say they're unwilling to leave the children in the care of strangers. "I just don't believe someone else should be raising our kids, that's all."

Some have tried a variety of child-care arrangements, only to have them fail in a moment of need. "We tried a whole bunch of things, and maybe they work for a little while," says Faye Ensey, a black twenty-eight-year-old office worker. "But what happens when your kid gets sick? Or when the baby sitter's kids get sick? I lost two jobs in a row because my kids kept getting sick and I couldn't go to work. Or else I couldn't take my little one to the baby sitter because her kids were sick. They finally fired me for absenteeism. I didn't really blame them, but it felt terrible anyway. It's such a hassle, I sometimes think I'd be glad to just stay home. But we can't afford for me not to work, so wc had to figure out something else."

For such families, that "something else" is the decision to take jobs on different shifts—a decision made by one-fifth of the families in this study. With one working days and the other on swing or graveyard, one parent is home with the children at all times. "We were getting along okay before Daryl junior was born, because Shona, my daughter, was getting on. You know, she didn't need somebody with her all the time, so we could both work days," explains Daryl Adams, a black thirty-year-old postal clerk with a ten-year-old daughter and a nine-month-old son. "I used to work the early shift—seven to three—so I'd get home a little bit after she got here. It worked out okay. But then this here big surprise came along." He stops, smiles down fondly at his young son and runs his hand over his nearly bald head.

"Now between the two of us working, we don't make enough money to pay for child care and have anything left over, so this is the only way we can manage. Besides, both of us, Alesha and me, we think it's better for one of us to be here, not just for the baby, for my daughter, too. She's growing up and, you know, I think maybe they need even more watching than when they were younger. She's coming to the time when she could get into all kinds of trouble if we're not here to put the brakes on."

But the cost such arrangements exact on a marriage can be very high. When I asked these husbands and wives when they have time to talk, more often than not I got a look of annoyance at a question that, on its face, seemed stupid to them. "Talk? How can we talk when we hardly see each other?" "Talk? What's that?" "Talk? Ha, that's a joke."

Mostly, conversation is limited to the logistics that take place at shift-changing time when children and chores are handed off from one to the other. With children dancing around underfoot, the incoming parent gets a quick summary of the day's or night's events, a list of reminders about things to be done, perhaps about what's cooking in the pot on the stove. "Sometimes when I'm coming home and it's been a hard day, I think: Wouldn't it be wonderful if I could just sit down with Leon for half an hour and we could have a quiet beer together?" thirty-one-year-old Emma Guerrero, a Latina baker, says wistfully.

But it's not to be. If the arriving spouse gets home early enough, there may be an hour when both are there together. But with the pressures of the workday fresh for one and awaiting the other, and with children clamoring for parental attention, this isn't a promising moment for any serious conversation. "I usually get home about forty-five minutes or so before my wife has to leave for work," says Ralph Jo, a thirty-six-year-old Asian repairman whose children, ages three and five, are the product of a second marriage. "So we try to take a few minutes just to make contact. But it's hard with the kids and all. Most days the whole time gets spent with taking care of business—you know, who did what, what the kids need, what's for supper, what bill collector was hassling her while I was gone—all the damn garbage of living. It makes me nuts."

Most of the time even this brief hour isn't available. Then the ritual changing of the guard takes only a few minutes—a quick peck on the cheek in greeting, a few words, and it's over. "It's like we pass each other. He comes in; I go out; that's it."

Some of the luckier couples work different shifts on the same days, so they're home together on weekends. But even in these families there's so little time for normal family life that there's hardly any room for anyone or anything outside. "There's so much to do when I get home that there's no time for anything but the chores and the kids," says Daryl's wife, Alesha Adams. "I never get to see anybody or do anything else anymore and, even so, I'm always feeling upset and guilty because there's not enough time for them. Daryl leaves a few minutes after I get home, and the rest of the night is like a blur—Shona's homework, getting the kids fed and down for the night, cleaning up, getting everything ready for tomorrow. I don't know; there's always something I'm running around doing. I sometimes feel like—What do you call them?—one of those whirling dervishes, rushing around all the time and never getting everything done.

"Then on the weekends, you sort of want to make things nice for the kids—and for us, too. It's the only time we're here together, like a real family, so we always eat with the kids. And we try to take them someplace nice one of the days, like to the park or something. But sometimes we're too tired, or there's too many other catch-up things you have to do. I don't even get to see my sister anymore. She's been working weekends for the last year or so, and I'm too busy week nights, so there's no time.

"I don't mean to complain; we're lucky in a lot of ways. We've got two great kids, and we're a pretty good team, Daryl and me. But I worry sometimes. When you live on this kind of schedule, communication's not so good."

For those whose days off don't match, the problems of sustaining both the couple relationship and family life are magnified enormously. "The last two years have been hell for us," says thirty-five-year-old Tina Mulvaney, a white mother of two teenagers. "My son got into bad company and had some trouble, so Mike and I decided one of us had to be home. But we can't make it without my check, so I can't quit.

"Mike drives a cab and I work in a hospital, so we figured one of us could transfer to nights. We talked it over and decided it would be best if I was here during the day and he was here at night. He controls the kids, especially my son, better than I do. When he lays down the law, they listen." She interrupts her narrative to reflect on the difficulty of raising children. "You know, when they were little, I used to think about how much easier it would be when they got older. But now I see it's not true; that's when you really have to begin to worry about them. This is when they need someone to be here all the time to make sure they stay out of trouble."

She stops again, this time fighting tears, then takes up where she left off. "So now Mike works days and I work graveyard. I hate it, but it's the only answer; at least this way somebody's here all the time. I get home about 8:30 in the morning. The kids and Mike are gone. It's the best time of the day because it's the only time I have a little quiet here. I clean up the house a little, do the shopping and the laundry and whatever, then I go to sleep for a couple of hours until the kids come home from school.

"Mike gets home at five; we eat; then he takes over for the night, and I go back to sleep for another couple of hours. I try to get up by 9 so we can all have a little time together, but I'm so tired that I don't make it a lot of times. And by 10, he's sleeping because he has to be up by 6 in the morning. So if I don't get up, we hardly see each other at all. Mike's here on weekends, but I'm not. Right now I have Tuesday and Wednesday off. I keep hoping for a Monday–Friday shift, but it's what everybody wants, and I don't have the seniority yet. It's hard, very hard; there's no time to live or anything," she concludes with a listless sigh.

Even in families where wife and husband work the same shift, there's less time for leisure pursuits and social activities than ever before, not just because both parents work full-time but also because people work longer hours now than they did twenty years ago.[4] Two decades ago, weekends saw occasional family outings, Friday-evening bowling, a Saturday trip to the shopping mall, a Sunday with extended family, once in a while an evening out without the children. In summer, when the children weren't in school, a week night might find the family paying a short visit to a friend, a relative, or a neighbor. Now almost everyone I speak with complains that it's hard to find time for even these occasional outings. Instead, most off-work hours are spent trying to catch up with the dozens of family and household tasks that were left undone during the regular work week. When they aren't doing chores, parents guiltily try to do in two days a week what usually takes seven— that is, to establish a sense of family life for themselves and their children.

"Leisure," snorts Peter Pittman, a twenty-eight-year-old African-American father of two, married six years. "With both of us working like we do, there's no time for anything. We got two little kids; I commute better than an hour each way to my job. Then we live here for half rent because I take care of the place for the landlord. So if somebody's got a complaint, I've got to take care of it, you know, fix it myself or get the landlord to get somebody out to do it if I can't. Most things I can do myself, but it takes time. I sometimes wonder what this life's all about, because this sure ain't what I call living. We don't go anyplace; we don't do anything; Christ, we hardly have time to go to the toilet. There's always some damn thing that's waiting that you've got to do."

Clearly, such complaints aren't unique to the working class. The pressures of time, the impoverishment of social life, the anxieties about child care, the fear that children will live in a world of increasing scarcity, the threat of divorce—all these are part of family life today, regardless of class. Nevertheless, there are important differences between those in the higher reaches of the class structure and the families of the working class. The simple fact that middle-class families have more discretionary income is enough to make a big difference in the quality of their social life. For they generally have enough money to pay for a baby-sitter once in a while so that parents can have some time to themselves; enough, too, for a family vacation, for tickets to a concert, a play, or a movie. At $7.50 a ticket in a New York or San Francisco movie house, a working-class couple will settle for a $3.00 rental that the whole family can watch together.

Finding time and energy for sex is also a problem, one that's obviously an issue for two-job families of any class. But it's harder to resolve in working-class families because they have so few resources with which to buy some time and privacy for themselves. Ask about their sex lives and you'll be met with an angry, "What's that?" or a wistful, "I wish." When it happens, it is, as one woman put it, "on the run"—a situation that's particularly unsatisfactory for most women. For them, the pleasure of sex is related to the whole of the interaction—to a sense of intimacy and connection, to at least a few relaxed, loving moments. When they can't have these, they're likely to avoid sex altogether—a situation the men find equally unsatisfactory.

"Sex?" asks Lisa Scranton, a white twenty-nine-year-old mother of three who feigns a puzzled frown, as if she doesn't quite know the meaning of the word. "Oh yeah, that; I remember now," she says, her lips smiling, her eyes sad. "At the beginning, when we first got together, it was WOW, real hot, great. But after a while it cools down, doesn't it? Right now, it's down the toilet. I wonder, does it happen to everybody like that?" she asks dejectedly.

"I guess the worst is when you work different shifts like we do and you get to see each other maybe six minutes a day. There's no time for sex. Sometimes we try to steal a few minutes for ourselves but, I don't know, I can't get into it that way. He can. You know how men are; they can do it any time. Give them two minutes, and they can get off. But it takes me time; I mean, I like to feel close, and you can't do that in three minutes. And there's the kids; they're right here all the time. I don't want to do it if it means being interrupted. Then he gets mad, so sometimes I do. But it's a problem, a real problem."

The men aren't content with these quick sexual exchanges either. But for them it's generally better than no sex at all, while for the women it's often the other way around. "You want to talk about sex, huh?" asks Lisa's husband, Chuck, his voice crackling with anger. "Yeah, I don't mind; it's fine, only I got nothing to talk about. Far as I'm concerned, that's one of the things I found out about marriage. You get married, you give up sex. We hardly ever do it anymore, and when we do, it's like she's doing me a favor.

"Christ, I know the way we've got to do things now isn't great," he protests, running a hand through his hair agitatedly. "We don't see each other but a few minutes a day, but I don't see why we can't take five and have a little fun in the sack. Sure, I like it better when we've got more time, too. But for her, if it can't be perfect, she gets all wound and uptight and it's like . . . " He stops, groping for words, then explodes, "It's like screwing a cold fish."

She isn't just a "cold fish," however. The problems they face are deeper than that. For once such conflicts arise, spontaneity takes flight and sex becomes a problem that needs attention rather than a time out for pleasure and renewal. Between times, therefore, he's busy calculating how much time has passed: "It's been over two weeks"; nursing his wounds: "I don't want to have to beg her"; feeling deprived and angry: "I don't know why I got married." When they finally do come together, he's disappointed. How could it be otherwise, given the mix of feelings he brings to the bed with him—the frustration and anger, the humiliation of feeling he has to beg her, the wounded sense of manhood.

Meanwhile, she, too, is preoccupied with sex, not with thoughts of pleasure but with figuring out how much time she has before, as she puts it, "he walks around with his mouth stuck out. I know I'm in real big trouble if we don't do it once a week. So I make sure we do, even if I don't want to." She doesn't say those words to him, of course. But he knows. And it's precisely this, the knowledge that she's servicing him rather than desiring him that's so hard for him to take.

The sexual arena is one of the most common places to find a "his and her" marriage—one marriage, two different sex lives.[5] Each partner has a different story to tell; each is convinced that his or her version is the real one. A husband says mournfully, "I'm lucky if we get to make love once a week." His wife reports with irritation, "It's two, sometimes three times a week." It's impossible to know whose account is closest to the reality. And it's irrelevant. If that's what they were after, they could keep tabs and get it straight. But facts and feelings are often at war in family life. And nowhere does right or wrong, true or false count for less than in their sexual interactions. It isn't that people arbitrarily distort the truth. They simply report their experience, and it's feeling, not fact, that dominates that experience; feeling, not fact, that is their truth.

But it's also true that, especially for women, the difference in frequency of sexual desire can be a response—sometimes conscious, sometimes not—to other conflicts in the marriage. It isn't that men never withhold sex as a weapon in the family wars, only that they're much more likely than women to be able to split sex from emotion, to feel their anger and still experience sexual desire. For a man, too, a sexual connection with his wife can relieve the pressures and tensions of the day, can make him feel whole again, even if they've barely spoken a word to each other.

For a woman it's different. What happens—or, more likely, what doesn't happen—in the kitchen, the living room, and the laundry room profoundly affects what's possible in the bedroom. When she feels distant, unconnected, angry; when her pressured life leaves her feeling fragmented; when she hasn't had a real conversation with her husband for a couple of days, sex is very far from either her mind or her loins. "I run around busy all the time, and he just sits there, so by the time we go to bed, I'm too tired," explains Linda Bloodworth, a white thirty-one-year-old telephone operator.

"Do you think your lack of sexual response has something to do with your anger at your husband's refusal to participate more fully in the household?" I ask.

Her eyes smoldering, her voice tight, she snaps, "No, I'm just tired, that's all." Then noticing something in my response, she adds, "I know what you're thinking; I saw that look. But really, I don't think it's *because* I'm angry; I really am tired. I have to admit, though, that I tell him if he helped more, maybe I wouldn't be so tired all the time. And," she adds defiantly, "maybe I wouldn't be."

Some couples, of course, manage their sexual relationship with greater ease. Often that's because they have less conflict in other areas of living. But whether they accommodate well or poorly, for all two-job families, sex requires a level of attention and concern that leaves most people wanting much of the time. "It's a problem, and I tell you, it has to be well planned," explains thirty-four-year-old Dan Stolman, a black construction worker. "But we manage okay; we make dates or try to slip it in when the baby's asleep and my daughter's out with a friend or something. I don't mean things are great in that department. I'm not always satisfied and neither is Lorraine. But what can you do? We try to do the best we can. Sex isn't all there is to a marriage, you know. We get along really well, so that makes up for a lot.

"What I really miss is that we don't ever make love anymore. I mean, we have sex like I said, but we don't have the kind of time you need to make love. We talk about getting away for an overnight by ourselves once in a while. Lorraine's mother would come watch the kids if we asked her; the problem is we don't have any extra cash to spare right now."

Time and money—precious commodities in short supply. These are the twin plagues of family life, the missing ingredients that combine to create families that are both frantic and fragile. Yet there's no mystery about what would alleviate the crisis that now threatens to engulf them: A job that pays a living wage, quality child-care facilities at rates people can pay, health care for all, parental leave, flexible work schedules, decent and affordable housing, a shorter work week so that parents and children have time to spend together, tax breaks for those in need rather than for those in greed, to mention just a few. These are the policies we need to put in place if we're to have any hope of making our families stable and healthy.

What we have, instead, are families in which mother goes to work to relieve financial distress, only to find that time takes its place next to money as a source of strain, tension, and conflict. Time for the children, time for the couple's relationship, time for self, time for social life—none of it easily available for anyone in two-job families, not even for the children, who are hurried along at every step of the way.[6] And money! Never enough, not for the clothes children need, not for the doctor's bill, not for a vacation, not even for the kind of child care that would allow parents to go to work in peace. But large as these problems loom in the lives of working-class families, difficult as they are to manage, they pale beside those they face when unemployment strikes, especially if it's father who loses his job.

6

"WHEN YOU GET LAID OFF, IT'S LIKE YOU LOSE A PART OF YOURSELF"

For Larry Meecham, "downsizing" is more than a trendy word on the pages of the *Wall Street Journal* or the business section of the *New York Times*. "I was with the same company for over twelve years; I had good seniority. Then all of a sudden they laid off almost half the people who worked there, closed down whole departments, including mine," he says, his troubled brown eyes fixed on some distant point as he speaks. "One day you got a job; the next day you're out of work, just like that," he concludes, shaking his head as if he still can't believe it.

Nearly 15 percent of the men in the families I interviewed were jobless when I met them.[1] Another 20 percent had suffered episodic bouts of unemployment—sometimes related to the recession of the early 1990s, sometimes simply because job security is fragile in the blue-collar world, especially among the younger, less experienced workers. With the latest recession, however, age and experience don't count for much; every man feels at risk.[2]

Tenuous as the situation is for white men, it's worse for men of color, especially African-Americans. The last hired, they're likely to be the first fired. And when the axe falls, they have even fewer resources than whites to help them through the tough times. "After kicking around doing shit work for a long time, I finally got a job that paid decent," explains twenty-nine-year-old George Faucett, a black father of two who lost his factory job when the company was restructured—another word that came into vogue during the economic upheaval of the 1990s. "I worked there for two years, but I didn't have seniority, so when they started to lay guys off, I was it. We never really had a chance to catch up on all the bills before it was all over," he concludes dispiritedly.

I speak of men here partly because they're usually the biggest wage earners in intact families. Therefore, when father loses his job, it's likely to be a crushing blow to the family economy. And partly, also, it's because the issues unemployment raises are different for men and for women. For most women, identity is multi-faceted, which means that the loss of a job isn't equivalent to the loss of self. No matter how invested a woman may be in her work, no matter how much her sense of self and competence are connected to it, work remains only one part of identity—a central part perhaps, especially for a professional woman, but still only a part. She's mother, wife, friend, daughter, sister—all valued facets of the self, none wholly obscuring the others. For the working-class women in this study, therefore, even those who were divorced or single mothers responsible for the support of young children, the loss of a job may have been met with pain, fear, and anxiety, but it didn't call their identity into question.

For a man, however, work is likely to be connected to the core of self. Going to work isn't just what he does, it's deeply linked to who he is. Obviously, a man is also father, husband, friend, son, brother. But these are likely to be roles he assumes, not without depth and meaning, to be sure, but not self-defining in the same way as he experiences work. Ask a man for a statement of his identity, and he'll almost always respond by telling you first what he does for a living. The same question asked of a woman brings forth a less predictable, more varied response, one that's embedded in the web of relationships that are central to her life.[3]

Some researchers studying the impact of male unemployment have observed a sequenced series of psychological responses.[4] The first, they say, is shock, followed by denial and a sense of optimism, a belief that this is temporary, a holiday, like a hiatus between jobs rather than joblessness. This period is marked by heightened activity at home, a burst of do-it-yourself projects that had been long neglected for lack of time. But soon the novelty is gone and the projects wear thin, ushering in the second phase, a time of increasing distress, when inertia trades places with activity and anxiety succeeds denial. Now a jobless man awakens every day to the reality of unemployment. And, lest he forget, the weekly trip to the unemployment office is an unpleasant reminder. In the third phase, inertia deepens into depression, fed by feelings of identity loss, inadequacy, hopelessness, a lack of self-confidence, and a general failure of self-esteem. He's tense, irritable, and feels increasingly alienated and isolated from both social and personal relationships.

This may be an apt description of what happens in normal times. But in periods of economic crisis, when losing a job isn't a singular and essentially lonely event, the predictable pattern breaks down.[5] During the years I was interviewing families for this book, millions of jobs disappeared almost overnight. Nearly everyone I met, therefore, knew someone—a family member, a neighbor, a friend—who was out of work. "My brother's been out of a job for a long time; now my brother-in-law just got laid off. It seems like every time I turn around, somebody's losing his job. I've been lucky so far, but it makes you wonder how long it'll last."

At such times, nothing cushions the reality of losing a job. When the unbelievable becomes commonplace and the unexpected is part of the mosaic of the times, denial is difficult and optimism impossible. Instead, any layoff, even if it's defined as temporary, is experienced immediately and viscerally as a potentially devastating, cataclysmic event.

It's always a shock when a person loses a job, of course. But disbelief? Denial? Not for those who have been living under a cloud of anxiety—those who leave work each night grateful for another day of safety, who wonder as they set off the next morning whether this is the day the axe will fall on them. "I tell my wife not to worry because she gets panicked about the bills. But the truth is, I stew about it plenty. The economy's gone to hell; guys are out of work all around me. I'd be nuts if I wasn't worried."

It's true that when a working-class man finds himself without a job he'll try to keep busy with projects around the house. But these aren't undertaken in the kind of holiday spirit earlier researchers describe.[6] Rather, building a fence, cleaning the garage, painting the family room, or the dozens of other tasks that might occupy him are a way of coping with his anxiety, of distracting himself from the fears that threaten to overwhelm him, of warding off the depression that lurks just below the surface of his activity. Each thrust of the saw, each blow of the hammer helps to keep the demons at bay. "Since he lost his job, he's been out there hammering away at one thing or another like a maniac," says Janet Kovacs, a white thirty-four-year-old waitress. "First it was the fence; he built the whole thing in a few days. Then it was fixing the siding on the garage. Now he's up on the roof. He didn't even stop to watch the football game last Sunday."

Her husband, Mike, a cement finisher, explains it this way: "If I don't keep busy, I feel like I'll go nuts. It's funny," he says with a caustic, ironic laugh, "before I got laid off my wife was always complaining about me watching the ball games; now she keeps nagging me to watch. What do you make of that, huh? I guess she's trying to make me feel better."

"Why didn't you watch the game last Sunday?" I ask.

"I don't know, maybe I'm kind of scared if I sit down there in front of that TV, I won't want to get up again," he replies, his shoulders hunched, his fingers raking his hair. "Besides, when I was working, I figured I had a right."

His words startled me, and I kept turning them over in my mind long after he spoke them: "When I was working, I figured I had a right." It's a sentence any of the unemployed men I met might have uttered. For it's in getting up and going to work every day that they feel they've earned the right to their manhood, to their place in the world, to the respect of their family, even the right to relax with a sporting event on TV.

It isn't that there are no gratifying moments, that getting laid off has no positive side at all. When unemployment first hits, family members usually gather around to offer support, to buoy a man's spirits and their own. Even in families where conflict is high, people tend to come together, at least at the beginning. "Considering that we weren't getting along so well before, my wife was really good about it when I got laid off," says Joe Phillips, an unemployed black truck driver. "She gave me a lot of support at first, and I appreciate it."

"You said 'at first.' Has that changed?" I ask.

"Hell, yes. It didn't last long. But maybe I can't blame it all on her. I've been no picnic to live with since I got canned."

In families with young children, there may be a period of relief—for the parents, the relief of not having to send small children off to child care every day, of knowing that one of them is there to welcome the children when they come home from school; for the children, the exhilarating novelty of having a parent, especially daddy, at home all day. "The one good thing about him not working is that there's someone home with the kids now," says twenty-five-year-old Gloria Lewis, a black hairdresser whose husband has been unemployed for just a few weeks. "That part's been a godsend. But I don't know what we'll do if he doesn't find work soon. We can't make it this way."

Teenagers, too, sometimes speak about the excitement of having father around at first. "It was great having my dad home when he first got laid off," says Kevin Sollars, a white fourteen-year-old. "We got to do things together after school sometimes. He likes to build ship models—old sailing ships. I don't know why, but he never wanted to teach me how to do it. He didn't even like it when I just wanted to watch; he'd say, 'Haven't you got something else to do?' But when he first got laid off, it was different. When I'd come home from school and he was working on a ship, he'd let me help him."

But the good times usually don't last long. "After a little while, he got really grumpy and mean, jumped on everybody over nothing," Kevin continues. "My mom used to say we had to be patient because he was so worried about money and all that. Boy, was I glad when he went back to work."

Fathers may also tell of the pleasure in getting to spend time with their children, in being a part of their daily life in ways unknown before. "There's a silver lining in every cloud, I guess. I got to know my kids like I never did before," says Kevin's father, who felt the sting of unemployment for seven months before he finally found another job. "It's just that being out of work gets old pretty fast. I ran out of stuff to do around the house; we were run-

ning out of money; and there I was sitting on my keister and stew-
ing all day long while my wife was out working. I couldn't even
enjoy building my little ships."

Once in a while, especially for a younger man, getting laid off
or fired actually opens up the possibility of a new beginning. "I
figured, what the hell, if I'm here, I might as well learn how to
cook," says twenty-eight-year-old Darnell Jones, a black father of
two who, until he was laid off, had worked steadily but always at
relatively menial, low-paying jobs in which he had little interest
or satisfaction. "Turned out I liked to cook, got to be real good at
it, too, better than my wife," he grins proudly. "So then we
talked about it and decided there was no sense in sitting around
waiting for something to happen when there were no good jobs
out there, especially for a black man, and we figured I should go
to cooking school and learn how to do it professionally. Now I've
got this job as a cook; it's only part-time, right now, but the pay's
pretty good, and I think maybe I'll go full-time soon. If I could
get regular work, maybe we could even save some money and I
could open my own restaurant someday. That's what I really
want to do."

But this outcome is rare, made possible by the fact that Darnell's wife has a middle-management position in a large corporation
that pays her $38,000 a year. His willingness to try something new
was a factor, of course. But that, too, was grounded in what was
possible. In most young working-class families of any color or ethnic group, debts are high, savings are nonexistent, and women
don't earn nearly enough to bail the family out while the men go
into a training program to learn new skills. A situation that doesn't
offer much encouragement for a man to dream, let alone to believe
his dream could be realized.[7]

As I have already indicated, the struggles around the division
of labor shift somewhat when father loses his job. The man who's
home all day while his wife goes off to work can't easily justify
maintaining the traditional household gender roles. Therefore,
many of the unemployed men pick up tasks that were formerly left
to their wives alone. "I figure if she's working and I'm not, I ought
to take up some of the slack around here. So I keep the place up,
run the kids around if they need it, things like that," says twenty-

nine-year-old Jim Andersen, a white unemployed electrician.

As wives feel their household burdens eased, the strains that are almost always a part of life in a two-job family are somewhat relieved. "Maybe it sounds crazy to you, but my life's so much easier since he's out of work, I wish it could stay this way," says Jim's wife, Loreen, a twenty-nine-year-old accounting clerk. "If only I could make enough money, I'd be happy for him to stay home and play Mr. Mom."

But it's only a fantasy—first because she can't make enough money; second, and equally important, because while she likes the relief from household responsibilities, she's also uneasy about such a dramatic shift in family roles. So in the next breath, Loreen says, "I worry about him, though. He doesn't feel so good about himself being unemployed and playing house."

"Is it only him you worry about? Or is there something that's hard for you, too?" I ask.

She's quiet for a moment, then acknowledges that her feelings are complicated: "I'm not sure what I think anymore. I mean, I don't think it's fair that men always have to be the support for the family; it's too hard for them sometimes. And I don't mind working; I really don't. In fact, I like it a lot better than being home with the house and the kids all the time. But I guess deep down I still have that old-fashioned idea that it's a man's job to support his family. So, yeah, then I begin to feel—I don't know how to say it— uncomfortable, right here inside me," she says, pointing to her midsection, "like maybe I won't respect him so much if he can't do that. I mean, it's okay for now," she hastens to reassure me, perhaps herself as well. "But if it goes on for a real long time like with some men, then I think I'll feel different."

Men know their wives feel this way, even when the words are never spoken, which only heightens their own anxieties about being unemployed. "Don't get me wrong; I'm glad she has her job. I don't know what we'd do if she wasn't working," says Jim. "It's just that . . . ," he hesitates, trying to frame his thoughts clearly. "I know this is going to sound pretty male, but it's my job to take care of this family. I mean, it's great that she can help out, but the responsibility is mine, not hers. She won't say so, but I know she feels the same way, and I don't blame her."

It seems, then, that no matter what the family's initial response is, whatever the good moments may be, the economic and psychological strains that attend unemployment soon overwhelm the good intentions on all sides. "It's not just the income; you lose a lot more than that," says Marvin Reed, a forty-year-old white machinist, out of work for nearly eight months. He pauses, reflects on his words, then continues."When you get laid off, it's like you lose a part of yourself. It's terrible; something goes out of you. Then, on top of that, by staying home and not going to work and associating with people of your own level, you begin to lose the sharpness you developed at work. Everything gets slower; you move slower; your mind works slower.

"It's a real shocker to realize that about yourself, to feel like you're all slowed down and ... ," he hesitates again, this time to find the words. "I don't know how to explain it exactly, maybe like your mind's pushing a load of mud around all the time," he concludes, his graying head bowed so as not to meet my eyes.

"Everything gets slower"—a sign of the depression that's so often the unwelcome companion of unemployment. As days turn into weeks and weeks into months, it gets harder and harder to believe in a future. "I've been working since I was fourteen," says Marvin, "and I was never out of work for more than a week or two before. Now I don't know; I don't know when I'll get work again. The jobs are gone. How do you find a job when there's none out there anymore?"

The men I talked with try to remind themselves that it's not their fault, that the layoffs at the plant have nothing to do with them or their competence, that it's all part of the economic problems of the nation. But it's hard not to doubt themselves, not to wonder whether there's something else they could have done, something they might have foreseen and planned for. "I don't know; I keep thinking I could have done something different," says Lou Coltrane, a black twenty-eight-year-old auto worker, as he looks away to hide his pain. "I know it's crazy; they closed most of the plant. But, you know, you can't help thinking, maybe this, maybe that. It keeps going round and round in my head: Maybe I should have done this; maybe I should have done that. Know what I mean?"

But even when they can accept the reality that they had no control over the situation, there's little surcease in the understanding. Instead, such thoughts increase their feelings of vulnerability and helplessness—feelings no one accepts easily. "I worked nineteen years for this damned company and how do they pay me back?" asks Eric Hueng, a forty-four-year-old unemployed Asian factory worker, as he leaves his chair and paces the room in a vain attempt to escape his torment. "They move the plant down to some godforsaken place in South America where people work for peanuts and you got no choice but to sit there and watch it happen. Even the government doesn't do a damn thing about it. They just sit back and let it happen, so how could I do anything?" he concludes, his words etched in bitterness.

For American men—men who have been nurtured and nourished in the belief that they're masters of their fate—it's almost impossible to bear such feelings of helplessness. So they find themselves in a cruel double bind. If they convince themselves that their situation is beyond their control, there's nothing left but resignation and despair. To fight their way out of the hopelessness that follows, they begin to blame themselves. But this only leaves them, as one man said, "kicking myself around the block"—kicks that, paradoxically, allow them to feel less helpless and out of control, while they also send them deeper into depression, since now it's no one's fault but their own.

"I can't believe what a fool I was," says Paul Santos, a forty-six-year-old Latino tool and die maker, his fingers drumming the table nervously as he speaks. "I was with this one company for over fifteen years, then this other job came along a couple of years ago. It seemed like a good outfit, solid, and it was a better job, more money and all. I don't know what happened; I guess they got overextended. All I know is they laid off 30 percent of the company without a day's notice. Now I feel stupid; if I had stayed where I was, I'd still be working."

Shame, too, makes an appearance, adding to the self-blame, to Paul's feeling that he did something wrong, something stupid—that if he'd somehow been better, smarter, more prescient, the outcome would be different. And the depression deepens. "I've been working all my life. Now it's like I've got nothing left," Paul explains, his eyes downcast, his voice choked with emotion. "When you work, you associate with a group of people you respect. Now you're not part of the group anymore; you don't belong anywhere. Except," he adds with disgust, "on the unemployment line."

"Now that's a sad sight, all these guys shuffling around, nobody looking at anybody else. Every time I go there, I think, *Hey, what the hell am I doing here? I don't belong here, not with these people. They're deadbeats.* Then I think, *Yeah, well you're here, so it looks like you're no better than them, doesn't it?*"

Like so many other men, Paul hasn't just lost a job; he's lost a life. For his job meant more than a living wage. It meant knowing he had an identity and a place in the world—a place where his competence was affirmed, where he had friends who respected and admired him, men with whom he could share both the frustrations and satisfactions of life on the job.

It's not just for men that the job site is a mirror in which they see themselves reflected, a mirror that reflects back an image that reassures them that they're valued contributors to the social world in which they live. It functions this way for all of us. But it's particularly important for men because when the job disappears, all this goes too, including the friendships that were so important in the validation of the self.[8]

In my earlier research on friendship, the men I interviewed spoke repeatedly about how, once they left the job, they lost contact with the friends they had made at work.[9] Sometimes these men acknowledged that it was "out of sight, out of mind." But others insisted that, even though they might never see each other again, these friendships represented lasting bonds. "Maybe they don't continue to see each other once the activity [or job] doesn't keep them together," said one man I interviewed then, "but that doesn't mean they don't share very deep and lasting bonds, does it?"[10] Perhaps. But the bonds, if they exist, can't replace the face-to-face interactions that are so important to the maintenance of the self.

"I don't see anybody anymore," mourns Bill Costas, a thirty-four-year-old unemployed white meat packer who had worked in the same plant for nine years. "The guys I worked with were my buddies; after all those years of working together, they were my friends. We'd go out after work and have a beer and shoot the bull. Now I don't even know what they're doing anymore."

For wives and children, it's both disturbing and frightening to watch husband and father sink ever deeper into despair. "Being out of work is real hard on him; it's hard to see him like this, so sad and jumpy all the time," laments Bill's wife, Eunice, a part-time bank teller who's anxiously looking for full-time work. "He's always been a good provider, never out of work hardly a day since we got married. Then all of a sudden this happens. It's like he lost his self-respect when he lost that job."

His self-respect and also the family's medical benefits, since Eunice doesn't qualify for benefits in her part-time job. "The scariest part about Bill being out of a job is we don't have any medical insurance anymore. My daughter got pneumonia real bad last winter and I had to borrow money from my sister for the doctor bill and her medicine. Just the medicine was almost $100. The doctor wanted to put her in the hospital, but we couldn't because we don't have any health insurance."

Her husband recalls his daughter's illness, in a voice clogged with rage and grief. "Do you know what it's like listening to your kid when she can't breathe and you can't send her to the hospital because you lost your benefits when you got laid off?"

In such circumstances, some men just sit, silent, turned inward, enveloped in the gray fog of depression from which they can't rouse themselves. "I leave to go to work in the morning and he's sitting there doing nothing, and when I come home at night, it's the same thing. It's like he didn't move the whole day," worries thirty-four-year-old Deidre Limage, the wife of a black factory worker who has been jobless for over a year.

Other men defend against feeling the pain, fear, and sadness, covering them over with a flurry of activity, with angry, defensive, often irrational outbursts at wife and children—or with some combination of the two. As the financial strain of unemployment becomes crushing, everyone's fears escalate. Wives, unable to keep silent, give voice to their concerns. Their husbands, unable to tolerate what they hear as criticism and blame—spoken or not—lash out. "It seems like the more you try to pull yourself up, the more you get pushed back down," sighs Beverly Coleride, a white twenty-five-year-old cashier with two children, whose husband has worked at a variety of odd jobs in their seven-year marriage. "No matter how hard we try, we can't seem to set everything right. I don't know what we're going to do now; we don't have next month's rent. If Kenny doesn't get something steady real quick, we could be on the street."

"We could be on the street"—a fear that clutches at the hearts and gnaws at the souls of the families in this study, not only those who are unemployed. Nothing exemplifies the change in the twenty years since I last studied working class families than the fear of being "on the street." Then, homelessness was something that happened somewhere else, in India or some other far-off and alien land. Then, we wept when we read about the poor people who lived on the streets in those other places. *What kind of society doesn't provide this most basic of life's needs?* we asked ourselves. Now, the steadily increasing numbers of homeless in our own land have become an ever-present and frightening reminder of just how precarious life in this society can be. Now, they're in our face, on our streets, an accepted category of American social life—"the homeless."

Just how readily accepted they are was brought home to me recently when my husband, who volunteers some time in the San Francisco schools, reported his experience with a sixth-grade class there. He had been invited to talk to the children about career opportunities and, in doing so, talked about his own past as a restaurateur. The students listened, engrossed. But instead of the questions he had expected when he finished, they were preoccupied with how he managed the problem of the homeless. Did he feed homeless people when they asked for food, they wanted to know. He explained that at the time he had restaurants in the Bay Area, there were no homeless on the streets. Undaunted, they wanted to know what he did when he found a homeless person sleeping in the doorway of the restaurant. He reminded them that he had just told them that homelessness wasn't an issue when he was in business. They listened, he said, but they couldn't really grasp the idea of a world without the homeless. How could it be otherwise? At their age, homelessness is so much a part of their daily world that they take it for granted, a phenomenon not of their time but of all times.

As homelessness has increased, even those of us who remember when it was unthinkable have become inured to the sight of the men and women who make their home on the streets. Inured, and also anxious. We recoil as we walk by, trying not to see, unable to meet their eyes, ashamed of our own good fortune, anger and sympathy tugging us in opposite directions. Neither feels good. The anger is a challenge to our belief that we're kind, humane, caring. But the sympathy is even more threatening. To allow ourselves to feel compassion is to open the floodgates of our own vulnerability, of our denied understanding of how delicately our lives and fortunes are balanced.

For Beverly Coleride, as for the other women and men I met, sustaining the denial has become increasingly difficult. No matter how much they want to obliterate the images of the homeless from consciousness, the specter haunts them, a frightening reminder of what's possible if they trip and fall. Perhaps it's because there's so much at stake now, because the unthinkable has become a reality, that anxieties escalate so quickly. So as Beverly contemplates the terror of being "on the street," she begins to blame her husband. "I keep telling myself it's not his fault, but it's real hard not to let it get you down. So then I think, well, maybe he's not trying hard enough, and I get on his case, and he gets mad, and, well, I guess you know the rest," she concludes with a harsh laugh that sounds more like a cry of pain.

She doesn't *want* to hurt her husband, but she can't tolerate feeling so helpless and out of control. If it's his fault rather than the workings of some impersonal force, then he can do something about it. For her husband, it's an impossible bind. "I keep trying, looking for something, but there's nothing out there, leastwise not for me. I don't know what to do anymore; I've tried everything, every place I know," he says disconsolately.

But he, too, can't live easily with such feelings of helplessness. His sense of his manhood, already under threat because he can't support his family, is eroded further by his wife's complaints. So he turns on her in anger: "It's hard enough being out of work, but then my wife gets on my case, yakking all the time about how we're going to be on the street if I don't get off my butt, like it's my fault or something that there's no work out there. When she starts up like that, I swear I want to hit her, anything just to shut her mouth," he says, his shoulders tensed, his fists clenched in an unconscious expression of his rage.

"And do you?" I ask.

The tension breaks; he laughs. "No, not yet. I don't know; I don't want to," he says, his hand brushing across his face. "But I get mad enough so I could. Jesus, doesn't she know I feel bad enough? Does she have to make it worse by getting on me like that? Maybe you could clue her, would you?"

"Maybe you could clue her"—a desperate plea for someone to intervene, to save him from his own rageful impulses. For Kenny Coleride isn't a violent man. But the stress and conflict in families where father loses his job can give rise to the kind of interaction described here, a dynamic that all too frequently ends in physical assaults against women and children.

Some kind of violence—sometimes against children only, more often against both women and children—is the admitted reality of life in about 14 percent of the families in this study.[11] I say "admitted reality" because this remains one of the most closely guarded secrets in family life. So it's reasonable to assume that the proportion of families victimized by violence could be substantially higher.

Sometimes my questions about domestic violence were met with evasion: "I don't really know anything about that."

Sometimes there was outright denial, even when I could see the evidence with my own eyes: "I was visiting my sister the other day, and I tripped and fell down the steps in front of her house."

And sometimes teenage children, anguished about what they see around them, refused to participate in the cover-up. "I bet they didn't tell you that he beats my mother up, did they? Nobody's allowed to talk about it; we're supposed to pretend like it doesn't happen. I hate him; I could kill him when he does that to her. My mom, she says he can't help it; it's because he's so upset since he got fired. But that's just her excuse now. I mean, yeah, maybe it's worse than it was before, but he did it before, too. I don't understand. Why does she let him do it to her?"

"Why does she let him do it to her?" A question the children in these families are not alone in asking, one to which there are few satisfactory answers. But one thing is clear: The depression men suffer and their struggle against it significantly increase the probability of alcohol abuse, which in turn makes these kinds of eruptions more likely to occur.[12]

"My father's really changed since he got laid off," complains Buddy Truelman, the fifteen-year-old son of an unemployed white steel worker. "It's like he's always mad about something, you know, ready to bite your head off over nothing. I mean, he's never been an at-ease guy, but now nothing you do is okay with him; he's always got something to say, like he butts in where it's none of his business, and if you don't jump to, he gets mad as hell, carries on like a crazy man." He pauses, shifts nervously in his chair, then continues angrily, "He and my mom are always fighting, too. It's a real pain. I don't hang around here any more than I have to."

Buddy's mother, Sheila, a thirty-four-year-old telephone operator, echoes her son. "He's so touchy; you can't say anything without him getting mad. I don't mind so much if he takes it out on me, but he's terrible to the kids, especially to my son. That's when I get mad," she explains, passing a hand over her worried brow. "He's got no right to beat up on that kid the way he does."

"Do you mean he actually hits him?" I ask.

She hesitates and looks away, the torment of memory etched on her face. Finally, brushing away the tears that momentarily cloud her vision, she replies, "Yeah, he has. The last time he did it, he really hurt him—twisted his arm so bad it nearly broke—and I told him I'd leave if he ever hit Buddy again. So it's been okay for a while. But who knows? He has a few beers and it's like he goes crazy, like he can't control himself or something."

Many of the unemployed men admit turning to alcohol to relieve the anxiety, loneliness, and fear they experience as they wait day after day, week after week for, as one man put it, "something to happen." "You begin to feel as if you're going nuts, so you drink a few beers to take the edge off," explains thirty-seven-year-old Bill Anstett, a white unemployed construction worker.

It seems so easy. A few beers and he gets a respite from his unwanted feelings—fleeting, perhaps, but effective in affording some relief from the suffering they inflict. But a few beers often turn out to be enough to allow him to throw normal constraints to the wind. For getting drunk can be a way of absenting the con-

scious self so that it can't be held responsible for actions undertaken. Indeed, this may be as much his unconscious purpose as the
need to rid himself of his discomfort. "I admit it, sometimes it's
more than a few and I fall over the edge," Bill grants. "My wife, she
tells me it's like I turn into somebody else, but I don't know about
that because I never remember."

With enough alcohol, inhibitions can be put on hold; con-
science can go underground. "It's the liquor talking," we say when
we want to exempt someone from responsibility for word or deed.
The responsibility for untoward behavior falls to the effects of the
alcohol. The self is in the clear, absolved of any wrongdoing. So it
is with domestic violence and alcohol. When a man gets drunk, the
inner voice that speaks his failure and shame is momentarily stilled.
Most men just relax gratefully into the relief of the internal quiet.
But the man who becomes violent needs someone to blame, someone onto whom he can project the feelings that cause him such
misery. Alcohol helps. It gives him license to find a target. With
enough of it, the doubts and recriminations that plague him are no
longer his but theirs—his wife's, his children's; "them" out there,
whoever they may be. With enough of it, there's nothing to stay his
hand when his helpless rage boils over. "I don't know what happens. It's like something I can't control comes over me. Then afterward I feel terrible," Peter DiAngelo, an unemployed thirty-two-
year-old truck driver, says remorsefully.

One-fifth of the men in this study have a problem with alcohol, not all of them unemployed. Nor is domestic violence perfectly correlated with either alcohol abuse or unemployment. But
the combination is a potentially deadly one that exponentially
increases the likelihood that a man will act out his anger on the
bodies of his wife and children. "My husband drinks a lot more
now; I mean, he always drank some, but not like now," says Inez
Reynoso, a twenty-eight-year-old Latina nurse's aide and mother
of three children who is disturbed about her husband's mistreat-
ment of their youngest child, a three-year-old boy. "I guess he
tries to drink away his troubles, but it only makes more trouble. I
tell him, but he doesn't listen. He has a fiery temper, always has.
But since he lost his job, it's real bad, and his drinking doesn't help
it none.

"I worry about it; he treats my little boy so terrible. He's always had a little trouble with the boy because he's not one of those big, strong kids. He's not like my older kids; he's a timid one, still wakes up scared and crying a lot in the night. Before he got fired, my husband just didn't pay him much attention. But now he's always picking on him; it's like he can't stand having him around. So he makes fun of him something terrible, or he punches him around."

The mother in me recoils at Inez's story. But the psychotherapist understands at least something of what motivates Ramon Reynoso's assault on his young son. For this father, this man who's supposed to be the pillar on which the family rests, who defines himself as a man by his ability to support his family, the sight of this weak and puny little boy is like holding up a mirror to his now powerless self. Unable to tolerate the feelings of self-hatred the image engenders, he projects them outward, onto the child, and rains blows down on him in an effort to distance himself from his own sense of loss and diminishment.

"Does he hit you, too?" I ask Inez.

She squirms in her chair; her fingers pick agitatedly at her jeans. I wait quietly, watching as she shakes her head no. But when she speaks, the words say something else. "He did a couple of times lately, but only when he had too many beers. He didn't mean it. It's just that he's so upset about being out of work, so then when he thinks I protect the boy too much he gets real mad."

When unemployment strikes, sex also becomes an increasingly difficult issue between wives and husbands. A recent study in Great Britain found that the number of couples seeking counseling for sexual problems increased in direct proportion to the rise in the unemployment rate.[13] Anxiety, fear, anger, depression—all emotions that commonly accompany unemployment—are not generators of sexual desire. Sometimes it's the woman whose ardor cools because she's frightened about the future: "I'm so scared all the time, I can't think about sex." Or because she's angry with her husband: "He's supposed to be supporting us and look where we are." More often it's the men who lose their libido along with their jobs—a double whammy for them since male identity rests so heavily in their sexual competence as well as in their work.[14]

This was the one thing the men in this study couldn't talk about. I say "couldn't" because it seemed so clearly more than just "wouldn't." Psychologically, it was nearly impossible for them to formulate the words and say them aloud. They had no trouble complaining about their wives' lack of sexual appetite. But when it was they who lost interest or who become impotent, it was another matter. Then, their tongues were stilled by overwhelming feelings of shame, by the terrible threat their impotence posed to the very foundation of their masculinity.

Their wives, knowing this, are alarmed about their flagging sex lives, trying to understand what happened, wondering what they can do to be helpful. "Sex used to be a big thing for him, but since he's been out of work, he's hardly interested anymore," Dale Meecham, a white thirty-five-year-old waitress says, her anxiety palpable in the room. "Sometimes when we try to do it, he can't, and then he acts like it's the end of the world—depressed and moody, and I can't get near him. It's scary. He won't talk about it, but I can see it's eating at him. So I worry a lot about it. But I don't know what to do, because if I try to, you know, seduce him and it doesn't work, then it only makes things worse."

The financial and emotional turmoil that engulfs families when a man loses his job all too frequently pushes marriages that were already fragile over the brink.[15] Among the families in this study, 10 percent attributed their ruptured marriages directly to the strains that accompanied unemployment. "I don't know, maybe we could have made it if he hadn't lost his job," Maryanne Wallace, a twenty-eight-year-old white welfare mother, says sadly. "I mean, we had problems before, but we were managing. Then he got laid off, and he couldn't find another job, and, I don't know, it was like he went crazy. He was drinking; he hit me; he was mean to the kids. There was no talking to him, so I left, took the kids and went home to my mom's. I thought maybe I'd just give him a scare, you know, be gone for a few days. But when I came back, he was gone, just gone. Nobody's seen him for nearly a year," she says, her voice limping to a halt as if she still can't believe her own story.

Economic issues alone aren't responsible for divorce, of course, as is evident when we look at the 1930s. Then, despite the economic devastation wrought by the Great Depression, the divorce rate didn't rise. Indeed, it was probably the economic privations of that period that helped to keep marriages intact. Since it was so difficult to maintain one household, few people could consider the possibility of having to support two.

But these economic considerations exist today as well, yet recent research shows that when family income drops 25 percent, divorce rises by more than 10 percent.[16] Culture and the institutions of our times make a difference. Then, divorce was a stigma. Now, it's part of the sociology and psychology of the age, an acceptable remedy for the disappointment of our dreams.

Then, too, one-fourth of the work force was unemployed—an economic disaster that engulfed the whole nation. In such cataclysmic moments, the events outside the family tend to overtake and supersede the discontents inside. Now, unemployment is spottier, located largely in the working class, and people feel less like they're in the middle of a social catastrophe than a personal one. Under such circumstances, it's easier to act out their anger against each other.

And finally, the social safety net that came into being after the Great Depression—social security, unemployment benefits, public aid programs targeted specifically to single-parent families—combined with the increasing numbers of women in the work force to make divorce more feasible economically.

Are there no families, then, that stick together and get through the crisis of unemployment without all this trauma? The answer? Of course there are. But they're rare. And they manage it relatively well only if the layoff is short and their resources are long.

Almost always, these are older families where the men have a long and stable work history and where there are fewer debts, some savings, perhaps a home they can refinance. But even among these relatively privileged ones, the pressures soon begin to take their toll. "We did okay for a while, but the longer it lasts, the harder it gets," says forty-six-year-old Karen Brownstone, a white hotel desk clerk whose husband, Dan, lost his welding job nearly six months ago. "After the kids were grown, we finally managed to put some money by. Dan even did some investments, and we made some money. But we're using it up very fast, and I get real scared. What are we going to do when his unemployment runs out?[17]

"I tell him maybe he has to get in a different line of work because maybe they don't need so many welders anymore. But he just gets mad and tells me I don't know what I'm talking about. Then there's no point talking to him at all; he just stamps around and hollers. Or else he leaves, gets in the car and goes screeching away. But I *do* know what I'm talking about. I read in the paper about how these companies are cutting back, and they're not going to need so many workers anymore. He knows it, too; he reads the paper all the time. He just won't try something else; it's like he's too proud or something."

When I talk with Karen's husband, Dan, he leans forward in his chair and says angrily, "I can't go out and get one of those damn flunky jobs like my wife wants me to. I've been working all my life, making a decent living, too, and I got pride in what I do. I try to tell her, but she won't listen." He stops, sighs, puts his head in his hands and speaks more softly: "I'm the only one in my whole family who was doing all right; I even helped my son go to college. I was proud of that; we all were. Now what do I do? It's like I have to go back to where I started. How can you do that at my age?"

He pauses again, looks around the room with an appraising eye, and asks: "What's going to happen to us? I know my wife's scared; that's why she's on my case so much. I worry, too, but what can I do if there's no work? Even she doesn't think I should go sling hamburgers at McDonald's for some goddamn minimum wage."

"There's something between minimum wage jobs and the kind you had before you were laid off, isn't there?" I remark.

"Yeah, I know; you sound like her now," he says, his features softening into a small smile. "But I can't, not yet. I feel like I've got to be ready in case something comes up. Meanwhile, it's not like I'm just sitting around doing nothing. I've hustled up some odd jobs, building things for people, so I pick up a little extra change on the side every now and then. It's not a big deal, but it helps, especially since it doesn't get reported. I don't know, I suppose if things get bad enough, I'll have to do something else. But," he adds, his anger rising again, "dammit, why should I? The kind of jobs you're talking about pay half what I was making. How are we supposed to live on that, tell me that, will you?"

Eventually, men like Dan Brownstone who once held high-paying skilled jobs have no choice but to pocket their pride and take a step down to another kind of work, to one of the service jobs that usually pay a fraction of their former earnings—that is, if they're lucky enough to find one. It's never easy in our youth-oriented society for a man past forty to move to another job or another line of work. But it becomes doubly difficult in times of economic distress when the pool of younger workers is so large and so eager. "Either you're overqualified or you're over the hill," Ed Kruetsman, a forty-nine-year-old unemployed white factory worker, observes in a tired voice.

But young or old, when a man is forced into lower-paying, less skilled work, the move comes with heavy costs—both economic and psychological. Economically, it means a drastic reduction in the family's way of life. "Things were going great. We worked hard, but we finally got enough together so we could buy a house that had enough room for all of us," says thirty-six-year-old Nadine Materie, a white data processor in a bank clearing center. "Tina, my oldest girl, even had her own room; she was so happy about it. Then my husband lost his job, and the only thing he could find was one that pays a lot less, *a lot less.* On his salary now we just couldn't make the payments. We had no choice; we had to sell out and move. Now look at this place!" she commands, with a dismissive sweep of her hand. Then, as we survey the dark, cramped quarters into which this family of five is now jammed, she concludes tearfully, "I hate it, every damn inch of it; I hate it."

For Tina Materie, Nadine's fifteen-year-old daughter, her father's lost job has meant more than the loss of her room. The comforts and luxuries of the past are gone, and the way of life she once took for granted seems like a dream. For a teenager whose sense of self and place in the world is so heavily linked to peer group acceptance and to, in Tina's own words, "being like the other kids," the loss is staggering. "We can't afford anything anymore; and I mean *anything*," she announces dramatically. "I don't even go to the mall with the other kids because they've got money to buy things and I don't. I haven't bought a new record since we moved here. Now my mom says I can't get new school clothes this year; I have to wear my cousin's hand-me-downs. How am I going to go to school in those ugly things? It's bad enough being in this new school, but now . . . ," she stops, unable to find the words to express her misery.

Worst of all for the children in the Materie family, the move from house to apartment took them to a new school in a distant neighborhood, far from the friends who had been at the center of their lives. "My brother and me, we hate living here," Tina says, her eyes misting over as she speaks. "Both of us hate the kids who live around here. They're different, not as nice as the kids where we used to live. They're tough, and I'm not used to it. Sometimes I think I'll quit school and get a job and go live where I want," she concludes gloomily.

Psychologically, the loss of status can be almost as difficult to bear as the financial strain. "I used to drive a long-distance rig, but the company I worked for went broke," explains Greg Northsen, a thirty-four-year-old white man whose wife is an office worker. "I was out of work for eleven and a half months. Want to know how many days that is? Maybe how many hours? I counted every damn one," he quips acidly.

"After all that time, I was ready to take whatever I could get. So now I work as an orderly in a nursing home. Instead of cargo, I'm hauling old people around. The pay's shit and it's damn dirty work. They don't treat those old people good. Everybody's always impatient with them, ordering them around, screaming at them, talking to them like they're dumb kids or something. But with three kids to feed, I've got no choice."

He stops talking, stares wordlessly at some spot on the opposite wall for a few moments, then, his eyes clouded with unshed tears, he rakes his fingers through his hair and says hoarsely, "It's goddamn hard. This is no kind of a job for a guy like me. It's not just the money; it's . . . ." He hesitates, searching for the words, then, "It's like I got chopped off at the knees, like . . . aw, hell, I don't know how to say it." Finally, with a hopeless shrug, he concludes, "What's the use? It's no use talking about it. It makes no damn difference; nothing's going to make a difference. I don't understand it. What the hell's happening to this country when there's no decent jobs for men who want to work?"

Companies go bankrupt; they merge; they downsize; they restructure; they move—all reported as part of the economic indicators, the cold statistics that tell us how the economy is doing. But each such move means more loss, more suffering, more families falling victim to the despair that comes when father loses his job, more people shouting in rage and torment: "What the hell's happening to this country?"

7

SHATTERED DREAMS

"Used to be you worked hard, you figured you got someplace. Not anymore," says thirty-eight-year-old George Karvick, a white father of three who worked for years in an automobile parts factory and now has a job in the maintenance division of a real estate management company. "We did everything we were supposed to do—worked hard, saved some money, tried to raise our kids to be decent law-abiding people—and what do we get?" he asks, his words biting, his eyes burning with indignation. "The goddamn company goes belly-up and look at me now.

"Maintenance, they call it; I'm nothing but a goddamn janitor," he says, spitting out the words as if they sear his tongue. "I worked hard to get where I was, and it's damn hard to go backward."

It is, indeed, "damn hard to go backward," harder still to believe in a future when things might be different again. "Life's never been some kind of a picnic, but now, every day there's more bad news," says George's wife, Anna. "It's so scary. I worry all the time. How bad will it get? It's like you work your whole life to be something, you know, so your kids will grow up and be something, and look what happens. Now I don't know; what are we working for now?"

The hope that sustained working-class people through bad

times twenty years ago, the belief that if they worked hard and played by the rules they would eventually grab a piece of the American dream, has been shattered. And with good reason. The 1973 recession marked the beginning of a long decline for American workers—a slide whose worst effects were obscured by the rise of two-income families and cushioned by the spending binge of the 1980s. By the time that decade was gone, the government had more than tripled the national debt, and the IOUs of both industry and consumers had more than doubled.[1]

In the 1990s the bill came due. But when the economy slumped this time, there were no reserves, nothing to break the fall—not in industry, not in the government, not in personal checking or savings accounts. Instead, both the nation and its people were left with a ruinous load of debt that required drastic cutbacks in both the public and private sectors. For industry this meant a dramatic restructuring of American business that took millions of jobs, at least half of which are gone for good, according to the best estimates of labor experts and the executives heading up the corporate makeovers.[2] Even the service sector, which saw fairly high levels of growth during the 1980s and which provided a paycheck—although a less than satisfactory one—for workers displaced from manufacturing, has suffered a shakeout that no one expects to end soon.[3]

Reflecting on these changes in the economy, Janet Norwood, the former U.S. Commissioner of Labor Statistics, said: "We've never been in a situation quite like this. It used to be that when we had a recession, everyone waited to be rehired. But the psychology now is that many of these jobs are not going to come back."[4]

For many younger workers who are trying to get a foothold on the ladder, therefore it's not going backward that worries them but whether there's any possibility of moving forward. "It's not like it was when my folks were my age," complains Ed Demovic, a twenty-five-year-old white stock clerk, married four years with two small children. "My parents didn't have it easy, and neither did Linda's. I listen to my dad talk; he didn't have any gravy train, but there was a chance to get ahead. You know, if you were willing to work hard, you could do okay. When one of us kids complained, he'd always tell us how we were living a lot better than he did when he was a kid, so we had no gripes coming. Not anymore! I'm not going to be able to say that to my own kids. From where I stand, it looks like we're going to be worse off. And God knows how bad things'll be by the time their turn comes."

The changed realities of the job market, the belief—a reasonable one until recently—that a college education would pay off heavily in increased lifetime earnings, has sent working-class youth into the college classroom in larger numbers than ever before.

Yet our optimistic statistics about the benefits of a college education obscure fundamental truths about class and gender differences. In 1990 men with four years of college earned, on average, $44,554 a year compared to $28,043 for male high-school graduates. Women college graduates, however, earned only $28,911— virtually the same as men who only went to high school—while women with high-school diplomas earned $18,954—nearly $10,000 less than men with the same education.[5]

The same income tables that show an increase in earnings of college graduates over those with four years of high school make no distinction between the kind of low-prestige school a working-class youth is likely to attend and the elite college or university that educates the child of a professional family. But it's clear to anyone who is not blinded by our myth of classlessness that the education is superior and the opportunities for mobility greater with a degree from Harvard or Princeton than one from Clearview State. If the average earnings of college graduates were broken down by school—which would, by and large, reflect a breakdown by class— the annual income of the Clearview graduate would be significantly less than the one from Princeton. As I wrote in *Worlds of Pain*, "Even when the children of working-class families go to a four-year college, most go to schools that, at best, will track them into lower-middle-class jobs through which they will live lives only slightly better than their parents'."[6]

Ironically, even that meager promise has now been broken. As of the late 1980s over three million people with some college education were working at full-time jobs that paid less than $11,000 a year.[7] By now that number undoubtedly is considerably higher. And even those college graduates who have enjoyed the prosperity their education promised now face diminished prospects. From

1979 to 1989, for example, the average earnings of people with a college degree rose by 2 percent after adjustment for inflation. Over the next three years these same college graduates saw their wages drop by 1.6 percent.[8]

At the same time that wages were falling, the average cost of a college education at a four-year public institution—the only kind a working-class student can possibly afford—soared from $599 a year in 1975 to $2,006 in 1990, while funds for student aid decreased. At those prices, a working-class youth needs not only a high level of motivation but a job, a student loan, and a room at home with Mom and Dad. "I couldn't go to school if I didn't live at home," explained Susanna Dionne, a black nineteen-year-old student and part-time worker. "I work twenty-four hours a week, and I've got some student loans, but it's not enough to pay for rent and food. Mostly between my job and my loan, I have enough to pay for my tuition and books and have a little left over for clothes and expenses like that. I'm lucky, though; I've got it better than a lot of my friends. I only pay my parents board, no rent."

With all her "luck," by the time Susanna graduates from college, she'll be between $10,000 and $12,000 in debt with no certainty of the kind of job her degree would have bought in rosier economic times. If she goes on to graduate or professional school, she'll add another $8,000 or so to her debt burden. Asked how she expects to pay off such debts, she answers worriedly, "I don't know; I worry about it all the time. I'd like to go to social work school and get my master's, but I get scared when I think about owing all that money. But the problem is, when I read the paper and see how hard it is to get a decent job, then I think maybe I have to. I mean, what choice will I have? Go to college all these years for some stupid job at Kmart?"

In an economy where unemployment is high, where media headlines announce that college graduates face the "worst job market in thirty years,"[9] and where the wages of the college educated haven't kept up with inflation for the last several years, Susanna and her peers have something to worry about. "I feel like I can't win, and I keep wondering what I'm doing," she continues. "I'm going to owe all this money and if I have to go to graduate school to get a decent job, it'll be even more. How am I ever going to pay it back?

No matter what I do, I'll be in debt for years and years. What am I going to do, live with my parents forever so I can pay off my debts?"

Susanna's parents brood, too. "How's she going to pay off all the money she'll owe?" asks her father, Raymond, a forty-five-year-old semiskilled worker. "What kind of a way is that to start out a life, having such big debts?" Her mother, Louise, a forty-year-old clerical worker, seconds her husband's words and adds her own concerns as well: "Don't get me wrong," she warns. "I don't want to push my kids out the door, but I've been Mom for a long time. My oldest son's got a job and a girlfriend, but he still lives here because he doesn't make enough money to get married and move out. And I've got another girl coming up behind Susanna. What's going to happen if these kids can't get off on their own like grown children are supposed to do? How long do we have to turn our lives over to them?" she asks, looking intently at me, as if expecting an answer.

It's a question that troubles many parents today as, in this era of decreasing wages and rising unemployment, more than a quarter of all adults under thirty-five are living under the parental roof.[10] True, as I said earlier, adult children in working-class families have always lived at home until they married. But until recently, they generally married in their teens, as the working-class women and men I interviewed twenty years ago did. Today, however, with so many young people deferring marriage into their twenties and beyond, their presence in the household becomes a noticeable burden to parents who are ready to move on to the next stage of life. "Our parents didn't have a chance to get tired of us being around," laughs Regina Whitehead, a white forty-seven-year-old receptionist. "I was eighteen, just out of high school, and Danny was nineteen, almost twenty, I guess, when we got married. It's different today. With kids not wanting to get married, and they can't afford to live on their own, they hang around a long time, and it's like you wonder when you're going to get to live your own life."

For the mothers, especially, almost all of whom work full-time outside the home, the full nest, not the empty one, is the problem. "We've got two of my kids still living with us. They're good kids; I even like having them here sometimes," continues Regina. "But it's hard; there's always something extra to do, lots of extra laundry all the time, things like that. And you know, if it was just me and my husband, I wouldn't be worrying so much all the time about what to cook for supper. It's a lot different when you've got them around. I come home from work, and there's always some kind of mess to clean up. Just once before I die I'd like to know what it's like to come home and the house would be just the way I left it," she concludes with a sigh.

Women like Regina Whitehead not only have a different sense of themselves than their mothers did, but a different set of expectations for this stage of life. Two decades ago many of the young families I met left their children in a grandmother's care while mother went off to a part-time job. It's true that these grandmothers usually were paid for their child-care services. But it was also a labor of love, something grandmothers expected to do, indeed would have been glad to do without charge if their financial situations permitted. Today, however, Grandma is likely to have her own full-time job. "I sometimes feel guilty because I can't help my kids out like my mother helped me," says Regina. "But I can't work and take care of the grandbabies, too."

It isn't just that she can't, however; it's also that she doesn't want to. "You say you 'can't,' which suggests it's what you'd like to do if you could afford to stay home," I remark.

She laughs. "Guess you caught me there, didn't you? Don't get me wrong, I love being Grandma, but my life's important to me, too, and so is my job. It may not be some big-time job like yours, but I like doing it."

Even fathers, most of whom cling to the old traditions more tightly than mothers—especially for their daughters—are ready for their adult children to leave the nest. "It's one thing you don't want the kids out on their own when they're eighteen, nineteen. But twenty-five?" exclaims Dan Whitehead acerbically. "If my girls had tried to leave when they were eighteen, I would have broken their legs. But I don't know; now I think: *Christ, how long?* I mean, what I really want is for them to get married and settle down in a place of their own. But if they're not going to do that, well, I don't know, maybe it's time for them to go anyway."

In all families an adult child living at home poses a dilemma: How will these adults, who are also and always parent and child, relate to each other? What happens to the old family rules? What kind of responsibilities can parents expect the children to assume? These are difficult issues for families to resolve. But for middle-class families the return of adult children doesn't create the kind of economic burden that working-class parents experience, nor does it generally mean a change in their life plans.

For the older families in this study, retirement—or if not actual retirement some other significant life change, such as a move from the city to the country—is high on the list of things they dream about, talk about, plan for. "All I've been thinking about is retiring and getting out of this stinking city," says Walt Mobley, a fifty-three-year-old white security guard. "My wife and me, we talk about it all the time."

But as their children continue to need their help, such talk comes to seem more like a fantasy than a realistic plan for the future. "Crazy, isn't it?" he continues. "Here we are with the kids all grown up; we should be making our plans. But what happens? I can't because I have to take care of them. My son's got a shitload of debts from college, so he can't go anywhere until he pays some of that off. That bum my daughter was married to walked out on her, so now she's here with her two kids. God knows when she'll get her life together again."

It isn't only the needs of adult children, however, that stand in the way of the older generation realizing its dreams. Few working-class families have the kind of pensions or investments that would allow them to retire in reasonable comfort. Their largest and most significant asset is the house they live in, the house that they always assumed would provide the nest egg for their old age. "The one thing we knew we had was the equity in this house; it was our security blanket." But after years of rising property values, most of these families awakened one day to find that their homes had lost a sizable portion of their value. According to a report in the *Wall Street Journal*, home equity dropped an unprecedented 16.6 percent in 1990, causing a decline in average household net worth for only the second time since World War II.[11]

In Southern California, the site of the greatest and most sustained level of housing price appreciation in history, the bust has been so severe that, in one three-month period during 1992, nearly

18 percent of homes sold for less than their purchase price.[12] A figure that would be much higher if most sellers hadn't taken their houses off the market rather than suffer the loss. "We paid $240,000 for this place seven years ago," says May Yau, a forty-nine-year-old Asian office worker who lives in a small city near Los Angeles. "A couple of years later, it was worth over $300,000. If we had sold even two, three years ago, when we first thought about it, that's what we could have gotten. Now it's too late; the best offer we've had was $215,000. So we're stuck here for a while anyway." Unfortunately for the Yaus and others like them, it may be a very long while, since California housing economists predict that home prices will plunge another 20 percent before leveling off.[13]

Translated into human terms, this means, among other things, that plans for the future have to be reconsidered. "Work's so damn slow, it'd be a good time to call it quits and get out of here," says Don Lermen, a fifty-five-year-old white mechanic. "But with the economy the way it is, nobody's buying houses in this city right now. We had the place up for sale for eight months and didn't have a nibble. The real estate agent said when a place hangs around that long, it gets stale. So we took it off the market. You know, even if we could sell it right now, with prices what they are—so low, I mean—we wouldn't get enough out of it. So it comes down to, I can't afford to retire."

Equally important, it means also that people who felt safe in their affluence now experience themselves at risk. "Until a couple of years ago, I had this plan," explains Paul Terrones, a fifty-year-old white appliance repair man. "We've got some savings, see, some investments that could bring in some money. So I figured we'd sell this house, and buy a little place up in the mountains. I don't mean where the tourists go; some small town where you could buy something cheap so I could put the rest of the money from the house into something that would bring in some more income. Between that, and maybe I'd do a few odd jobs on the side—you know, building or fixing things for people in town—we could live a good life. But no more; I can't even think about it anymore. This house is down about 25 percent in the last two years. And with interest rates where they are, you've got to be a lot richer than I'm ever going to be to live off investments.

"So what am I going to do now? Hell, I don't know, and I don't like not knowing. Me and my wife, we both feel kind of nervous all the time now, you know, uptight about what's going to happen, how we'll manage. Christ!" he explodes, slamming his fist against the arm of his chair. "I thought we had it made, and look at us all of a sudden worrying about what's going to happen tomorrow."

It's one of the great ironies of this era that while the older generation worries about falling housing prices, their children find themselves priced out of the housing market. Twenty years ago a young working-class family had a chance of making the dream of owning a home come true. "It's what we worked for, to have a nice house for the kids to grow up in," explains Serena Wycoff, a forty-five-year-old white hairdresser. "It was hard; we were young, and we had babies right away. And it took quite a few years for my husband to settle down in a job. He floated around at first, trying this and that. But when he saw nothing else really worked, he got on at Ford, and he's been there ever since. God willing, he'll stay there until he retires. But with the economy the way it is and everybody getting laid off, you can't be sure of anything these days, can you?" she concludes, shaking her head as if to push the unwanted thoughts away.

The Wycoffs' house, like the homes of most working-class people of their generation, is small, unpretentious, modestly furnished, the pride of ownership visible in the many loving little touches that say: *This is mine, the achievement of a lifetime.* But even the falling prices and lowered mortgage rates haven't brought such a home within the reach of most young working-class families.[14] Those in the top income tier might be able to support the mortgage payments, but the down payment is a daunting obstacle. In the last two decades, therefore, the proportion of young families who own their own homes dropped from 51.4 percent to 44.3 percent,[15] while the average age of first-time home buyers leaped astonishingly—from twenty-seven to thirty-five in the ten years between 1980 and 1990.[16]

The few families in this study who have managed to become homeowners have been forced into the very low end of the housing market, which means that their houses have even less space and fewer comforts than the unassuming homes in which they grew up.

"Believe me, I didn't grow up in no mansion, but it was a lot nicer house than this one, bigger, too," says Luanne Roberts, a thirty-one-year-old white cashier, who surveys her living room with a critical eye.

Or the only housing they can afford is in distant fringe cities, leaving them with long commutes that add not only to the daily stress but also to the time pressure that husbands and wives both complain about so bitterly. "The driving back and forth is a killer; traffic's murder," explains Burt Reimerson, a thirty-three-year-old white warehouse worker who lives in a small city on the edge of a metropolitan area in the Midwest. "I get off work at 5 and don't get home until 6, 6:30. By then I'm dead beat. But can I just take a load off and take it easy? Hell, no. First there's the kids; then the wife's always got something for me to do. Christ, there's no time to live; it's work and shit, that's all, work and shit. But what can I do? No way could we afford a house closer to the city—no way."

Stress and time, however, aren't the only expenses of the commute to suburb or exurb. When the Reimersons lived in the city, Burt's wife, Leona, was a secretary making over $20,000 a year. Now with the mortgage payment higher than the rent they used to pay and the additional expense of a long-distance commute, her earnings are more important to the family economy than ever before. But being so far away from the children proved to be too anxiety provoking. "At first we thought I'd commute, too, like Burt does," she explains. "I tried it for a couple of months, but it didn't work. It's not good for both of us to be over an hour away from the kids. I worried the whole time I was gone. Suppose they need something? Or one of them gets sick? Or maybe it's snowing and I can't get home. Burt didn't like it either, so we talked and decided I should quit and look for something closer to home."

But she hasn't been able to find a comparable job in or near the town where they now live. "I guess there never were that many places to work around here, but with the recession and nobody's hiring and companies going out of business and all . . . ," she explains, her words trailing off, her hands thrust forward, palms up in a gesture of helplessness. "I looked and looked but I couldn't find a secretary's job like the one I had, and things were getting tighter and tighter. We needed the money real bad, so I couldn't hold out anymore. I gave up and took this job in the bakery, working for $4.50 an hour. Can you believe it?" she asks, shaking her head and pausing to let the words sink in. Then she continues, a note of pride in her voice: "I worked my way up after about a year, so now I manage the shop. But I still only get $6.25 an hour, not near what I was making before. It's something like $8,000 a year less. Boy, what a difference that would make in our life right now. This move cost us so much, I sometimes wonder whether it was worth it. We both do," she concludes wistfully.

Yet the Reimersons and the others like them are the lucky ones. For the rest, the dream of owning a home seems like a mirage. "It pisses me off," exclaims Dale Streets, a twenty-nine-year-old black UPS driver. "I grew up in a house, but I don't think my kids will. And I'm one of the lucky ones. I got a steady job; I make a pretty good living, and with what my wife brings in, we're doing okay. But you've got to be rich to buy a house these days, and that ain't going to happen," he concludes unhappily.

It's true that with housing prices so high buying a home is a problem for young families in any class. But parents in the middle- and upper-income brackets are far more likely than those below to be able to offer all or part of a down payment to their children. For the working-class young, such outside help rarely is available. "Have you seen the prices of houses around here?" asks Delia Johnson, a black twenty-eight-year-old bridge toll taker. "I'm not talking about anything fancy, just a plain old little house. Even with both of us working as hard as we can, we're never going to be able to save enough to buy one. I mean, we talk about it; we even go out looking sometimes. But it's not going to happen. Where would we ever get the money for a down payment?" she asks, her body slumping in discouragement.

It's not only while they're alive that middle-class parents help out their adult children, but after they die as well. No one talks much about this nearly taboo subject, but the prospect of an inheritance is a reality of life that most young middle-class adults don't forget.[17] For it provides both a financial and a psychological safety net to know that one day they'll come into enough money to ease at least some of their financial burdens. The working-class young see no possibility for such relief. Indeed, most of them will be lucky if they don't have to support their parents in their old age.

In addition to whatever help or inheritance they may get from their well-off parents, the adult children of middle- and upper-middle-class families earn more money, therefore have far more options than those in the working class. In her inquiry into the downward mobility of middle-class baby boomers, Katherine Newman writes at length about the housing misfortunes of young adults who grew up in an affluent town in New Jersey. Unable to afford homes in the community of their childhood or its stylish equivalents, they settle for housing in less prosperous towns, where houses are smaller than those they're accustomed to; community services, conveniences, and comforts are fewer; and neighbors are more diverse.

"Communities that have lower housing costs often lack the amenities that make a well-heeled community like Pleasanton so desirable: parks, pools, and the like," writes Newman. "They are also more likely to be mixed income towns where racial and class tension is in the air. Whatever the current economic status of Pleasanton's boomers, there is no escaping the fact that they were raised in a lily-white town, where the schools were good, and the diction, world-view, and style of the middle to upper-middle class became part and parcel of their personalities. People raised in Pleasanton stick out when they 'integrate' these modest communities and often find they have little in common with their older, less educated neighbors. Housing, it seems, is not all they were after: a community of like-minded souls is no less important and it may be a long time in coming," Newman concludes.[18]

Small wonder that working-class families are so irate today. They watch the neighborhoods they love being taken over by people who "stick out," who are contemptuous of them and their lifestyle, and worst of all, who move there as a last resort and for whom the need to do so is one of life's misfortunes. For what to Newman's middle-class families seems like deprivation would be a gift of abundance to the working-class families in this study. Indeed, it's at least partly the migration of young professional middle-class families into these communities that has priced the working class out. For the older families who live in these neighborhoods, there's some benefit. As the professionals move in and gentrify the area, property values go up. But the children of the working-class will suffer the cost, since they'll never by able to buy a house in the neighborhood they grew up in.

The parents of the young families in this study watch the struggle of their adult children in pain and puzzlement. "What happened?" they ask themselves. "Where did it all go wrong?" they wonder. They did what was expected, willingly sacrificing their own comforts and gratifications in their earlier years in the belief that it would ensure a better, easier life for their children in the later ones. Hasn't this been the unique and quintessential American promise—that each generation would surpass the one before it? "You always expected that you'd sacrifice but it would be worth it because your kids will have it better than you did," says Leona Reimerson's mother, a forty-nine-year-old sales clerk whose husband, Joe, has worked on the assembly line for twenty-three years. "What else did you work all your life for?"

For the parental generation—men and women who are old enough to have been wage earners twenty years ago—nothing seems to make much sense anymore. When they were their children's age, median family income (in 1972 dollars) hovered around $12,000 a year; now it has nearly tripled to just over $34,000. For those who managed on $12,000 two decades ago, the idea that they could make over $30,000 and still feel poor is almost impossible to comprehend. As Mike Fillman, a white forty-nine-year-old machinist, exclaimed: "Dammit, I don't get it. Between me and the wife we make $38,000 a year, and we're always behind. I remember when I thought that was a fortune. If anybody'd ever told me I wouldn't be rich on that kind of money, I'd have told him he was nuts. Back when I was making twelve or thirteen grand a year, I used to think if I could just get up to twenty I'd have it made. Now thirty-eight doesn't make it. How do you figure it?"

It is hard indeed to "figure it," to integrate the fact that dollars no longer mean the same thing, that he can make what once seemed like "a fortune" to him and still have trouble paying the bills. He knows that everything costs more, that taxes are higher, that they take a bigger cut out of his paycheck now than they did before. He has heard and read enough to know that, after taking inflation into account, his $38,000 isn't worth much more than his

$12,000 was two decades ago. And he knows, too, that the average pay for men in his line of work fell by about 4 percent in 1991.[19]

But this cognitive knowledge lies alongside a deeply embedded sensibility born in the past, making it difficult to incorporate fully the new reality. So when he comes up against the economic squeeze he feels in the present, he's caught, not quite able to understand why he's hurting financially when the numbers tell him he *ought* to feel rich. Just so, when he sees his grown children unable to make it on incomes that would have seemed grand when he was their age, the picture doesn't make sense. "I don't get it, that's all; I just don't get it. It's all unreal; nothing makes any sense anymore. How did we get to this place in this country? What the hell's gone wrong?"

Partly what's gone wrong is that while the numbers seem large, when inflation is factored in, adults thirty-five and younger earn less now than people in the same age group did thirty years ago. Moreover, although federal income taxes haven't risen substantially, and in some cases may even be less than they were before, other taxes—such as state income taxes, payroll taxes, property taxes, sales taxes, social security, and various local taxes and use fees— have taken an increasing share of the weekly paycheck of most workers.

During the 1960s, for example, real wages were increasing by 1 or 2 percent a year, while taxes were taking about one-third of the extra income. So long as people were improving their living standard, the tax burden wasn't an issue. But in the 1970s real wages began to stagnate or decline at the same time that many taxes were increasing, which meant that taxes were taking a greater portion of people's already diminishing income—a situation that laid the basis for the tax revolts that in recent years have made headlines in communities across the country.

But while the increasing tax burden is the manifest target of working-class anger, the discontinuity between past and present realities sustains and nourishes their discontent. "At first when I started to work it seemed like we were making so much money," says Mike's wife, Marlen. "I mean, $38,000! That's a lot, isn't it? We really felt rich, like now we could have all those nice things we couldn't afford before. We bought a new refrigerator—the old one was *really* old—and new carpet and a sofa for the living room, things like that. And Mike bought a new car. It was the first brand new car he ever bought. We tried to help out the kids, too; they were having a real hard time. Then all of a sudden, the bills piled up on us. Sure, it was easy to charge all that stuff, but pretty soon we were having trouble paying the interest on our credit cards. We learned pretty fast that we weren't rich," she concludes ruefully.

The result has been a peculiar disjunction between the belief that they ought to be affluent juxtaposed against the end-of-the-month shortfall, leaving people perplexed and uncertain about just how to feel and whom to blame. "What the hell's happening to this country?" they shout. "Nothing makes sense anymore," they cry. But since no one lives comfortably in a world in which "nothing makes sense," they make sense in whatever way they can, which often means blaming "them." Sometimes "they" are an abstraction—the government, the politicians, the bureaucrats, the feds, the Congress. But there's little satisfaction in raging against these distant, lifeless, and immovable bodies. So they turn instead on those in their line of vision—the aliens in their midst, most of whom these days are people of color.

3

RACE AND THE RISE OF ETHNICITY

8

PAST HISTORY/PRESENT REALITY

The Bardolinos

"I'm Italian," says Tony Bardolino. "My grandparents came over from the old country before the first world war from this little village in Italy and until the day they died, it was still home to them. After all those years here, my grandmother could hardly speak any English. If you lived in one of those Italian neighborhoods back East like they did, I guess you didn't have any reason to learn English. Everybody talked Italian.

"I hardly remember them. My father was the youngest of twelve kids, so they were pretty old when I was born, and I was still a little kid—I don't know, maybe about ten or eleven—when they died. I just remember that being Italian was a big deal; everything was always 'In Italy this' and 'Italian that.' You know how that is, people think everything they've got is always the best.

"I guess my old man must have had a bellyful of it because he left New York and moved to California. He was stationed out here in World War II, and he never went back there, at least not to live, after he got out of the army. He's the only one of the twelve kids who did that; the rest mostly still live back East."

"Do you speak Italian?" I ask Tony.

"No. I mean, I know a few words I picked up from when I was a kid, but that's all. Even my father and mother don't really know it anymore. I mean, they did when they were growing up. My father says he had to talk Italian when he was a kid because his folks didn't know English. But he's been away from there a long time, and I haven't heard them talk Italian since we were kids and they didn't want us to understand what they were saying. Well, that's not exactly right. They can still put on a show if they have to, like if we're in an Italian restaurant with them, they'll talk Italian to the people there. But even if you didn't know anything, you could tell they're not so good at it. I mean, they know a lot more than me or my kids know. Ha, that's a joke. My kids, they don't know anything; they're just plain old vanilla California kids, that's all."

"Does that bother you?"

"I don't exactly know. Me and my wife, we talk about it sometimes. It seems like a shame that they don't know anything about their background. But then I think, *Why? What's such a shame?* I mean, what would I want them to know? They know they're Italian. If you ask them, that's what they'll tell you. But maybe it would be nice if they could speak the language; maybe they'll study it when they get to high school."

"Did you?"

"Nope. I didn't get into any of that. I wasn't interested then, but when I think about it now, I guess I sort of wish I did. I don't know why; it just seems like it would be nice to know it."

"Can you say how being Italian affects your life?

He leans forward in the chair and shrugs: "I don't know; I guess it doesn't. It's just there; you know, like something that was there before I was born, and it'll be there after I'm gone." He pauses, gazes past me for a moment, then says, "But that's something, isn't it? My kids' kids, they'll be Italian, and their kids, too.

"But what does being Italian mean to you?"

"You mean besides pizza and pasta?" he asks laughing. Then more seriously, "Hell, I don't know exactly how to answer that. Well, it means family, I guess; that's the big thing with Italians— family. When I was a kid, we'd go back East—you know, where my father's family still lives—and I'd think, *Gee, this is nice, all the cousins around, always somebody to play with.* It was like real warm and friendly because everybody knows everybody and people care about each other."

I know the neighborhood he's talking about because I interviewed the family of one of Tony's many cousins there. It was the eastern Bardolinos, in fact, who referred me to the California side of the family. As I listen to Tony speak I remember walking the streets of that small section of the city where they live and feeling as if I'd entered an Italian village. The geography and topography are different, but the ambience is much the same.

As evening fell and the day's work was done, the streets came to life, women shouting their greetings, men strolling over to the café for an espresso and a game of cards. Instead of Joe and Paul and Ben, however, these men were called Giuseppe and Pasquale and Benito. None of the adults was speaking in English. Only among the children, whose shrill calls pierced the soft air of an Indian summer evening, did I hear the sounds of both English and Italian.

The café is the center of community life, just as it is in the villages of Italy. There, local gossip is exchanged; news of the old country passed from one to another. On the evening of my visit, they were talking about a sick child in the village back home. It's now two or three generations since the immigrants came, but everyone, even the young people who were born here, still refer to that Italian community as "my home village." Although I couldn't understand the words, I could hear the urgency that underlay them as they made plans to collect money to help pay the medical bills of a child in Italy that few of them knew.

"Will everyone give money?" I asked twenty-two-year-old Giuseppe Bardolino, who was my guide and interpreter on that evening.

He looked at me bewildered. "What do you mean?"

I wasn't sure how to respond since my question seemed so clear. So I tried again. "I mean, not everyone knows this child, and I'd guess most families around here don't have a lot of extra money. So won't there be some who won't want to give anything?"

"No. She's a *paesan*, a kid from our home village; sure they'll give," he replied, as if that information alone was enough to explain the community response.

With these images of his eastern family floating around in my head, I pull myself back to the present and ask Tony: "Do you ever wish you could live in a neighborhood like the one your cousins still live in and be surrounded by family and by so much that's distinctly Italian?"

He smiles and shrugs: "No, I don't think so. It looked good when I was a kid, but even then I didn't like it so much that anybody on the street could act like my father or mother. I mean, once you went out of the house any grown-up had a right to tell you what to do, and if you didn't listen with respect—that's a big Italian thing, respect—you'd get it when you got home. I mean, sure people care about each other, but that's not always so great either. There's no privacy; everybody knows everybody's business. It's like you can't get away from them; you're surrounded.

"And then there's all those feuds. That's the other thing about Italians—the blood feuds. Who wants to live with that crap? People don't talk to each other because of some stupid thing that made somebody mad a hundred years ago. My father used to tell us stories he heard from his folks about the feuds in Italy. People actually killed each other there. It's kind of crazy stuff, but like the song says, 'that's Italian,'" he concludes, a wry note of pride in his voice.

*   *   *

Although some analysts argue that regional differences don't exist,[1] I have long had the impression that the accouterments of white ethnic culture, and the identity and attachment that go along with them, are more important in the eastern part of the country than in the West. It's clear that, the recent resurgence of ethnicity notwithstanding, its waning is a national phenomenon. But it's equally plain to even a casual observer that both ethnic culture and identification are a more visible fact of life in the East than in the West.

Partly perhaps this is a class phenomenon. The Irish neighborhoods of South Boston are bound together as much by the common experience of privation as by their ethnic heritage. True, the two probably are interactive. Since the intensity of ethnic bonds wanes among those who move out of the old neighborhood and into the middle class, it's reasonable to assume that the experience of shared deprivation reinforces the ties among those who can't escape. But in a nation where myth has it that everyone is middle class, and where the conventional wisdom says that their class position is a product of their own inadequacies, it's also psychologically easier and safer for people to see ethnicity as the binding force rather than to acknowledge the commonality of their working-class status.

The class distinction holds in the West as well. But the social structures that historically reinforced white ethnic group solidarity and identity—the shared status that resulted from the channeling of group members into particular occupations; the residential concentration that helped to preserve elements of the institutions, associations, and language of the mother country—didn't exist when the West was opened up. Certainly, some aspects of these communities were recreated in western cities. But for both sociological and psychological reasons, they didn't have the same cohesive power as those in the East.

Sociologically, there wasn't a continuing flow of immigrants to shore up the European ethnic communities as there was in cities like New York, Buffalo, Boston, Philadelphia, or Chicago.[2] Moreover, opportunities for social and economic mobility were greater in the West where, because of its newness, the social hierarchy was more fluid than in the more established eastern cities.

Psychologically, too, there were differences between the immigrants who remained huddled together in their eastern ghettos and those who left the relative safety of the community and the life they knew to pursue a vision of something else. For these people, some level of psychological separation from the extended clan must already have been in place, and their ethnic attachments, if not their identity, at least somewhat attenuated. Once they left, therefore, they may have been happy to put behind them the demands for conformity these ethnic communities exerted, therefore reluctant to establish new ones in the image of the old.

Whatever the cause, the separate and distinct enclaves of ethnic whites that still are visible in the large cities of the Northeast and Midwest are almost nonexistent in the West. San Francisco has its famous North Beach, it's true—a center-city neighborhood filled with Italian coffeehouses, restaurants, and shops that cater to the city's love affair with Italian food. There, it's still possible on a Sunday afternoon to watch old men play bocce ball and to hear Italian spoken on the street, as families take their after-dinner stroll around the park. But it's increasingly uncommon. For North Beach long ago lost most of its Italian population, who, along with other white ethnics, left the heart of the city for its outlying districts or for the suburbs.

But even the ethnic enclaves in the East aren't likely to remain intact for long, as young people become restless with the limited opportunities and the social constraints. Giuseppe Bardolino ("Joe" in the world outside the neighborhood) is a good example. "My father only wants me to stay here and work with him in the café, but I've got to get out. I tried to do what he wants, but I can't. Don't get me wrong, I have a lot of respect for these people, but I can't live this life. It chokes you. So last year I figured if I really wanted to get out, I better go to college so I can get a decent job. It's my second year now, and I'm doing real good. But if you listen to my father, you'd think I was a criminal or something. Who knows?" he adds sardonically, "I sometimes think he'd like that better."

A short while later I sit at a table in the corner of the café with Giuseppe's father, Italian-born Benito Bardolino, and listen as he asks: "Why does he have to go to college? What's book learning going to get him? Let him go out and get a job like a real man if he doesn't want to work here with me."

To Giuseppe/Joe, caught between the two worlds symbolized by his two names, his father seems narrow in vision and mean in spirit. But the reality is more complicated. Partly Benito's resistance to his son's aspirations rests in the fact that the world he seeks seems a frightening one—a world where life is unpredictable, where alien values hold sway. "My son says he wants a different life. What does that mean?" he asks uncomprehendingly. "He wants to give up the family, the community, his *paesanos?* Without that you're nothing. Doesn't he understand that's his history?"

When he talks about his history, Benito doesn't just mean the village with its ancient ways and myriad family and social connections. He wants his son to remember also the struggles of his forebears when they first came to the land of golden opportunity. For it was neither golden nor safe for those Mediterranean migrants, who learned quickly about America's revulsion to dark skin. Some who ventured into the South became victims of the southern obsession with race and, mistaken for American blacks, found themselves on the wrong end of the hangman's rope. But even in the North, life was hard and acceptance excruciatingly slow. "All my life I heard how hard it was for Italians when they first came to this country. It wasn't easy for me either," recalls Benito. "I was only eight when we came, but I still remember what it was like, I mean, feeling out of place and people making fun of you, and you got no place to hide except around your own kind. Now my son wants to forget all that, like it didn't happen."

Partly, also, Benito worries that he'll not only lose his son but his grandchildren as well. "He goes to college like he's better than everybody else, and what'll he have? No family, no *paesanos*, nothing. That's a life? What? He'll move someplace far away and come see his family on Christmas and Easter? Is that what he wants? His kids won't even know the language. We see it here all the time; these kids move away, then come back with grandchildren who can hardly say an Italian word."

And partly the father fears that if his son surpasses him, he'll forfeit his respect. "I've seen these kids who go to college, they get swell heads and they think they know it all. My son, he already thinks he's smarter than the old man. He gets any more fancy ideas in his head, I won't be able to talk to him at all."

But with all the bluster, the same father who derogates his son's "book learning," who complains about his "fancy ideas," also takes a certain pride in his achievements. "He's a smart kid," he tells me proudly. "He's getting good grades, not like his brother who didn't finish high school."

There are, of course, well-recognized differences among ethnic groups, with some, like the Jews and the Chinese, pushing their children onto the mobility path. In these communities family pride and status depend upon the children's successful climb. But there also are costs both to the family and to the ethnic group—costs that people in these communities begin to count only in retrospect.

The gap between relatively uneducated parents and their highly educated children affects both intergenerational and ethnic group solidarity. The more educated the children, the greater the social and intellectual distance from their parents. With advanced education, horizons broaden and opportunities expand, which means that their work is likely to take them far from the home they grew up in, both metaphorically and geographically. And the more highly they are educated, the higher the probability that they'll marry outside the ethnic group.

Whether they seek to promote their children's mobility or to retard it, then, working-class parents find themselves in a bind. Those who foster it risk losing their children to an alien way of life. Those who want to slow it down foresee the problem and respond fearfully. So the father who's a laborer listens to his college-student son repeat something a professor said in class earlier in the day and lashes out: "Yeah, what makes you think that pansy teacher of yours knows anything? Just because he went to college don't mean he's smart." And the mother whose dream is to see her daughter married with children of her own and living down the street watches her twenty-year-old daughter studying for tomorrow's exam and finds something for her to do. "Will you get your nose out of that damn book and help me get these kids to bed?"

The children get angry, finding their parents' behavior all but incomprehensible. "I hear her talking to my aunts, and you'd think I was discovering the moon the way she brags," complains the daughter. "But she makes me crazy. Every time she sees me studying, she finds a way to interrupt me. I got a C on a midterm last week; I never got a C before. It was all because I didn't have any time to study; she had me running all week."

In his moving autobiography, Richard Rodriguez—the Mexican-American boy who spoke only Spanish until he entered school and went on to earn a Ph.D. in English literature; the boy whose parents still have trouble with both the American culture and its language—gives eloquent testimony to the high price the family pays for the mobility of its children.[3] When worlds separate so profoundly, every visit home is fraught with difficulty. For the child, there's always the question: What will we talk about when I get there? For the parents, this child they raised, nurtured, and loved comes back a stranger, interested in matters they know nothing about, doing things they find baffling. "You mean people tell a psychiatrist about their personal lives?" Rodriguez's mother asks aghast when he tries to explain the process to her.[4]

How do you explain your life to parents who can't even imagine what you do for a living? Long after I got my doctorate, my illiterate immigrant mother still couldn't figure out what I do. "You sit and talk to people and they pay you for *that?*" Nor could she see any reason why I had earned the title "Doctor." "You can't give me a prescription, so what kind of doctor are you?" she'd sniff dismissively.

But it isn't only that she can't fathom what I do; it's that she doesn't want to. For my professional gain is, in her view, her loss. In all these years, she has never spoken a word of pride or praise for any of my accomplishments, at least not to me. She may brag to friends and neighbors about her "daughter, the doctor" and round them up to watch TV when she knows I'm doing a guest appearance on some national show. But when, in hurt and exasperation, I once asked why she'd never told me she was proud of what I had achieved, she answered angrily: "Proud? What do I get out of it? It's like I don't have a daughter. I see my friends' daughters taking care of them; they go to lunch; they take them shopping. What do I have? You live three thousand miles away, and even if you didn't, what would I have? You're too busy."

These difficult and disturbing costs go unrecognized in our celebration of upward mobility. But my mother knows them, as do all the mothers and fathers whose children have climbed up and out—out of the family, the class, and the ethnic group. And so do the children who find themselves separated from both the family and their past.

The Tomalsons

"That's a funny question. I'm black, of course," says Gwen Tomalson impatiently when I ask about ethnicity.

"Why is it so funny? Many black people now prefer to think of themselves as African-American," I reply.

"Yeah, well, that's all a little fancy for me," she says with irritation. Then, more thoughtfully, "Maybe I'm African-American, too;

I guess I am. My people were dragged here from Africa, so that makes me African-American, but it doesn't mean anything to me.

"My sister's different; she likes the idea of being African-American. I say it doesn't do anything for us, so what's the difference? She says it means something to her because it's part of our history, and it makes her feel she's part of all those Africans all over the world. That's okay; I don't have any problem with it if it makes her feel better to think that. I just don't feel that way. What difference does it make how many black people there are in Africa? It doesn't change anything here, and this is where I live.

"The fact is, I'm not African; I'm American, more American than lots of white people who can't even talk English. But nobody cares about that. Generations of my family were born here in this country, but that doesn't make any difference, does it? There's still all this prejudice and discrimination against us. Is that going to go away because we decide we want to be African-Americans instead of black? I don't think so."

"Can you tell me something about your family's past?"

"It's a pretty common story for a black family," she sighs. "My great-great-great-grandparents, I guess it was—no, I'm not sure how many 'greats'—but they were slaves on a plantation in Georgia. When I think about it, it makes me sick. The whole idea of slavery, it's disgusting what white people did. How could they do it, selling people's children like that? I think it must be why black people treasure children so much. Not that we really remember, but just knowing black children were sold and their parents never saw them again; it makes you grateful you have your kids and you know you're going to keep them. I don't know, I sometimes think maybe it's why so many black girls who get pregnant have the baby instead of getting an abortion. I mean, when you have a history like that, keeping your child seems very important.

"Don't get me wrong. I don't think these kids should be having babies the way they're doing. They're not ready to take care of them; they're just kids themselves. But when I think about it, and think about how black people feel about children, I just wonder if that isn't one reason."

She pauses and says, laughing, "It's hard to keep me on track, huh? What was it you asked me? Oh yeah, about my family. I guess they were all sharecroppers or something like that after they got freed. Lots of them are still down there, especially the older folks, like my grandparents' generation. Everybody's always been pretty poor, I guess you'd say. I don't know, I think it's harder down there. We went to visit a few times when I was younger and I didn't like it. God knows, my family never had it easy here, but it's different being poor here and there."

"How is it different?"

"It's hard to describe. Poor there seems—How can I say it?—it seems dirtier. Lots of times you don't even have a toilet," she says with a shudder.

"When did your family leave the South?"

"It was during World War II. My grandparents on my mom's side came up here because they thought there'd be more opportunities in the North. My mother was just a baby when they came. I think they went to Detroit first, but then after the war when all the white soldiers came back, they couldn't get work there anymore. So they moved here to New York. One of my grandmother's sisters was living here by then, and I guess she wanted to be near her, too.

"My father's family came earlier, but I'm not sure when. I never knew his parents; they died when he was about fifteen, I think. So we don't know a lot about his side."

"So you grew up in New York City?"

"Yeah, in Harlem. It's hard to describe what it was like then. My sister still lived there until a few years ago, and when I'd go back to visit her, it didn't seem like the same place. Nobody knows anybody anymore; everybody's scared all the time. The street I used to live on is like a war zone, with drugs and crime. Most of the buildings on my old block are boarded up and abandoned now. It's terrible."

She stops abruptly, shakesher head, and says, "Listen to me; you'd think this place is some great shakes or something. There's plenty of trouble here, too, with drugs and guns and all that; it's everywhere now. But it's not like what's happening in Harlem where I used to live. Or, I don't know, maybe I think that because it was so different when I was growing up there. It was like living anywhere else. You never thought about being afraid to go out on the street; you knew everybody and they knew you. We didn't even lock our doors most of the time, and people looked out for each other. If you were outside and getting rowdy or something, a neighbor would step in and tell you to behave. And if you didn't do like you were told, they'd tell your parents. It was sort of like having lots of aunts and uncles right there. It was a nice feeling. If your parents weren't home, somebody was always there to take care of you if you needed it."

Again she pauses, her gaze seeming to turn inward, as if caught in a reverie about her childhood. Then she continues, "When I hear myself talk like this, I think: *Hey, you're making it sound like some kind of a paradise.* It wasn't; people were poor. There were drugs in Harlem then, too. But it wasn't the same. I don't know why. Maybe it wasn't so widespread, and it wasn't kids selling drugs and carrying guns like today."

"Tell me about the family you grew up in."

"It wasn't easy. My mother worked six days a week cleaning other people's houses. Sometimes she'd go to two different places in one day, and wouldn't come home until 8 or 9 at night. My father worked as a janitor in a couple of buildings downtown, so he had two jobs, too. You couldn't call them fun to be around when they came home. I guess they were too tired to want to have much to do with us. All mom wanted to do was go to bed, and my father, well, he had a drinking problem. But I have to say, I don't think he ever missed a day's work because of it.

"In a way, we were luckier than a lot of kids on the block, at least until my father died. We didn't have a lot, but we never really wanted for anything either. There was always enough food; we had decent clothes—nothing fancy, but decent—and the rent got paid.

"After my dad died, it was different; it was really hard then. I wanted to quit school to help out, but my mama wouldn't let me. She kept saying my father would turn over in his grave if he knew I wasn't getting my education. He used to say to me, 'Girl, you're smart enough to go to college and be something, so do it.' But with him gone, somebody had to help my mother, and my sister was too young, only fourteen."

"What happened?"

"Mama won. I didn't quit. I got a job as a salesgirl at Woolworth's and worked and went to school. It didn't do my grades any good, and it was no life for a sixteen-year-old. There was no time for any fun at all. I think I was pretty mad for a while, and I kept threatening to quit school, but my mama was tough," she says tenderly. "She was right, too. Having that high school diploma made it a lot easier for me to decide to go to college now. If I had to first get my GED, I don't think I'd have done it. This way, I could get right into the nursing program. It's still hard, you know, having a family and working and going to school. But we're managing, and George helps a lot."

"What was it like to grow up black in New York?"

"It's funny; when you live in Harlem, everybody's black, so you don't really think too much about it when you're very little. Then, from the time I was about five until I was in the sixth grade, I wanted to be white. I used to watch the Mickey Mouse Club and all I wanted to be was mouseketeer. I'd tell my mother that I was going to be a mouseketeer, and she'd always say that's silly, but she never said why. Now I know it's because she didn't know how to tell me that I wasn't good enough because I was black. But at the time I couldn't figure out why she thought it was so ridiculous. Then, when I was about five, I figured it out because I began to see that there were no kids like me who were mouseketeers."

"Can you say what that understanding meant to you then?" I ask.

"It was devastating," she says, swallowing hard to contain her feelings as the memory sweeps over her. "It was like somebody standing right there in front of me and saying you're not good enough because you're the wrong color. You have to remember that I was growing up in a world of blond Barbie dolls, so I already knew white was beautiful and black wasn't. But this really made it real. I remember after that playing with white dolls and pretending I was white, and saying to my mother that I wanted to be white because white people had all the fun.[5]

"People say, well, we have black dolls now, so it's different. But it's not. It's still the same. A child looks around at the world and it seems like white people have everything. When Julia was about five, she started to walk around with a shirt on her head and hanging down her back. At first I didn't pay any attention. But when she kept doing it, I asked her what she was doing. She said she was pretending she had long blond hair and that she wanted to be white because black people didn't have any fun.

"Imagine, all these years later, and a black child still wants to be white. Maybe I should have known it was coming, but I was stunned. I thought it would be different for my kids because we tried so hard to make them very, very aware of being black and how they should be proud of it. But how can you fight it? She gets her ideas about the world from TV, and what's there to make you feel good about being black?" she concludes bitterly, as she wipes away the tears she can't control.

As I listen to her, I remember all the black parents—one-third of those I spoke with—who reported such incidents. A father told me how pained he was to hear his nine-year-old daughter tell him that a black model was "too dark" to be pretty. A mother talked about finding her daughter putting talcum powder on her face to see what she'd look like if she were white. "Can you imagine a little white girl wanting to black up her face?" she asked caustically.[6] "But what do you expect? Kids aren't dumb. They know being pretty means you've got white skin, a nice little nose, and thin lips."[7]

The subject of beauty—that is, who's attractive, who's not—is not a trivial one. A society's definition of beauty and attractiveness goes a long way in determining who's in and who's out, not just in the private social world but in public life as well. And while it was no surprise to me that most whites don't think black features or skin color are attractive, I was taken aback to find that, as they sought to articulate their racial feelings, the subject of beauty arose spontaneously in well over a third of their interviews.

"I don't think I'm a racist, but I just don't like the way black people look," says Ann Smollen, a seventeen-year-old white high school student. "I can't help it. If a person is black, I'm not attracted to them because they just don't look good to me." She hesitates, weighing her words, then says, "You know, sometimes when I see black people I wonder what it feels like for them. It must be hard. I can't imagine anyone wanting to be black, can you? Maybe that's wrong or something, but there's nothing I can do about it, is there?" she concludes helplessly, as if her response were natural, something imprinted in the genes.

*   *   *

When people ask about ethnicity, I think first about being a Jew, second about national origins. Because Jews are a people who have been driven from land to land without finding full acceptance anywhere, the country of my parents' birth—the one they fled *because* they were Jews—has little claim on my inner life. Instead, the long history of anti-Semitism has made being a Jew a central and defining feature of my identity, the one I can't forget, perhaps don't dare to forget, while my Russian ancestry serves only to remind me of the dangers of being Jewish.

The same is true for native American blacks. I don't mean that the experiences of Jews and blacks are the same. Far from it. In a land where race prejudice is so deeply rooted, the fact that Jews usually are white makes a very big difference in their life experience. But the histories of blacks and Jews also reveal some common threads. Both are peoples who were forced out of their homelands—one by exile, the other by captivity. Both have a long history of oppression—one because of religion, the other because of race. Such circumstances bind a people together in an almost elemental or tribal way—a connection that's born of the shared misery of persecution and subjugation—and identity lies with the group rather than with national origins. On the issue of ethnic identification, therefore, American blacks and Jews have more in common with each other than blacks do with other people of color.

The difference between African-Americans and others is clear when we look at the various peoples from Central and South America, Mexico, Asia, and the Caribbean. No matter how long they may have been here, no matter how far removed from the ethnic culture their immigrant forebears brought with them, when I asked about ethnicity they responded with the homeland of their ancestors. For Americans of African descent, it's different. Although Africa may be the land of their ancestors, and *African-American* the recently preferred term, when I asked about their ethnic background they almost always looked puzzled, as if wondering whether I was blind, then answered simply, "Black."

Yet the distinction between race and ethnicity has been lost in the racial politics of the last two decades. It's true, of course, that the two can be intimately intertwined, that both race and ethnicity may be important aspects of group and personal life. And it's also true that, in this historical moment, it's impossible to talk about the rise of ethnicity without reference to race. Nevertheless, the two are separate phenomena and should be kept analytically distinct.

My reason for insisting on this separation is simple: Race is one of the most enduring categories of American social thought, an idea buried deep in our social consciousness. Indeed, race may be second only to gender as the deepest and most long-lasting division in American social life. With the exception of gender, all other differences—differences of class, of ethnicity, even of religion—pale next to the differences most Americans attribute to race. Indeed, when we think "race," we think "difference"—not difference in some neutral way, in the way we might think about ethnic variations, but difference we measure as in inferior and superior, difference that says people of color don't match up to those who are white.

True, many of us can point to a neighbor, a workmate, an acquaintance of some kind who violates the racial stereotypes we carry inside. But that's different from thinking about race in the abstract. Then the stereotypes dominate. It's true also that whites and people of color both may live in enclaves or ghettos and give allegiance to a more or less distinct set of subcultural norms. But for whites it's a choice; they have the option to "pass."

For America's racial minorities it's different. No matter what their ethnic identities may be, it's their color that counts, that dictates how white society relates to them, that foretells their life chances. We need only look at the blacks from the various Caribbean countries to see how powerfully the racial definition holds in this society. They may define themselves in ethnic terms—as Antiguan, Jamaican, Haitian, Guyanese, and so on, all distinct cultures with norms, values, and lifeways of their own. But the American eye doesn't see their ethnic differences; the ear doesn't attend to the variation in the patterns of their speech or to the characteristic cadence and lilt of the words that mark their different origins. We see only black.

The same can be said about Asians and Latinos as well. Indeed, the very words we use—*Asian, Latino, Hispanic*—obscure the separate groups who fall under these umbrella terms and violate the ways in which they identify themselves. Nevertheless, there's an important distinction between the way white America relates to blacks and its relationship to all other racial groups.

In her brilliant and provocative series of essays about the interplay between whiteness and blackness, Toni Morrison writes: "The concept of freedom did not emerge in a vacuum. Nothing highlighted freedom—if it did not in fact create it—like slavery."[8] The same may be said about whiteness. Throughout our history, nothing has highlighted our belief in the superiority of our whiteness like a poor and uneducated black population in our midst.[9] Nor has anything else allowed us so easily to look away from our unease about ourselves, to project onto this dark presence our own shadow side, to maintain the belief in our moral superiority. For the consciousness of white America is shaped by the presence of and comparison with this racial other with whom we have always had, in Morrison's memorable words, a "curiously intimate and unhingingly separate" relationship.[10]

It's true that at other times and in particular places different racial or ethnic groups have played a part in framing that consciousness—the Indians in the nineteenth century, the Asians in California at the end of the last century and the first part of this one, the Mexicans in the Southwest. And even today, there are regional variations in our racial preoccupations. But our national obsession with race, the one that supersedes all the historical and regional differences, has had a black face since the first slave set foot on American soil.

The history of blacks and whites, then, is an exceptional one, marked by forced passage, by slavery, by the incredible intimacy in which we have lived while at the same time maintaining an almost unbridgeable separation. Yes, we stole the land from the Mexicans; killed the Native Americans; worked the Chinese to death in the mines and on the railroads, then refused them entry into the country; denied the rights of citizenship to the Japanese and threw them into American-style concentration camps. And while I want nothing I say to diminish the horror of these atrocities or the racism that made them possible, I will also insist upon the uniqueness of the black–white relationship.

Whatever their color, except for Native Americans, the others were also immigrants—the outlanders, the foreigners; separate, remote, impenetrable; speaking another language, bringing with them another culture. The task, as whites saw it, was to Americanize them— to teach them "our language" and "our ways"; to try, at least, to bring them into the fold. Only blacks of African descent were "ours" in the literal and metaphoric sense—ours, and also a despised other; an integral part of our history, yet separate; among us but not of us.[11] Only they have stood in this peculiar relationship to white America, profoundly American—more so, perhaps, than most whites precisely because they have been part of the land for 350 years—and at the same time an alien other; tightly bound by centuries of shared experience, by ties of history, culture, language, and proximity, yet agonizingly separate and apart, like members of a feuding family who can neither come together nor remain apart and indifferent. A *danse macabre* in which neither dancer takes any pleasure, yet neither can stop the dance.

The Riveras

"My father came first. He was an illegal; he crossed the border in Texas—El Paso—and worked in the oil fields, picked fruit, whatever he could get, and sent money home to my mother and the kids," explains Rick Rivera, the youngest of nine children in his family. "It was a hard life. My father was here all by himself, killing himself so he could support the family back there. And my mother had all these kids to take care of and feed, and hardly any money to do it with. They lived like that for about ten years. My father would come home for a few days or weeks a couple of times a year, and each time he crossed the border, he didn't know if he'd get back."

He pauses reflectively, "When I talk about it like this, I wonder how they lived that way. What kind of family life is that? Funny thing is they didn't talk much about it; my mother was always talking about Mexico and the family there, things like that. And my father didn't talk hardly at all about anything. I wasn't born yet then; I'm the only one in the family born in this country. But I used to hear the stories from my brothers and sisters when I was a little kid.

"I think they wanted me to know how lucky I was. They're a lot older than me, and they had a real hard life in Mexico, working from the time they were little kids. It wasn't any better when they got here either, because the family was so poor. None of them ever got through high school, even after they came here. I'm the first one in the family to get a high school diploma," he says proudly. "And now my daughter's going to go to college. I wish my father was around to see it."

"How did the whole family finally get here?" I ask Rick.

"I'm not sure exactly. I think it was after my father became an American citizen, then he could bring them all here. I guess by then they saved up enough money to make the trip; I don't really know. One of my sisters told me once that my mother didn't want to come by then. She says it broke my mother's heart that she had to leave her family and her town in Mexico and come to this strange place. But she didn't have a choice, I guess, not once my father said she should come. His word was the law. My sister says some of the kids didn't want to go either. They hardly knew my father, and they didn't speak English, and they were scared about coming here."

"Was Spanish your first language?"

"Yeah, that's all we spoke in the house. I had to know Spanish. I was like the bridge to America for them. My father knew some English, but I don't think he ever got comfortable talking it. It was like he was putting on another front when he had to talk in English; his voice even sounded different. And my mother, she never really learned it.

"Some of my brothers and sisters learned to talk pretty good, but they were so much older, none of them were living at home by the time I was five or six years old. So I was the one who'd go with my mother if she had to go to the clinic. It wasn't like now when there are doctors who speak Spanish. Then the doctors were all Anglos who didn't know any Spanish. She was okay if she stayed in the neighborhood, the *barrio*, because everybody spoke Spanish in the stores and all. But if she had to go somewhere else, I'd have to go with her."

"Do you speak Spanish at home now?"

"No. Matter of fact, I don't talk it a lot anymore, especially since my folks died. To the day she died, my mother made me talk Spanish in her house, or even when she came here to my house. It was okay after I grew up, but when I was a kid, I resented it. Once I went to school and learned English, I wanted to be like the American kids. I wanted to talk like them; I even wanted to eat like them. But I couldn't talk English in my house, not even to my sisters or brothers. If I did, my mother would tell me in Spanish, 'If you want to talk English, go live with the Anglos.' I hated it. You know how kids are; they don't want to be different.

"I mean, who wanted to be a 'greaser' or a 'spic'? That's what you got called in school. So like I said, I wanted to be an American. I was always uncomfortable if I'd be with my mother on the bus or train and people would hear us talking Spanish. Ana says the same thing. She never let her mother come to school because she was ashamed of her accent. And if you had white friends, you couldn't bring them home because they wouldn't know what anybody was talking about. It's not good," he concludes vehemently. "A lot of Mexican families still do that; it's not good for the kids. They need to know English if they're going to make something of themselves."

His words are a penetrating reminder of my own childhood, and of the many ways I tried to distance myself from my immigrant background, of how much I, too, didn't want to be who I was. So I listen to him and wince at the memory of my cruelty—a child's cruelty, to be sure, but nevertheless a cruel rejection of the family that nurtured me. If my mother spoke Yiddish in public, I looked away, pretended not to know her, refused to respond. But she couldn't win. I was equally embarrassed when she spoke English, cringing every time I heard her accent, barely hiding my scorn when she mispronounced a word, wishing I had a mother who was a *real* American. What must it be like, I wonder, to grow up comfortable in your own skin, to feel fully at home in the world, to know you belong, to take for granted your place in society? What must it be like for parents to feel their children's shame?

I push the thoughts out of my mind and return to my task. "What about your children?" I ask Rick. "Do they speak Spanish?"

"No, not really. Ana and me, we both wanted the kids to talk English right when they went to school, so we mostly talked English in the house, except," he adds with a smile, "when we didn't want them to understand something. I guess we thought if we all talked English and they grew up more like American kids, they wouldn't have the kind of feelings we had. I mean, they know they're Mexican, but they're also real Americans."

For Rick Rivera, as for so many others who grew up in immigrant families, the wish for his children to be "real Americans" is born in the hope that he can spare them the anguish of feeling different, of being outcast because they aren't seen as "real Americans." But it's a particularly difficult passage for people of color to negotiate, as the words of Rick's eighteen-year-old son, Robert, reminded me when I spoke with him earlier in the day. "We're Chicano," he announced angrily when I asked about ethnicity. "*Mis padres* don't like that word. They'll tell you they're Mexican, but me, I'm Chicano."

"What's the difference?" I asked him.

"Chicano means something. I'm not Mexican; I was born here, and so were my parents. So why should I say I'm Mexican? How many generations does it take to become an American if you speak Spanish and have dark skin? Do you know the answer to that? No, you probably don't because you're Anglo," he said, flinging the words at me as if they were missiles. "Well, I'll tell you. You can't count them, that's how many. It's time we Chicanos stood up for ourselves because nobody else is going to do it."

Recalling Robert's words and the intensity with which they were spoken, I remark to his father, "Robert doesn't feel much like a real American. He calls himself Chicano. How do you feel about that?"

"I don't know; I don't know anything anymore," he replies in a voice suddenly sapped of energy. "What's the difference what the name is? Now it seems like it was all a dream, but how could we know? Ana and me, we really believed if we followed all the rules, our kids would grow up like everybody else in this country, you know, have the same chances like any Anglo kid."

He stops talking and stares out the window for what seems like a long time. Then he turns back to me and says numbly, "Now I don't know; we're really scared. The young people, they're mad. I don't blame them, but I worry about what's going to happen."

He pauses again, shifts his body in the chair, sighs, and continues: "What can I say about Robert? All of a sudden he wants to study Spanish so he can know his culture better. It's all because he's disillusioned with this country. How can I blame him? Everybody's got their hand in the till but us. We're the last ones anybody thinks about. Black people, they make noise, so they get something. Don't get me wrong, I got nothing against them, at least not against the people who are willing to work for a living and don't look for handouts. But they're not the only ones who've suffered. There's plenty of prejudice against us, too, but who gets to go to the Supreme Court? Some black guy who everybody knows isn't even smart."

*   *   *

Race—it's the great divide in our society, dividing people of color from each other, separating whites from them all. Indeed, it's almost impossible not to trip over the divisions and the differences, even among people of good will. Some time ago I had a conversation with a black friend in which we were talking about women's experience, trying to sort out what's different and what's the same for women who occupy different places in the class and status hierarchy of American life. I was arguing more strongly for the similarities, or at least for finding the common ground; she wanted to insist on the differences. Finally, exasperated because she couldn't convince me, she asked: "When you look in the mirror, what do you see?"

Perplexed, I wondered aloud, "What does that have to do with this conversation?"

"Just tell me and you'll see," she demanded.

"I see a woman, of course," I replied.

"When I look," she said, half triumphantly, half angrily, "I see a black woman."

Her words hit me like a hammer blow—not just a woman, a

black woman. But it wasn't only the words she spoke that were so compelling, it was the way she spoke them—*a black woman*—the words inseparable, fused together, her identity embodying them both as if they were one. When, I wondered, had I ever thought of myself self-consciously as a *white* woman? A Jewish woman, perhaps, but not a white woman. That I took for granted.

Months later, when I was interviewing Ana Rivera and we were talking about race and ethnicity, I asked her the same question. "When you look in the mirror, what do you see?"

She looked at me inquiringly for a moment, as if trying to figure out what was behind the question, then said hesitantly, "A Mexican woman."

"Why did you hesitate?"

"Because I wasn't sure whether to say *Mexican* or not."

"And why did you?"

"Because in this country, they don't let you forget, even if you want to."

Hearing Ana's words reminded me also of the time when a student with whom I worked closely came into my office, flopped into a chair, and sat looking at me morosely. "What's the matter?" I asked.

"I'm so damn tired of being reminded all the time that I'm black," she answered, the words tumbling from her lips. "Just once, I'd like to know what it's like to feel like just a person, not a black person, but just an ordinary, regular person." By which, of course, she meant a white person. For who else is "ordinary" and "regular" in this land of ours? Who else can take their color for granted?

Writing about feminism, race, and legal theory, law professor Angela Harris tells of a meeting attended by a sophisticated and diverse group of feminists who were asked to pick two or three words to describe who they were. "None of the white women mentioned their race; all of the women of color did."[12] *All of the women of color*—not just black women but Asian women and Latinas as well. How could it be otherwise when the color of their skin has defined them and their life chances for as long as this nation has existed?

So long as race remains so pivotal in this society, racial identity will be burned into the consciousness of a person of color. My own relationship to my Jewishness helped me to understand that, since the force of my identity as a Jew lies as much in the anti-Semitism that still exists as in any intrinsic statement about myself as Jew. The difference between me and my black friend, however—or, for that matter, between me and Robert and Ana Rivera, whose dark, Indian features mark them as aliens in the land of their birth—is great. Being Jewish isn't immediately visible in the world, a difference that has saved me from much of the suffering and humiliation people of color have experienced for so long.

For the whites I spoke with, the world looks different. Not one person thought about color in responding to my question about ethnicity. They didn't need to because, as Harris notes, "It is only white people who have the luxury of 'having no color.'"[13]

The Kwans

"Obviously I'm Chinese," says Carol Kwan. Then with shrug and a smile, she adds, "Well, maybe it's not so obvious since Americans always say they can't tell the difference between us Asians."

"You speak beautifully, but it doesn't sound as if English was your first language," I say.

"It wasn't. I was born in China, and left there with my father and older sister when I was about five years old. I don't remember a lot, only going on a train and being very excited and then in a little while wanting my mother. I couldn't understand why she and my little sister couldn't come with us."

"You mean your father took two children and left your mother and one child in China?"

"Yes, that's the way it happens a lot in China. You see, when a family applies for immigration, the government doesn't usually let the whole family go at one time. They'll say this one can go and that one can't. No reason; it's just the way they do it. About half the families in the village my parents come from are in the same situation. The husband is in Hong Kong or Macao or maybe even here in the United States—they go wherever they have relatives—and maybe he took one or two children with him, maybe not. The rest of the family is in China, and they won't let them leave.

"My father applied for the whole family and after waiting a

long time, they said he could leave, but my mother couldn't go. So he took the two older children and left thinking that once he was out, he'd be able to get them out easier. But it didn't work that way. We left China in 1960, and my mother and sister didn't get out until 1979."

"Where did you go when you left?"

"We went to Hong Kong. At first we stayed with my father's relatives, but then he got a job and we lived by ourselves. My father didn't have any education, so he worked at different jobs—in a restaurant as a kitchen helper, as a janitor, things like that. My sister and I went to school, and we sort of lived a normal life. We lived there for about seven years.

"I guess we were poor, but you know how kids are. If there's enough to eat and you have a place to sleep and decent clothes, you don't really notice. Besides, Hong Kong was an exciting city after that village in China. There was so much to do and see. Actually, when we finally got to go to the U.S., my sister and I didn't want to go. We didn't know any English, and we were scared."

"Why did you leave Hong Kong?"

"My father always wanted to go to the United States. He had a brother here, and he was trying to get us over for a long time. But we couldn't get a visa for all those years. Then when they changed the immigration laws here, we could get one, so my uncle sent some money and we left.

"Coming here was really hard for us. The first few weeks in school, we were totally lost. We didn't understand anything people were saying. We were in junior high school. That's when you go to different rooms for your classes, and we didn't understand about that. It was all so confusing. Fortunately, there were a couple of Chinese kids in the school who had only been here for a year or so, and they took care of us. They explained about going to different rooms, and they showed us where we were supposed to go to eat, things like that."

"How did you manage to learn English?"

"You just learn it because you have to. For a little while we had an ESL [English as a Second Language] class, and that was helpful. All the other classes, like math and music and history and those things, we did with the other kids. ESL was only for English class.

The classes were smaller and everything was simpler and slower, so it was easier to catch on to. The teacher spoke Chinese, too, but she didn't use it unless there was no other way to make us understand, you know, just a few words to guide you along. It's a good system to ease a foreign child into English. Better than the bilingual education everybody's talking about now. What good would it have been for me to go to a Chinese class? I already knew Chinese; I needed to learn English.

"Anyway the big problem for kids isn't learning English. How can they help learning it when it's all around them? But pretty soon we began to speak English and my father still spoke only Chinese. Even my uncle and his wife spoke mostly Chinese. That gets kind of hard. You know, kids want to be like everyone else. We wanted to speak English, but they demanded that we speak Chinese. My cousins—they were born here—and my sister and me, we'd always talk English when we were by ourselves. But if they caught us, they didn't like it. They didn't get mad exactly, because they knew we had to speak English to do well in school, and that was very important. It was really drummed into us. But it was hard because they worried that we'd forget the language altogether."

"Was there a Chinese neighborhood in Seattle then?"

"You mean like Chinatown in San Francisco? No. But we did live in a Chinese community where everyone spoke Chinese and there were Chinese stores all around."

"Did being immersed in a Chinese community make the transition easier or did it delay your entry into American life?"

"I think it made it easier; you feel more at home. But you can't help getting to know the new country, too. You see other people and how they live all around you. You get on a bus, and it's there. You have to figure out how to pay the light bills, how to manage at the bank, things like that. You watch TV or go to the movies. You can't get away from it. But living in the Chinese community, you can at least relax a little more at home; you don't feel so alien and out of things. It's comforting.

"The real problem comes when kids begin to integrate and then they begin to feel ashamed of who they are. After a while when my English kept getting better and better, I just wanted to be like every American kid in school. Then it didn't feel comforting anymore; it was more like it was forcing me to stay an alien. I didn't want to talk Chinese; I wouldn't even take Chinese food for lunch; I only wanted to eat what they were eating. I'd go to the store and buy some of that awful white bread and make peanut butter and jelly or tuna fish sandwiches. I never liked it, but I made myself eat it so I'd be like one of them."

"When did your mother and sister finally get here?"

"They finally got out twenty years later. By then we had moved to this house, and my father had his own janitorial business. My sister and I used to help out there after school. When my mother and older sister came, it was a real shock to them. They spent their lives living in a hut and working in the village fields, and suddenly they came to this house. I don't think they ever saw a paved road or an indoor toilet before. And we didn't even live in a Chinese community anymore, so they didn't have anybody to talk to.

"It was very hard for everybody. My mother was very scared of everything here. Until she died, she never really got over her fears. And my sister, well, she just feels left out and cheated. Compared to how they had to live there, she thought we were like millionaires, so she feels like she missed out on a lot. And I guess she did. But it's hard for me and my older sister because my Chinese sister—that's how I think of her—wants us to feel guilty, like maybe we're supposed to make it up to her. But I don't know how. We lived such different lives, we can't really relate to each other."

"What about your relationship with your mother?"

"That was hard, too. She hadn't been my mother since I was a little girl, so she was like a stranger. I mean, she was this illiterate Chinese peasant, and she comes here to two daughters who are educated Americans. I used to feel sorry for her, but we couldn't communicate with each other because we had nothing in common. My sister and I tried to be nice and respectful, but she didn't know anything about how to live here. How could she be a real mother to us?

"It was awful with my father, too. After being separated for twenty years, they were strangers. When she first came, they would look at each other like they'd never met. They tried to be polite, but you could see that they were really uncomfortable and didn't have anything to say to each other. What could they say? They were separated in their twenties and didn't see each other again until their forties. And in between they were living such different lives.

"It was like a pretend family after they came; it wasn't real. The real family was my sister, my father, and me. It's really terrible, that kind of separation. But there are lots of families like that in the Chinese community. It's the only way they can get here; so the men still come alone and eventually maybe they bring their wives and children over."

"Do your children speak Chinese?"

"Not really. We send them to Chinese school because I think they should know the language and culture. But I don't think they'll go much longer. They're not interested, and it's a hassle to get them to keep going. My husband says we should just forget it; it's not worth fighting with them over it.

"They learned a little Chinese in school, but not much, and they speak as little as possible. If I ever talk to them in Chinese, they answer in English. They're really not particularly interested in anything Chinese; they're just typical American kids. When I look around at the American-born Chinese kids I know, I think it'll all be gone in another generation. Just look at all the intermarriage now."

"How do you feel about that?"

"I suppose deep down I'd rather my children married Chinese just because I think there's less conflict raising a family if people have the same background. But I don't expect it, and I know I won't be able to influence them. I just assume at least one of my children will marry a Caucasian. It's inevitable, isn't it, when you throw people together like we do in this country? Isn't that what the melting pot means?"

*   *   *

The melting pot—the metaphor that has dominated America's vision of itself for more than a century, a vision that has been hotly contested in recent years. As is common in such public debates, the arguments swing from one extreme to the other—one side contending that the melting pot is a fiction, the other insisting on its authenticity. In fact, it's neither myth nor reality. Instead, what we see depends on our angle of vision. Turn the prism one way and it looks real; shift it a little and we see the deep divisions that separate us.

There's little doubt that whites have melted. Certainly they still lay some claim to their ethnic past, but it has no significant effect on their daily lives or the opportunities available to them. For people of color it's different, although, as I've already said, there's also a distinction between the way white America relates to blacks and its relationship to other racial groups—a distinction that the interracial marriage statistics bring vividly to life.

The last decades have seen an enormous increase in Asian–white and Latino–white intermarriage. Exogamy among the Japanese in Seattle, for example, climbed from 17 percent in the early 1960s to 30 percent by the time the decade ended. By 1975, the rate of marriage outside that Japanese community stood at over 50 percent. Nationwide, nearly one-third of both Asians and Latinos married out in 1980, mostly to white mates.[14]

The only exception to this dramatic rise is the black–white marriage rate, which remains extremely low. In 1980 there were 167,000 black–white marriages, for a total of just $\frac{3}{10}$ of 1 percent of all married couples. By 1991 the number was 231,000, or $\frac{4}{10}$ of 1 percent.[15]

Some analysts make a persuasive argument that intermarriage facilitates the social transformation of race—an ostensibly immutable essence—into ethnicity—a malleable bundle of cultural forms. By which they mean that perceptions of racial difference change and that the classification of who's "white" and who's "colored" shifts with time and circumstance. Anthropologist Roger Sanjek writes that intermarriage is wholly unacceptable only when race stands for "biologically defined difference" and the possibility of any cultural resemblance between the groups is denied.[16] Given the large numbers of Asian–white and Latino–white marriages, this raises the question of whether the perception of difference is waning with respect to these groups. Will Asians and Latinos undergo a social conversion from race to ethnicity, leaving black Americans to stand alone as a separate "race"? Are African-Americans the one group about whom it's almost impossible for whites to see anything but biologically defined and cultural differences?

9

"IS THIS A WHITE COUNTRY, OR WHAT?"

"They're letting all these coloreds come in and soon there won't be any place left for white people," broods Tim Walsh, a thirty-three-year-old white construction worker. "It makes you wonder: Is this a white country, or what?"

It's a question that nags at white America, one perhaps that's articulated most often and most clearly by the men and women of the working class. For it's they who feel most vulnerable, who have suffered the economic contractions of recent decades most keenly, who see the new immigrants most clearly as direct competitors for their jobs.

It's not whites alone who stew about immigrants. Native-born black, too, fear the newcomers nearly as much as whites—and for the same economic reasons. But for whites the issue is compounded by race, by the fact that the newcomers are primarily people of color. For them, therefore, their economic anxieties have combined with the changing face of America to create a profound uneasiness about immigration—a theme that was sounded by nearly 90 percent of the whites I met, even by those who are themselves first-generation, albeit well-assimilated, immigrants.

Sometimes they spoke about this in response to my questions; equally often the subject of immigration arose spontaneously as people gave voice to their concerns. But because the new immigrants are dominantly people of color, the discourse was almost always cast in terms of race as well as immigration, with the talk slipping from immigration to race and back again as if these are not two separate phenomena. "If we keep letting all them foreigners in, pretty soon there'll be more of them than us and then what will this country be like?" Tim's wife, Mary Anne, frets. "I mean, this is *our* country, but the way things are going, white people will be the minority in our own country. Now does that make any sense?"

Such fears are not new. Americans have always worried about the strangers who came to our shores, fearing that they would corrupt our society, dilute our culture, debase our values. So I remind Mary Anne, "When your ancestors came here, people also thought we were allowing too many foreigners into the country. Yet those earlier immigrants were successfully integrated into the American society. What's different now?"

"Oh, it's different, all right," she replies without hesitation. "When my people came, the immigrants were all white. That makes a big difference."

"Why do you think that's so?"

"I don't know; it just is, that's all. Look at the black people; they've been here a long time, and they still don't live like us—stealing and drugs and having all those babies."

"But you were talking about immigrants. Now you're talking about blacks, and they're not immigrants."

"Yeah, I know," she replies with a shrug. "But they're different, and there's enough problems with them, so we don't need any more. With all these other people coming here now, we just have more trouble. They don't talk English; and they think different from us, things like that."

Listening to Mary Anne's words I was reminded again how little we Americans look to history for its lessons, how impoverished is our historical memory. For, in fact, being white didn't make "a big difference" for many of those earlier immigrants. The dark-skinned Italians and the eastern European Jews who came in the late nineteenth and early twentieth centuries didn't look very white to the fair-skinned Americans who were here then. Indeed, the same people we now call white—Italians, Jews, Irish—were seen as another race at that time. Not black or Asian, it's true, but an alien other, a race apart, although one that didn't have a clearly defined name. Moreover, the racist fears and fantasies of native-born Americans were far less contained then than they are now, largely because there were few social constraints on their expression.

When, during the nineteenth century, for example, some Italians were taken for blacks and lynched in the South, the incidents passed virtually unnoticed. And if Mary Anne and Tim Walsh, both of Irish ancestry, had come to this country during the great Irish immigration of that period, they would have found themselves defined as an inferior race and described with the same language that was used to characterize blacks: "low-browed and savage, grovelling and bestial, lazy and wild, simian and sensual."[1] Not only during that period but for a long time afterward as well, the U.S. Census Bureau counted the Irish as a distinct and separate group, much as it does today with the category it labels "Hispanic."

But there are two important differences between then and now, differences that can be summed up in a few words: the economy and race. Then, a growing industrial economy meant that there were plenty of jobs for both immigrant and native workers, something that can't be said for the contracting economy in which we live today. True, the arrival of the immigrants, who were more readily exploitable than native workers, put Americans at a disadvantage and created discord between the two groups. Nevertheless, work was available for both.

Then, too, the immigrants—no matter how they were labeled, no matter how reviled they may have been—were ultimately assimilable, if for no other reason than that they were white. As they began to lose their alien ways, it became possible for native Americans to see in the white ethnics of yesteryear a reflection of themselves. Once this shift in perception occurred, it was possible for the nation to incorporate them, to take them in, chew them up, digest them, and spit them out as Americans—with subcultural variations not always to the liking of those who hoped to control the manners and mores of the day, to be sure, but still recognizably white Americans.

Today's immigrants, however, are the racial other in a deep and profound way. It's true that race is not a fixed category, that it's no less an *idea* today than it was yesterday. And it's also possible, as I have already suggested, that we may be witness to social transformation from race to ethnicity among some of the most assimilated—read: middle-class—Asians and Latinos. But even if so, there's a long way to go before that metamorphosis is realized. Meanwhile, the immigrants of this era not only bring their own language and culture, they are also people of color—men, women, and children whose skin tones are different and whose characteristic features set them apart and justify the racial categories we lock them into.[2] And integrating masses of people of color into a society where race consciousness lies at the very heart of our central nervous system raises a whole new set of anxieties and tensions.

It's not surprising, therefore, that racial dissension has increased so sharply in recent years. What is surprising, however, is the passion for ethnicity and the preoccupation with ethnic identification among whites that seems suddenly to have burst upon the public scene. Responding to this renewed emphasis on our ancestral past, students of ethnicity have been engaged in a lively debate about its meaning—a debate cast in terms of assimilation versus pluralism.[3]

The assimilationists rest their argument in structural realities, insisting that it's impossible to maintain ethnic group unity in the face of continuing social, residential, and occupational mobility. If people no longer live together, work together, marry each other, these theorists contend, ethnic solidarity ceases to exist anyplace but in the imagination.

The pluralists challenge the structural hypothesis, claiming instead that evidence for the importance of ethnicity lies in the persisting behavioral and attitudinal differences among ethnic groups. Italians, Irish, Germans, Jews, and so on, they maintain, all exhibit subcultural variations that derive from the culture their ancestors brought with them to these shores.

But even a casual comparison of the culture in the mother country and its expression here shows some very large differences. Sometimes these subcultural variations are so mixed with Americanisms that they seem only distantly related to the original culture, especially to an observer from the native land. And sometimes the immigrant generation clings tenaciously to the culture it left, enacting cultural forms and abiding by norms that are frozen in time, while the home country culture grows and changes. In this case, it doesn't take long before the group's culture in the new land looks more like a parody of the native culture than an emulation or a variation of it. Nor is this adaptation likely to survive the immigrant generation.

As further evidence for their premise, pluralists point to survey data that show that the vast majority of Americans identify themselves as ethnics. It's certainly true that when asked a question about ethnic background, most people respond with their ancestors' country of origin.[4] But whether this answer reflects a statement about their personal identity as well as their ancestry is an open question. Even if it does say something about identity, it tells us nothing about its *meaning* to the person who makes the claim, gives us no clue to whether ethnicity is central or peripheral to the definition of self. Sociologist Mary Waters argues that people can have a strong sense of ethnic identity without attaching any specific meaning either to their ethnic heritage or to the identity they claim—a formulation about ethnicity and identity that is itself without meaning.[5]

What does being German, Irish, French, Russian, Polish mean to someone who is an American? It's undoubtedly different for recent immigrants than for those who have been here for generations. But even for a relative newcomer, the inexorable process of becoming an American changes the meaning of ethnic identification and its hold on the internal life of the individual. Nowhere have I seen this shift more eloquently described than in a recent op-ed piece published in the *New York Times*. The author, a Vietnamese refugee writing on the day when Vietnamese either celebrate or mourn the fall of Saigon, depending on which side of the conflict they were on, writes:

Although I sometimes mourn the loss of home and land, it's the American landscape and what it offers that solidify my hyphenated identity. . . . Assimilation, education, the English language, the American 'I'—these have carried me and many others further from that beloved tropical country than the C-

130 ever could. . . . When did this happen? Who knows? One night, America quietly seeps in and takes hold of one's mind and body, and the Vietnamese soul of sorrows slowly fades away. In the morning, the Vietnamese American speaks a new language of materialism: his vocabulary includes terms like career choices, down payment, escrow, overtime.[6]

A new language emerges, but it lives, at least for another generation, alongside the old one; Vietnamese, yes, but also American, with a newly developed sense of self and possibility—an identity that continues to grow stronger with each succeeding generation. It's a process we have seen repeated throughout the history of American immigration. The American world reaches into the immigrant communities and shapes and changes the people who live in them.[7] By the second generation, ethnic identity already is attenuated; by the third, it usually has receded as a deeply meaningful part of life.

Residential segregation, occupational concentration, and a common language and culture—these historically have been the basis for ethnic solidarity and identification. As strangers in a new land, immigrants banded together, bound by their native tongue and shared culture. The sense of affinity they felt in these urban communities was natural; they were a touch of home, of the old country, of ways they understood. Once within their boundaries, they could feel whole again, sheltered from the ridicule and revulsion with which they were greeted by those who came before them. For whatever the myth about America's welcoming arms, nativist sentiment has nearly always been high and the anti-immigrant segment of the population large and noisy.

Ethnic solidarity and identity in America, then, was the consequence of the shared history each group brought with it, combined with the social and psychological experience of establishing themselves in the new land. But powerful as these were, the connections among the members of the group were heightened and sustained by the occupational concentration that followed—the Irish in the police departments of cities like Boston and San Francisco, for example, the Jews in New York City's garment industry, the east central Europeans in the mills and mines of western Pennsylvania.[8]

As each ethnic group moved into the labor force, its members often became concentrated in a particular occupation, largely because they were helped to find jobs there by those who went before them. For employers, this ethnic homogeneity made sense. They didn't have to cope with a babel of different languages, and they could count on the older workers to train the newcomers and keep them in line. For workers, there were advantages as well. It meant that they not only had compatible workmates, but that they weren't alone as they faced the jeers and contempt of their American-born counterparts. And perhaps most important, as more and more ethnic peers filled the available jobs, they began to develop some small measure of control in the workplace.

The same pattern of occupational concentration that was characteristic of yesterday's immigrant groups exists among the new immigrants today, and for the same reasons. The Cubans in Florida and the Dominicans in New York,[9] the various Asian groups in San Francisco, the Koreans in Los Angeles and New York—all continue to live in ethnic neighborhoods; all use the networks established there to find their way into the American labor force.[10]

For the white working-class ethnics whose immigrant past is little more than part of family lore, the occupational, residential, and linguistic chain has been broken. This is not to say that white ethnicity has ceased to be an observable phenomenon in American life. Cities like New York, Chicago, and San Francisco still have white ethnic districts that influence their culture, especially around food preferences and eating habits. But as in San Francisco's North Beach or New York's Little Italy, the people who once created vibrant neighborhoods, where a distinct subculture and language remained vividly alive, long ago moved out and left behind only the remnants of the commercial life of the old community. As such transformations took place, ethnicity became largely a private matter, a distant part of the family heritage that had little to do with the ongoing life of the family or community.

What, then, are we to make of the claims to ethnic identity that have become so prominent in recent years? Herbert Gans has called this identification "symbolic ethnicity"—that is, ethnicity that's invoked or not as the individual chooses.[11] Symbolic ethnicity, according to Gans, has little impact on a person's daily life and, because it is not connected to ethnic structures or activities—except for something like the wearing of the green on St. Patrick's Day—it makes no real contribution to ethnic solidarity or community.

The description is accurate. But it's a mistake to dismiss ethnic identification, even if only symbolic, as relatively meaningless. Symbols, after all, become symbolic precisely because they have meaning. In this case, the symbol has meaning at two levels: one is the personal and psychological, the other is the social and political.

At the personal level, in a nation as large and diverse as ours—a nation that defines itself by its immigrant past, where the metaphor for our national identity has been the melting pot—defining oneself in the context of an ethnic group is comforting. It provides a sense of belonging to some recognizable and manageable collectivity—an affiliation that has meaning because it's connected to the family where, when we were small children, we first learned about our relationship to the group. As Vilma Janowski, a twenty-four-year-old first-generation Polish-American who came here as a child put it: "Knowing there's other people like you is really nice. It's like having a big family, even if you don't ever really see them. It's just nice to know they're there. Besides, if I said I was American, what would it mean? Nobody's just American."

Which is true. Being an American is different from being French or Dutch or any number of other nationalities because, except for Native Americans, there's no such thing as an American without a hyphen somewhere in the past. To identify with the front end of that hyphen is to maintain a connection—however tenuous, illusory, or sentimentalized—with our roots. It sets us apart from others, allows us the fantasy of uniqueness—a quest given particular urgency by a psychological culture that increasingly emphasizes the development of the self and personal history. Paradoxically, however, it also gives us a sense of belonging—of being one with others like ourselves—that helps to overcome some of the isolation of modern life.

But these psychological meanings have developed renewed force in recent years because of two significant sociopolitical events. The first was the civil rights movement with its call for racial equality. The second was the change in the immigration laws, which, for the first time in nearly half a century, allowed masses of immgrants to enter the country.

It was easy for northern whites to support the early demands of the civil rights movement when blacks were asking for the desegregation of buses and drinking fountains in the South. But supporting the black drive to end discrimination in jobs, housing, and education in the urban North was quite another matter—especially among those white ethnics whose hold on the ladder of mobility was tenuous at best and with whom blacks would be most likely to compete, whether in the job market, the neighborhood, or the classroom. As the courts and legislatures around the country began to honor some black claims for redress of past injustices, white hackles began to rise.

It wasn't black demands alone that fed the apprehensions of whites, however. In the background of the black civil rights drive, there stood a growing chorus of voices, as other racial groups—Asian-Americans, Latinos, and Native Americans—joined the public fray to seek remedy for their own grievances. At the same time that these home-grown groups were making their voices heard and, not incidentally, affirming their distinctive cultural heritages and calling for public acknowledgment of them, the second great wave of immigration in this century washed across our shores.

After having closed the gates to mass immigration with the National Origins Act of 1924, Congress opened them again when it passed the Immigration Act of 1965.[12] This act, which was a series of amendments to the McCarran-Walter Act of 1952, essentially jettisoned the national origins provisions of earlier law and substituted overall hemisphere caps. The bill, according to immigration historian Roger Daniels, "changed the whole course of American immigration history" and left the door open for a vast increase in the numbers of immigrants.[13]

More striking than the increase in numbers has been the character of the new immigrants. Instead of the large numbers of western Europeans whom the sponsors had expected to take advantage of the new policy, it has been the people of Asia, Latin America, and the Caribbean who rushed to the boats. "It is doubtful if any drafter or supporter of the 1965 act envisaged this result," writes Daniels.[14] In fact, when members of Lyndon Johnson's administration, under whose tenure the bill became law, testified before Congress, they assured the legislators and the nation that few Asians would come in under the new law.[15]

This is a fascinating example of the unintended consequences of a political act. The change in the law was sponsored by northern Democrats who sought to appeal to their white ethnic constituencies by opening the gates to their countrymen once again—that is, to the people of eastern and southern Europe whom the 1924 law had kept out for nearly half a century. But those same white ethnics punished the Democratic Party by defecting to the Republicans during the Reagan-Bush years, a defection that was at least partly related to their anger about the new immigrants and the changing racial balance of urban America.

During the decade of the 1980s, 2.5 million immigrants from Asian countries were admitted to the United States, an increase of more than 450 percent over the years between 1961 and 1970, when the number was slightly less than half a million. In 1990 alone, nearly as many Asian immigrants—one-third of a million— entered the country as came during the entire decade of the 1960s. Other groups show similarly noteworthy increases. Close to three-quarters of a million documented Mexicans crossed the border in the single year of 1990, compared to less than half a million during all of the 1960s. Central American immigration, too, climbed from just under one hundred thousand between 1961 and 1970 to more than triple that number during the 1980s. And immigrants from the Caribbean, who numbered a little more than half a million during the 1960s, increased to over three-quarters of a million in the years between 1981 and 1989.[16]

Despite these large increases and the perception that we are awash with new immigrants, it's worth noting that they are a much smaller proportion of the total population today, 6.2 percent, than they were in 1920, when they were a hefty 13.2 percent of all U.S. residents.[17] But the fact that most immigrants today are people of color gives them greater visibility than ever before.

Suddenly, the nation's urban landscape has been colored in ways unknown before. In 1970, the California cities that were the site of the original research for *Worlds of Pain* were almost exclusively white. Twenty years later, the 1990 census reports that their minority populations range from 54 to 69 percent. In the nation at large, the same census shows nearly one in four Americans with African, Asian, Latino, or Native American ancestry, up from one in five in 1980.[18] So dramatic is this shift that whites of European descent now make up just over two-thirds of the population in New York State, while in California they number only 57 percent. In cities like New York, San Francisco, and Los Angeles whites are a minority—accounting 38, 47, and 37 percent of residents, respectively. Twenty years ago the white population in all these cities was over 75 percent.[19]

The increased visibility of other racial groups has focused whites more self-consciously than ever on their own racial identification. Until the new immigration shifted the complexion of the land so perceptibly, whites didn't think of themselves as white in the same way that Chinese know they're Chinese and African-Americans know they're black. Being white was simply a fact of life, one that didn't require any public statement, since it was the definitive social value against which all others were measured. "It's like everything's changed and I don't know what happened," complains Marianne Bardolino. "All of a sudden you have to be thinking all the time about these race things. I don't remember growing up thinking about being white like I think about it now. I'm not saying I didn't know there was coloreds and whites; it's just that I didn't go along thinking, *Gee, I'm a white person.* I never thought about it at all. But now with all the different colored people around, you have to think about it because they're thinking about it all the time."

"You say you feel pushed now to think about being white, but I'm not sure I understand why. What's changed?" I ask.

"I told you," she replies quickly, a small smile covering her impatience with my question. "It's because they think about what they are, and they want things their way, so now I have to think about what I am and what's good for me and my kids." She pauses briefly to let her thoughts catch up with her tongue, then continues. "I mean, if somebody's always yelling at you about being black or Asian or something, then it makes you think about being white.

Like, they want the kids in school to learn about their culture, so then I think about being white and being Italian and say: What about my culture? If they're going to teach about theirs, what about mine?"

To which America's racial minorities respond with bewilderment. "I don't understand what white people want," says Gwen Tomalson. "They say if black kids are going to learn about black culture in school, then white people want their kids to learn about white culture. I don't get it. What do they think kids have been learning about all these years? It's all about white people and how they live and what they accomplished. When I was in school you wouldn't have thought black people existed for all our books ever said about us."

As for the charge that they're "thinking about race all the time," as Marianne Bardolino complains, people of color insist that they're forced into it by a white world that never lets them forget. "If you're Chinese, you can't forget it, even if you want to, because there's always something that reminds you," Carol Kwan's husband, Andrew, remarks tartly. "I mean, if Chinese kids get good grades and get into the university, everybody's worried and you read about it in the papers."

While there's little doubt that racial anxieties are at the center of white concerns, our historic nativism also plays a part in escalating white alarm. The new immigrants bring with them a language and an ethnic culture that's vividly expressed wherever they congregate. And it's this also, the constant reminder of an alien presence from which whites are excluded, that's so troublesome to them.

The nativist impulse isn't, of course, given to the white working class alone. But for those in the upper reaches of the class and status hierarchy—those whose children go to private schools, whose closest contact with public transportation is the taxi cab—the immigrant population supplies a source of cheap labor, whether as nannies for their children, maids in their households, or workers in their businesses. They may grouse and complain that "nobody speaks English anymore," just as working-class people do. But for the people who use immigrant labor, legal or illegal, there's a payoff for the inconvenience—a payoff that doesn't exist for the families in this study but that sometimes costs them dearly.[20] For while it may be true that American workers aren't eager for many of the jobs immigrants are willing to take, it's also true that the presence of a large immigrant population—especially those who come from developing countries where living standards are far below our own—helps to make these jobs undesirable by keeping wages depressed well below what most American workers are willing to accept.[21]

Indeed, the economic basis of our immigration policies too often gets lost in the lore that we are a land that says to the world, "Give me your tired, your poor, your huddled masses, yearning to breathe free."[22] I don't mean to suggest that our humane impulses are a fiction, only that the reality is far more complex than Emma Lazarus's poem suggests. The massive immigration of the nineteenth and early twentieth centuries didn't just happen spontaneously. America may have been known as the land of opportunity to the Europeans who dreamed of coming here—a country where, as my parents once believed, the streets were lined with gold. But they believed these things because that's how America was sold by the agents who spread out across the face of Europe to recruit workers—men and women who were needed to keep the machines of our developing industrial society running and who, at the same time, gave the new industries a steady supply of hungry workers willing to work for wages well below those of native-born Americans.

The enormous number of immigrants who arrived during that period accomplished both those ends. In doing so, they set the stage for a long history of antipathy to foreign workers. For today, also, one function of the new immigrants is to keep our industries competitive in a global economy. Which simply is another way of saying that they serve to depress the wages of native American workers.

It's not surprising, therefore, that working-class women and men speak so angrily about the recent influx of immigrants. They not only see their jobs and their way of life threatened, they feel bruised and assaulted by an environment that seems suddenly to have turned color and in which they feel like strangers in their own land. So they chafe and complain: "They come here to take advantage of us, but they don't really want to learn our ways," Beverly Sowell, a thirty-three-year-old white electronics assembler, grumbles irritably. "They live different than us; it's like another world how they live. And they're so clannish. They keep to themselves, and they don't even *try* to learn English. You go on the bus these days and you might as well be in a foreign country; everybody's talking some other language, you know, Chinese or Spanish or something. Lots of them have been here a long time, too, but they don't care; they just want to take what they can get."

But their complaints reveal an interesting paradox, an illuminating glimpse into the contradictions that beset native-born Americans in their relations with those who seek refuge here. On the one hand, they scorn the immigrants; on the other, they protest because they "keep to themselves." It's the same contradiction that dominates black–white relations. Whites refuse to integrate blacks but are outraged when they stop knocking at the door, when they move to sustain the separation on their own terms—in black theme houses on campuses, for example, or in the newly developing black middle-class suburbs.

I wondered, as I listened to Beverly Sowell and others like her, why the same people who find the lifeways and languages of our foreign-born population offensive also care whether they "keep to themselves."

"Because like I said, they just shouldn't, that's all," Beverly says stubbornly. "If they're going to come here, they should be willing to learn our ways—you know what I mean, be real Americans. That's what my grandparents did, and that's what they should do."

"But your grandparents probably lived in an immigrant neighborhood when they first came here, too," I remind her.

"It was different," she insists. "I don't know why; it was. They wanted to be Americans; these here people now, I don't think they do. They just want to take advantage of this country."

She stops, thinks for a moment, then continues, "Right now it's awful in this country. Their kids come into the schools, and it's a big mess. There's not enough money for our kids to get a decent education, and we have to spend money to teach their kids English. It makes me mad. I went to public school, but I have to send my kids to Catholic school because now on top of the black kids, there's all these foreign kids who don't speak English. What kind of an education can kids get in a school like that? Something's wrong when plain old American kids can't go to their own schools.

"Everything's changed, and it doesn't make sense. Maybe you get it, but I don't. We can't take care of our own people and we keep bringing more and more foreigners in. Look at all the homeless. Why do we need more people here when our own people haven't got a place to sleep?"

"Why do we need more people here?"—a question Americans have asked for two centuries now. Historically, efforts to curb immigration have come during economic downturns, which suggests that when times are good, when American workers feel confident about their future, they're likely to be more generous in sharing their good fortune with foreigners. But when the economy falters, as it did in the 1990s, and workers worry about having to compete for jobs with people whose standard of living is well below their own, resistance to immigration rises. "Don't get me wrong; I've got nothing against these people," Tim Walsh demurs. "But they don't talk English, and they're used to a lot less, so they can work for less money than guys like me can. I see it all the time; they get hired and some white guy gets left out."

It's this confluence of forces—the racial and cultural diversity of our new immigrant population; the claims on the resources of the nation now being made by those minorities who, for generations, have called America their home; the failure of some of our basic institutions to serve the needs of our people; the contracting economy, which threatens the mobility aspirations of working-class families—all these have come together to leave white workers feeling as if everyone else is getting a piece of the action while they get nothing. "I feel like white people are left out in the cold," protests Diane Johnson, a twenty-eight-year-old white single mother who believes she lost a job as a bus driver to a black woman. "First it's the blacks; now it's all those other colored people, and it's like everything always goes their way. It seems like a white person doesn't have a chance anymore. It's like the squeaky wheel gets the grease, and they've been squeaking and we haven't," she concludes angrily.

Until recently, whites didn't need to think about having to "squeak"—at least not specifically as whites. They have, of course, organized and squeaked at various times in the past—sometimes as ethnic groups, sometimes as workers. But not as whites. As whites they have been the dominant group, the favored ones, the ones who could count on getting the job when people of color could not. Now suddenly there are others—not just individual others but identifiable groups, people who share a history, a language, a culture, even a color—who lay claim to some of the rights and privileges that formerly had been labeled "for whites only." And whites react as if they've been betrayed, as if a sacred promise has been broken. They're white, aren't they? They're *real* Americans, aren't they? This is their country, isn't it?

The answers to these questions used to be relatively unambiguous. But not anymore. Being white no longer automatically assures dominance in the politics of a multiracial society. Ethnic group politics, however, has a long and fruitful history. As whites sought a social and political base on which to stand, therefore, it was natural and logical to reach back to their ethnic past. Then they, too, could be "something"; they also would belong to a group; they would have a name, a history, a culture, and a voice. "Why is it only the blacks or Mexicans or Jews that are 'something'?" asks Tim Walsh. "I'm Irish, isn't that something, too? Why doesn't that count?"

In reclaiming their ethnic roots, whites can recount with pride the tribulations and transcendence of their ancestors and insist that others take their place in the line from which they have only recently come. "My people had a rough time, too. But nobody gave us anything, so why do we owe them something? Let them pull their share like the rest of us had to do," says Al Riccardi, a twenty-nine-year-old white taxi driver.

From there it's only a short step to the conviction that those who don't progress up that line are hampered by nothing more than their own inadequacies or, worse yet, by their unwillingness to take advantage of the opportunities offered them. "Those people, they're hollering all the time about discrimination," Al continues, without defining who "those people" are. "Maybe once a long time ago that was true, but not now. The problem is that a lot of those people are lazy. There's plenty of opportunities, but you've got to be willing to work hard."

He stops a moment, as if listening to his own words, then continues, "Yeah, yeah, I know there's a recession on and lots of people don't have jobs. But it's different with some of those people. They don't really want to work, because if they did, there wouldn't be so many of them selling drugs and getting in all kinds of trouble."

"You keep talking about 'those people' without saying who you mean," I remark.

"Aw c'mon, you know who I'm talking about," he says, his body shifting uneasily in his chair. "It's mostly the black people, but the Spanish ones, too."

In reality, however, it's a no-win situation for America's people of color, whether immigrant or native born. For the industriousness of the Asians comes in for nearly as much criticism as the alleged laziness of other groups. When blacks don't make it, it's because, whites like Al Riccardi insist, their culture doesn't teach respect for family; because they're hedonistic, lazy, stupid, and/or criminally inclined. But when Asians demonstrate their ability to overcome the obstacles of an alien language and culture, when the Asian family seems to be the repository of our most highly regarded traditional values, white hostility doesn't disappear. It just changes its form. Then the accomplishments of Asians, the speed with which they move up the economic ladder, aren't credited to their superior culture, diligence, or intelligence—even when these are granted—but to the fact that they're "single minded," "untrustworthy," "clannish drones," "narrow people" who raise children who are insufficiently "well rounded."[23]

True, the remarkable successes of members of the Asian immigrant community have engendered grudging, if ambivalent, respect. "If our people were as hard working and disciplined as the Asians, we'd be a lot better off," says Doug Craigen, a thirty-two-year-old white truck driver.

But the words are barely out of his mouth before the other side surfaces and he reaches for the stereotypes that are so widely accepted. "I'm not a racist, but sometimes they give me the creeps. You've got to watch out for them because they'll do anything for a buck, anything. I guess the thing that bothers me most is you can't get away from them," he explains, as if their very presence is somehow menacing. "They're all over the place, like pushy little yellow drones. You go to the bank, they're working there. You go to a store, they're behind the counter. It's like they're gobbling up all the jobs in town."

The job market isn't the only place where Asians are competing successfully with whites. From grade school to college, Asian students are taking a large share of the top honors, leaving white parents in a state of anxious concern.[24] "I don't know if our kids can compete with those Chinese kids," worries Linda Hammer, a thirty-year-old white beautician who hopes to see her children in college one day. "My kids aren't bad students, but those Asian kids, that's all they live for. I don't think it's good to push kids so hard, do you? I mean, I hear some of those people beat their kids if they don't get A's. They turn them into little nerds who don't do anything but study. How can American kids compete with that?"

Whites aren't alone in greeting Asian successes so ambivalently. Like Doug Craigen, Lurine Washington, a black thirty-year-old nurse's aide, speaks admiringly of the accomplishments of her Asian neighbors. "I could get killed for saying this, but I don't care. The Asians are a lot more disciplined than blacks as a whole. That's not a racist statement; it's a fact because of their culture. Saying that doesn't mean I don't like my people, but I'm not blind either. All I know is if our kids worked as hard in school as theirs do, they could make something of themselves, too. And those families, all of them working together like that. You've got to respect that, don't you?"

Moments later, however, Lurine complains, "If we don't watch out, they'll take over everything. I mean, they already own half the country, even Rockefeller Center. You know what I mean. They're like ants; there's so many of them, and they're so sneaky and everything. And they think they're better than other people; that's what really makes me mad."

Not surprisingly, as competition increases, the various minority groups often are at war among themselves as they press their own particular claims, fight over turf, and compete for an ever-shrinking piece of the pie. In several African-American communities, where

Korean shopkeepers have taken the place once held by Jews, the confrontations have been both wrenching and tragic. A Korean grocer in Los Angeles shoots and kills a fifteen-year-old black girl for allegedly trying to steal some trivial item from the store.[25] From New York City to Berkeley, California, African-Americans boycott Korean shop owners who, they charge, invade their neighborhoods, take their money, and treat them disrespectfully.[26] But painful as these incidents are for those involved, they are only symptoms of a deeper malaise in both communities—the contempt and distrust in which the Koreans hold their African-American neighbors, and the rage of blacks as they watch these new immigrants surpass them.

Latino–black conflict also makes headlines when, in the aftermath of the riots in South Central Los Angeles, the two groups fight over who will get the lion's share of the jobs to rebuild the neighborhood. Blacks, insisting that they're being discriminated against, shut down building projects that don't include them in satisfactory numbers. And indeed, many of the jobs that formerly went to African-Americans are now being taken by Latino workers. In an article entitled, "Black vs. Brown," Jack Miles, an editorial writer for the *Los Angeles Times*, reports that "janitorial firms serving downtown Los Angeles have almost entirely replaced their unionized black work force with non-unionized immigrants."[27]

On their side of the escalating divide, the Latino community complains bitterly that they always take second place to black demands. "Nobody pays attention to us like they do to the blacks," protests Julio Martinez, a thirty-year-old Latino warehouseman. "There's a saying in Spanish: You scratch where it itches. There's plenty of problems all around us here," he explains, his sweeping gesture encompassing the Latino neighborhood where he lives, "but they don't pay attention because we don't make so much trouble. But people are getting mad. That's what happened in L.A.; they got mad because nobody paid attention."

But the disagreements among America's racial minorities are of little interest or concern to most white working-class families. Instead of conflicting groups, they see one large mass of people of color, all of them making claims that endanger their own precarious place in the world. It's this perception that has led some white ethnics to believe that reclaiming their ethnicity alone is not enough, that so long as they remain in their separate and distinct groups, their power will be limited. United, however, they can become a formidable countervailing force, one that can stand fast against the threat posed by minority demands. But to come together solely as whites would diminish their impact and leave them open to the charge that their real purpose is simply to retain the privileges of whiteness. A dilemma that has been resolved, at least for some, by the birth of a new entity in the history of American ethnic groups—the "European-Americans."[28]

Presently, this is little more than an idea in the minds of those who would mobilize white ethnics to organize under a common umbrella. But it's a powerful idea, one that's beginning to develop an organizational base, as is evident from the emergence of European-American clubs in various cities around the country. No one knows just how many of these clubs exist or what proportion of their membership is made up of working-class ethnics. But in the three clubs I visited during the course of this research, their members were drawn almost exclusively from the white working-class.

Although these European-American clubs probably aren't widespread yet, the outlines of things to come are visible. "It's time for European-Americans to defend themselves against all these minority people who are ruining the country," says Ben Wiltsey, a twenty-seven-year-old white construction worker who joined a European-American club a few months before we met. "We're getting people from all over the county joining up with us to call a halt. This multicultural business is garbage. White people need their own space to practice their culture."

While most of the people I talked with wouldn't put it so crudely, virtually all would give assent to the idea embodied in the words Ben spoke. They don't usually speak so self-consciously about themselves as European-Americans, either. But the notion of European-Americans as an ethnic group has permeated their consciousness, even if in a relatively inchoate way.[29] Consequently, they see themselves as people whose European immigrant heritage gives them some common ground, a socially acceptable place to stand in opposition to "them." "They all get together to fight for what they want, so why shouldn't we?" asks Tony Bardolino, with mounting irritation. "You can't just have a white organization anymore because they call you a racist, so maybe you need something else, like all the people who were once immigrants get together."

However it's framed and articulated, the idea has profound social and political significance. At the political level, an organization of European-Americans can provide the vehicle through which white ethnics can make their needs and wishes heard most effectively.[30] As one large confederation instead of a diverse collection of groups, each with its own agenda, European-Americans would have greater standing in the policy debates that have swept the nation in recent years. "We've left our chair at the multicultural table empty, and the multicultural table is where the debate is, where the deals are being made," explains the head of the European-American Study Group in one California city.

As European-Americans, whites remain hyphenated Americans, but rather than being divided by their various ancestries, they're united by virtue of their shared European origin. Never mind that the historical experience of the Irish in the potato fields, the Italians in the villages of southern Italy, and the Jews in the shtetls of eastern Europe were so different. Or that there had been, until recently, few common bonds between them in the New World. All this gets muted in favor of the similarity of the immigrant experience as it is embodied in the "we came, we suffered, we conquered" myth, which by now has gained legendary proportions. And all of it without a single reference to race. Instead, the quintessential American experience is defined in terms of immigration, its burdens, and the ability to overcome such burdens through sacrifice and hard work. These are the real Americans, the only ones worthy of the name. It just happens that they're all white.

"It has nothing to do with race," maintains Delia Kronin, a thirty-eight-year-old working-class woman of Hungarian ancestry who, with her German-American husband, recently joined a group calling themselves "The European-Americans." Other members of the group repeat Delia's words and contend that their purpose in joining together is simply to affirm the common bond of people of European extraction. "Why should we be the ones who feel like we have no place?" asks Ron Morgan, a forty-one-year-old police officer. "We come here and meet with other people like us. What's wrong with that? Nobody complains when black people or Asians or Hispanics go to their own clubs, so why can't we?"

It's undoubtedly true that one reason for the emergence of such alliances is that many whites now find themselves in social and political situations where they feel they are the outsiders. But it's disingenuous to maintain that race is not a relevant issue. Communities like Canarsie in Brooklyn, where Italians and Jews have banded together to keep blacks out, offer evidence of the growing tendency for whites of European ancestry to join together in common cause around racial issues.

Historically, these two ethnic groups have had little in common. And despite the fact that they share a neighborhood, Jonathan Rieder's account of life in Canarsie makes it clear that this has not changed.[31] The life-styles and values of that community's Jews and Italians are conspicuously different, and neither has much respect for the other. Italian conservatism, both political and cultural, clashes with the Jewish liberal and cosmopolitan worldview. The willingness of some Italian activists to risk violence frightens the more pacific Jews. But these differences pale when they're confronted with what they perceive to be an invasion of blacks. Then they come together, bound by their whiteness, to protect their turf.

It's generally not expressed in these terms, of course. Instead, the talk is of differences in culture, class, values, and life-styles. Yet professional middle-class black families—people with more education and higher class status than most Canarsie residents—are no more welcome there than those who are poor and working class. Sometimes whites explain this contradiction by saying they worry that the neighborhood will tip once the walls are breached. "Some black people, I wouldn't mind, you know, those who are decent people, the educated kind," says Jake Rosenbaum, a forty-year-old white taxi driver who, by his own account, barely made it through high school. "The problem is once one of them, even the nice ones, comes on the block, the whole neighborhood's gone, just like that," he explains, snapping his fingers on the word *that* for emphasis.

Others speak fearfully about who will come into the neighborhood once an acceptable black family moves in. "I don't know. I've got nothing against the nice ones; they're people just like us," says Janet Marcantonio, a white thirty-eight-year-old office worker. "But they've got these big families and who knows who they'll bring with them. I mean everybody's got people who come to visit, or maybe even stay for a while, things like that. But with them, even if they're okay themselves, you worry that they'll bring an element into the neighborhood that you don't want. And once they move in, you can't control who comes to their house, can you?

"I don't like what some people around here do and how they talk, but I had to move once before because they came in and it ruined the neighborhood. So now I think we've all got to be together on this, even if you don't like some of the people and how they talk and act."

Whatever they say, then, it's clear that it's minority demands for equal treatment, whether in housing, jobs, or education, that has brought whites together. Indeed, until racial minorities came to be seen as a serious threat, white ethnics didn't join with others to celebrate their European heritage. We need only look at the high school and college campuses of the nation to see the shift. There, where the relatively closed nature of these institutions allows a view not ordinarily available in the world outside, we see white students struggling to deal with the minority presence and to find legitimacy for the kind of public expression of their identity that, in the current climate, is readily acceptable for other racial groups but not for whites as whites.

So, for example, many of the white students who participated in a recent study of racial attitudes on the University of California's Berkeley campus worry that they will soon find themselves disadvantaged in the competition for jobs with minorities. Alongside this fear, and not unrelated to it, is their feeling of being left out, without an easily recognizable social identity.[32] The others are all part of a group; they have some basis for coming together, both socially and politically. But the whites are, well . . . just white—with no particular claim that anyone would honor. Indeed, to ask to be heard as a white person is to open oneself to the charge of racism.

I don't mean to suggest that racism, although often in coded form, isn't a central issue in the discourse of discontent in America today. Nevertheless, it's also true that in recent years there has been no escaping the indictment, regardless of the intent.

Now, as other racial groups on campus have found common cause and a shared social space—whether informally in the eating halls or other public spaces that have come to be their designated meeting places, or more formally in racially separated dormitories and theme houses—white students also want a place and an identity of their own. But since they can't comfortably ask for recognition as whites, they embrace their ethnic past and demand public acknowledgment of their newly acquired group status.

At the University of California at Berkeley, for example, white students and their faculty supporters insisted that the recently adopted multicultural curriculum include a unit of study on European-Americans. At Queens College in New York City, where white ethnic groups retain a more distinct presence, Italian-American students launched a successful suit to win recognition as a disadvantaged minority and gain the entitlements accompanying that status, including special units of Italian-American studies.

White high school students, too, talk of feeling isolated and, being less sophisticated and wary than their older sisters and brothers, complain quite openly that there's no acceptable and legitimate way for them to acknowledge a white identity. "There's all these things for all the different ethnicities, you know, like clubs for black kids and Hispanic kids, but there's nothing for me and my friends to join," Lisa Marshall, a sixteen-year-old white high school student explains with exasperation. "They won't let us have a white club because that's supposed to be racist. So we figured we'd just have to call it something else, you know, some ethnic thing, like Euro-Americans. Why not? They have African-American clubs."

Ethnicity, then, often becomes a cover for "white," not necessarily because these students are racist but because racial identity is now such a prominent feature of the discourse in our social world. In a society where racial consciousness is so high, how else can whites define themselves in ways that connect them to a community and, at the same time, allow them to deny their racial antagonisms?

Ethnicity and race—separate phenomena that are now inextricably entwined. Incorporating newcomers has never been easy, as our history of controversy and violence over immigration tells us.[33] But for the first time, the new immigrants are also people of color, which means that they tap both the nativist and racist impulses that are so deeply a part of American life. As in the past, however, the fear of foreigners, the revulsion against their strange customs and seemingly unruly ways, is only part of the reason for the anti-immigrant attitudes that are increasingly being expressed today. For whatever xenophobic suspicions may arise in modern America, economic issues play a critical role in stirring them up.

10

"THIS COUNTRY DON'T OWE NOBODY NOTHING!"

"At first I thought, sure, why not? Everybody should have an equal chance," says John Anstett, a thirty-four-year-old white short-order cook. "But then I began to see that people take advantage; they don't really do the job right, and they take a place from a white guy who's more qualified. That's not fair. So then I began to think, *Hey, wait a minute. This country don't owe nobody nothing!*"

"This country don't owe nobody nothing"—it's a quintessentially American notion, born in our history and idealized in our culture. But it's another of our myths. For, in fact, most of us, including John Anstett, do believe that our country owes us a certain amount of care and protection. And it's precisely because the government seems to have abandoned that responsibility—whether in assuring people of a decent job at a living wage or providing health care for their families—that people feel so vulnerable and, therefore, so angry.

"I don't know exactly how to say this, but what the hell, I might as well tell it like I feel it," says Bob Grenowski, a white forty-eight-year-old unemployed machine operator. "Everything's gone to hell lately. The government don't care about the working man anymore. They pay off everybody but hard-working people like us. You sweat your life away, and all they do is put their hands in your pocket so they can give it away to those lazy bums on welfare.

"You're probably one of those bleeding-heart liberals that thinks just because they're black, we owe them something. But let me tell you: This country doesn't owe them a damn thing. I worked for mine; my kids are working for theirs. Let them work like we do; then they'll have what we have."

I said in the opening pages of this book that "one of the surprising findings of this study is how much in common all these families have, how much agreement they would find among themselves . . . if they could put away the racial stereotypes and hostilities that separate them and listen to each other talk." Nowhere is this more true than on the very issues about which whites complain so long and so loudly—whether about the enormous cultural and economic changes of recent decades or about taxes, schools, welfare, and affirmative action. Indeed, there were many times when I wouldn't have been able to guess the race or ethnic background of the speaker if I had been listening with my eyes closed.

There are, of course, also important differences in the worldviews of blacks, Latinos, Asians, and whites, just as there's a wide range of opinion within each group. As immigrants, for example, Caribbean blacks tend to have a different view than native African-Americans on some issues, such as open immigration, while on others, like affirmative action, their shared racial oppression puts them on the same side. Similarly, there are differences among the various Spanish-speaking peoples. Because they usually come for economic rather than political reasons, and because their ancestral homelands are close enough to allow free flow back and forth across the borders, Mexican-Americans and Puerto Ricans are more likely than those who come from more distant lands to want their children to remain fluent in Spanish.[1] The different Asian nationalities, too, while allied on some issues, also bring their own perspective to programs designed to protect minority rights. Recent immigrants are more likely to be hesitant to claim those rights than people who have been here for a generation or two. Even relatively small class and status distinctions make a difference in how people respond to many of the issues before them.

Nevertheless, along with the differences within groups and among them, there are some broad areas of agreement across the groups that too often go unnoticed. Most working-class blacks, for example, are no more willing to defend the present welfare system than are whites. "I don't get it. Welfare encourages girls to have babies, then everybody sits around complaining about it," says Marvella Washington, a thirty-two-year-old African-American secretary.

Nor is it unusual for Latino and Asian parents to object to bilingual education programs and to refuse to allow a child to participate. "My kids talk Spanish at home; in school they should talk English. That's the only way they'll get ahead in this country," says Paul Ortiz, a thirty-four-year-old first-generation Latino immigrant who believes that his limited command of English stands in the way of his advancement.

It's hard to talk about bilingual education with any clarity because the words themselves encompass a broad range of programs—some good, others bad. At their best, these programs offer non-English-speaking children a supportive environment in which to learn English and help them move into mainstream classes expeditiously. But few can show such promising results. A two-year study of bilingual education in California, for example, found the programs across the state not only rife with problems but relatively ineffective.[2] When the investigators compared the progress of non-English-speaking students who were taught the basic school subjects in their own language with those who attended classes taught in English only, they found no significant difference in reading and language skills.

Most reasonable people agree that we need some kind of program to help ease students who don't speak English into our educational system. "I think it's good if the teacher knows Spanish when there's kids in school who can't talk English," says Rubén Jover, a thirty-year-old Mexican-American restaurant worker. "How are they going to learn if they don't understand what the teacher says? A lot of these kids come up here and get into school and they're lost, so somebody should help them, you know, not for long, maybe a couple of weeks or a month, something like that, just so they get their feet wet."

But there are serious and legitimate questions about which programs would be most effective, for whom and for how long—questions that, in this era of racial and ethnic discord, don't get a reasoned hearing. Conservatives blindly argue against bilingual education; liberals often are equally mindless in their defense. Alongside them stands an entrenched bilingual bureaucracy and its supporters in the Latino and Asian communities. The result is a contentious debate that demonizes the dissenter and stifles rational discourse.[3]

It's also true that the assault on bilingual education often is based in ignorance and leveled without regard to the quality of the program or the needs of the children. Almost all the whites in this study, for example, spoke adamantly against bilingual education, even though few knew anything about the program in their children's school, or even if the school had one. "I don't know if my kids' school has one; I just know it's not a good idea," John Bochus, a white thirty-year-old fry cook says doggedly.

"If you don't know anything about it, how do you know it's not a good idea?" I ask him.

He shrugs off my question and says shortly, "Those kids have to learn English, that's all. Nobody spent money putting my grandparents in any special classes and they learned. Why can't these kids? Why do we have to be coddling these people all the time?"

It's not just the bilingual education programs themselves that raise John's hackles. It's the very idea that foreigners can come here and tap scarce community resources, that their children are getting special attention and treatment at a time when his own are suffering the effects of the decline in funds for public education.[4] He can't move to the suburbs; he can't afford to put his children in private schools. He can only watch helplessly as more and more non-English-speaking students come into the school at the same time that the quality of public education deteriorates. For him, the link between the two seems clear: "They," with their special needs and demands, have caused the problem. Never mind that the federal and state governments crippled public education during the Reagan-Bush years. Or that the failure of the economy in recent years has eroded funding for education even further. He knows only what he sees.

Given the controversy these programs have stirred and the fiscal problems of public educational systems across the land, champions of bilingual education have reason to feel threatened. In such an atmosphere, it's common for advocates to close ranks and quash dissent, much as families do when under attack. Their credible fears notwithstanding, however, plain old-fashioned self-interest also plays a part in the acrimony on their side of the debate.

For both bureaucrats and community advocates, careers are at stake—jobs for bureaucrats, power for community leaders. Like the ward bosses in cities like New York, Chicago, Boston, and Philadelphia in the early part of the century, today's ethnic entrepreneurs derive authority and status from their role as spokespersons and favor brokers for their communities. Unfortunately, the heat with which they enter the debate helps to make sensible public discussion nearly impossible and social change much less likely. Tragically, the victims may be the very children they insist they want to save.

Despite the often hotly voiced public demands by those who claim to speak for the community, virtually none of the Asian or Latino families in this study, even those who are relatively recent immigrants, believe children should be placed in a special language program for anything but a very short time. And by "short" they mean weeks or at most a few months, certainly not the three years or more that most American bilingual programs advocate. "Children should learn English in school, period," Irene Wang, a twenty-nine-year-old Chinese seamstress, says uncompromisingly. "Maybe if kids can't speak or understand a word, they need some kind of a program at first to help them. But it should only be for the first couple of weeks or so. Kids learn quickly if they're encouraged and know they have to."

She pauses a moment, then continues reflectively. "You know, my first language was Chinese; that's what I spoke when I started school. But I picked up English fast and so did all the other Chinese kids I went to school with. It's not whether you want to or not; if you're living here you're bound to pick up English. It's keeping the Chinese that's hard. But that's not the school's problem; that's just the way it is when you live in a country that doesn't speak your family language."

For Irene, the acknowledgment of a reality: "That's just the way it is when you live in a country that doesn't speak your family language." But it's often accompanied by the pained understanding of the cost of giving up the first language, the mother tongue, the words and sounds that stand for the safety and security of the family. "I'm really tormented about bilingual education and I don't know what to think," says Maria Fuentes, a nineteen-year-old Latina college student whose first language was Spanish. "In some ways it would have been a help to me to be in a bilingual program when I was a little Spanish-speaking kid because along with your language goes your world. And when you give up your language, you also give up your world, or part of it at least. But then I think, I wouldn't have wanted it because all I wanted was to be like the other kids; that's who I wanted to identify with. With English I could fit in and make friends with the other kids. Being Spanish-speaking made me feel too isolated. I'll never let that happen to my kids."[5]

She stops, stares out the window as if gathering her thoughts, then continues. "Did you ever read Richard Rodriguez's book, the one about being a Mexican boy growing up here in the United States? This thing he wrote about the public world and the private world and how Spanish was the language of his private world. That's real for me; that's just the way I felt when I was little."

Then with a sigh, she adds, "Everything gets so complicated. I'm supposed to think he sold out as a Chicano because he's against affirmative action and bilingual education. But I don't. In a lot of ways I relate to him and his ideas. I can't help it; I just do. I guess it comes down to, if you live in a country, you have to speak the language and do it right, otherwise you'll never get anyplace."

Initially the goal of bilingual programs was quite simply to teach foreign-speaking students English. But as identity politics have become a more prominent part of our national life, there has been a shift in their mission. Advocates now call for these programs to become bicultural as well, their argument being that children's self-esteem, and with it their ability to learn, rests on the maintenance of their native culture.

For some this is a revolutionary idea. For others it's not even a call to a small insurrection. Rather, as African-American social critic Henry Louis Gates, Jr. writes, the idea that self-esteem or its failure determines life chances relies on the "pop-psychology vocabulary of the recovery movement." When conservatives worry that Afrocentrism is "dangerously politicized," Gates argues, "they've got it backward. The trick of Afrocentrism is to have supplanted real politics with a kind of group therapy. It seeks to redress the problem of poor self-esteem rather than the problem of poor life chances."[6]

Perhaps because they understand this intuitively, the idea that schools should be a place for the transmission of ethnic culture makes no more sense to most of the Asian and Latino families in this study than it does to the whites. "My husband and I teach the children about our culture," says Susan Gee, a thirty-five-year-old Chinese office worker. "My children go to Chinese school to learn their history and the Chinese language. I don't need the public school to teach them about those things; that's what the family is for. In public school kids should learn English and everything else they need to know so they can get along in this country and be successful."

This doesn't mean that the Gees, the Fuenteses, and others like them oppose a multicultural curriculum, if by that we mean one that would portray the variety of the American experience and present an honest examination of both the contributions and the trials of the various groups and cultures that make up the tapestry of American life. In fact, the same parents who speak scathingly about bilingual education and believe it's the family's job to teach children about their ethnic culture also wish the schools taught more about the history of their people in this country and of the social, economic, and cultural contributions they've made to it. "I don't think they have to teach about Mexican culture. It's the family's job to teach kids about where they came from. But I'd like it if they learned more about how Mexican people helped to build this country," Manny Torres, a thirty-nine-year-old Mexican repairman, says wistfully. "They never hear about that. Just like they don't hear about how bad Mexican people have been treated here. I think that should be part of the history they learn about, don't you?"

This complaint about what's missing from the historical education of American children isn't given to people of color only. The whites in this study also now say they would favor a multicultural education that takes their past into account. True, their response is a defensive one, designed to counter the demands that people of color are making on the educational system. But it's also part of an emerging understanding of the complexity of our country's history and a wish to have their part in the making of America acknowledged. "Yeah, I think kids should learn the true history of their country," says Tony Bardolino. "It's good for them to know all about the people that made this country so great. What I don't like is that they teach all this stuff about slavery and things like that, but they don't teach about Italians and everything they went through when they came here. Kids need to learn about it all, and not just Italian kids learning about Italians, but everybody should learn about everybody."

Affirmative action—the series of programs that were designed to make up for past discrimination by giving minorities and women preference in hiring and education—is not only the most controversial of all the issues that divide whites and people of color, it also generates the most complicated responses among the groups and within them.

At the most basic level, the idea of merit is deeply embedded in the hearts and minds of most Americans. "You get what you deserve," they say. "If people work hard and know their stuff, they'll do okay," they insist. Never mind that there's plenty of evidence for all to see that it's a myth, that merit doesn't always count. Most people still believe it does.

For whites the belief that they've earned their place through hard work and merit is, as political scientist Jennifer Hochschild has written, a double-edged sword.[7] On the positive side, it allows them to feel superior to those below them, to look down secure in the knowledge that they are the intellectual and moral betters of those in their view. Paradoxically, however, when they stumble and fall, the same idea that consoled them in good times corrodes their self-esteem in the bad ones. For if achievement and the good life are based on merit, when the dream fails they have no one to blame but themselves.

After listening to one white person after another denounce affirmative action programs because they violate the idea of a meritocracy, I asked: "Do you ever think that until now white people got the job because they were white?"

Nearly universally, the question was met with angry denials.

"Nobody ever gave us anything; we worked hard for everything we got," they insist. And they're right. No one ever did give them anything. Working-class men and women of any color have experienced more than their fair share of pain, oppression, and humiliation as they sought to make a living for their families. But it's also undeniable that in a society where race is one of the primary lines dividing its citizens, whiteness itself is a privilege. Whether they look for a job, a house, a school, or a home mortgage, being white gives them an edge.

To believe that, however, would undermine their conviction about merit and would diminish their accomplishments. So they resist any suggestion that being white has been an advantage in the job market. "Who says that?" Walt Maher, a twenty-nine-year-old white house painter demands angrily, when I raise the issue with him. "That never happened to me. Anytime I got a job it's because I was better than the other guy, that's all. These people, they just want something for nothing because they were once slaves. Well, hell, that's not my fault, and I don't think we owe them anything, not a damn thing."

"How do you account for the fact, then, that so many minority people have had trouble finding decent jobs or getting into your union?" I ask.

"What's the big deal? They're just not good enough, that's all. Or else they're lazy and don't really want to work."

It's temptingly easy to dismiss their denial of white privilege as a sham—a willful refusal to acknowledge the advantages that inhere in whiteness in this society. But it's more complicated than that. For people whose lives actually are privileged, it's possible to grasp the abstract idea that being white has advantaged them. To working-class families who struggle so hard just to manage each day, however, the notion that they're privileged seems absurd.

It isn't only the reality of working-class life that makes the idea of privilege so preposterous to them. Ideology and reality intersect here to facilitate the "not knowing." This nation has long conspired to keep white privilege a secret from itself—a remarkable accomplishment that rests on the widely accepted and deeply internalized belief in white superiority. Like most white Americans, the people in this study absorbed the ideology of white superiority with their mother's milk. To Walt Maher and others like him, the idea that so many men of color can't find decent jobs because "they're just not good enough" is an invariable truth born of his unflinching belief in the superiority of whiteness. If whites are exceptional, then the fact that he works when a black or Latino man doesn't has nothing to do with privilege. It's simply a statement of fact about the difference between them, about who's better, smarter, more industrious, more responsible, more morally advanced—in a word, superior.

In the characteristically circuitous reasoning that marks this worldview, there's no contradiction between the concept of white superiority and the American ideology of equal opportunity, which also is deeply embedded in the national psyche. The observed differences between whites and people of color simply are interpreted in ways that are consonant with the stated ideals of justice, fairness, and equality. Thus, the people I met insist they have no problem with the idea of equal opportunity; in fact, they applaud it. They just don't think the others are equal. "Look, I think fair's fair. It's okay with me if a black guy gets a job because he's really good," says Tony Bardolino. "But you know that's not the way it works. If you're white and the best, you still won't get the job because they'll give it to some black guy who's not even really qualified. They talk about everybody should be equal, but they don't mean it. I've got to be equal, but not him."

This definition of the situation serves whites psychologically as well as economically. It's bad enough to lose out to another white. But when the victor in the competition is a member of a despised racial minority—part of a group that hasn't even been allowed into the competition until recently—it becomes an even more bitter pill to swallow. By clinging to the belief that all affirmative action hires are unqualified, they can continue to believe in the idea of a meritocracy and avoid a confrontation with the one thing they could count on until now—the conviction that they're superior to people of color.

It's not whites alone who continue to hold to the idea that excellence will reap its own reward. Many of those who have been the victims of racial discrimination and know it also believe that merit counts. "I have a lot of trouble with quotas and things like that," Gloria Cameron, a thirty-six-year-old black claims adjuster, says heatedly. "People should be hired on merit and with these quotas, people who aren't qualified get the job just because of their color. I don't think anybody should ever have to hire a less qualified person for a job. That's not good for anybody, not the person or the company," she concludes firmly.

"Do you ever think that until now white people got the job because they were white?" I ask Gloria, just as I've asked others.

She shrugs the question off, her expression caught between laughter and impatience. "Of course I do; I wasn't born yesterday. But that's not right either. I think if you live in a country that says everybody should be equal and able to have a good life if they earn it, then that's the way it should be, whether you're black, white, or green."

As I listen to Gloria's words, I'm struck by the intensity of her response, by her insistence that merit must count. It makes sense. For blacks, who have been discriminated against for so long, a *real* meritocracy would finally allow them a level playing field on which to enter the game.

The range of opinions about affirmative action among people of color is wide—differences that are rooted in status, achievement, and gender. People who are unemployed, who are employed at very low-level jobs, or who believe they never got a break are most likely to be the strongest proponents of preferential hiring. "All I know is the black man don't stand a chance without somebody holding the door open, even if it's just a little bit," says Lutrell Patterson, a twenty-eight-year-old stock clerk. "So yeah, I'm for affirmative action or quotas or whatever you want to call it. Without the government pushing that door open, a lot more black men wouldn't have jobs today."

But it's not uncommon for those working-class men and women—whether black, Asian, or Latino—who have climbed just a rung or two up the employment ladder to distance themselves from affirmative action policies because they believe it depreciates their accomplishments.[8] "I don't like the idea because people keep thinking you don't deserve the job, and then you don't know if you really earned it yourself," says Joe Estevez, a thirty-seven-year-old Latino foreman in an oil refinery. "Like when I got made foreman, some of the guys on the shift were saying it's just because I'm Hispanic, you know, that they had to do it by the numbers. I mean, you can't enjoy it when you know people are saying things like that. It puts doubts in your mind about whether you really achieved something or not."

For Joe Estevez and others like him, then, the very presence of affirmative action programs threatens to deprive them of a sense of accomplishment. So they express their doubts and ambivalences. But it isn't necessarily because they believe there's something intrinsically wrong with the idea. Rather, it's the definition of the situation that's so damaging. For as the old sociological axiom says: "If men define the situation as real, then it is real in its consequences." In this case, the commonly accepted definition among whites is that affirmative action hires lack qualifications and competence. So when Joe Estevez is promoted to foreman, his white workmates mutter about doing it "by the numbers."

Partly they may do so as a way of defending against their own uneasiness about being passed over. If Joe got the job because the company needed to promote a minority person, then it's not because white men were considered and found wanting. But this interpretation of events consigns Joe to a world that assumes he's unqualified at best, incompetent at worst. A definition of the situation that exacts its cost in self-esteem. If he argues for affirmative action, it seems to him that he joins his workmates in demeaning his own achievement. To deal with this, he distances himself from affirmative action policies and joins with whites in criticizing the program and repeating the catechism that says no one should be hired unless fully qualified, implying, of course, that affirmative action hires are not.

For most people of color, then, affirmative action presents a difficult set of issues. Even Gloria Cameron, who spoke so resolutely in opposition to affirmative action hiring, soon revealed the complex set of fears and feelings that underlies her position. "The other thing I don't like about affirmative action is that some people take advantage. I mean, they get themselves hired because of this affirmative action but then maybe they're too lazy or don't know enough to do a really good job. They make it bad for the rest of us."

The fear that others will "make it bad for the rest of us" is a common one, especially among those who have moved up the class and status hierarchy. "This affirmative action thing is a hard one. You know, being a black man in this country is hard enough. Then when people who aren't so qualified get hired and screw up, it makes it worse for all of us," Daryl Jackson, a thirty-two-year-old black airline worker, says agitatedly.

"I worked damn hard to get where I am, and I do a hell of a lot better job than a lot of the guys I work with because I know my butt's on the line if I make any mistakes. Besides, if I screw up, I'll make it bad for all the other black people who are still trying to get in."

Whatever their misgivings—however they may feel about having their accomplishments devalued or about the face others of their group present to the world—most people of color also have significant disagreements with whites about whether there's a need for some kind of affirmative action policy, not to make up for the sins of yesterday but to deal with the discrimination that remains with us today. "The problem is," continues Daryl, "there's still a lot of prejudice around, so if it wasn't for affirmative action, a less qualified white person would get hired before a more qualified black person. That's the way it was for a long, long time, so that's why you need these kinds of programs.

"It's not fair; I know that. Some white people work hard and they can't get in because the company's got to hire a minority person. But life isn't fair, and all those people who can get in now couldn't get in for hundreds of years before. That wasn't fair either."

Parenthetically, the current lore about affirmative action is that it has helped middle-class people, while leaving the working-class and poor behind. But nothing could be further from the truth. The majority of the men and women who have been the beneficiaries of these programs were at the lower levels of the work hierarchy, if they had a job at all, before affirmative action gave them a hand up. But we have been blinded to this by the insistent repetition of a myth that has little to do with reality.

Partly this myth has been perpetuated by those who would discredit these programs. If opponents insist that affirmative action hasn't helped the poor and near poor, then the justification for the program's existence is called into question. Partly the myth lives because we Americans have so confounded the issue of class that anyone who has a job, a TV set and a VCR falls into the middle class. Partly it's sustained by the presence of an increasing number of high-profile black, Latino, and Asian professionals. And partly also the myth holds sway because of the visibility of the poor in our inner cities.

It's true that the proportion of minority families who live in poverty today is substantially higher than it was a few decades ago. Without affirmative action, however, there would be even more people whose lives are blighted by unemployment and underemployment; more men, women, and children whose life chances are constricted by their race and their place in the social and economic world.[9] The real problem, then, is not that we have skimmed the top but that, given the depth and breadth of the need, there simply have been too few opportunities available.

No matter what their reservations about preferential hiring, the one thing blacks and Latinos—but not Asians—agree on is the need for affirmative action in education. "It's different with school because black schools are terrible; everybody knows that," says Jewel Storiman, a twenty-nine-year-old black office worker, who moments earlier had spoken heatedly in opposition to affirmative action in the workplace. "This is a country that says everybody should have a chance at a good education, but then black kids have to go to the poorest schools, and that means they don't learn as much as white kids. So that puts them at a disadvantage. It's not their fault; it's society's fault because black schools are inferior. So it's right that they should make up for that by giving those kids a chance later on, like letting them into college even if their grades aren't as good as some of the other kids."

Asians, on the other hand, have a different view. They generally have no trouble with affirmative action on the job, but they feel victimized by it at the educational level. "They put higher standards on Asians and lower standards for the other nationalities, and I don't think that's right," complains Anna Wang, a twenty-nine-year-old Chinese office worker with two children. "People should be judged by their accomplishments, not by what color they are. They let black kids who don't have such good grades into college and keep out Chinese kids who have a lot higher grades. My niece had a 3.9 grade-point average and couldn't get into the school she wanted to go to, but some black kid with a 3.0 gets in. That's discrimination against the Chinese, but nobody makes a lot of noise about *that*."

Universally, Asian parents fear that every affirmative action admission means their own children won't have a place they earned by dint of hard work and high grades. So even those who might be somewhat sympathetic to the idea in the abstract are likely to argue for a more universal program, one that's not based on race. Such a program becomes acceptable at least partly because it gives Asian children, not all of whom come out of high school with 3.9 or 4.0 grade-point averages, a chance. "I realize that if everybody has to be a 4.0 to get into Berkeley, then only they'll get in," says Ralph Huie, a forty-year-old Asian draftsman whose son's 3.75 wasn't enough to get him into any of the top-rated colleges on his list. "So if there's some small number of places for people who don't do that well, it would give them a chance to get an education. That kind of program I'd support. But it would have to be only a small number of places, and it would have to be for more than just blacks. It should be for anybody who meets those lower standards."

Among whites, too, affirmative action evokes an intricate set of responses. At the most manifest level, no matter how their murmurings are cast—"It's a matter of qualifications"; "It's reverse discrimination"; "You have to earn your keep"; "I thought we believed in merit in this country"—the bottom line is that they find themselves faced with competition from unexpected quarters, and they don't like it. As Hochschild has noted: "The ideology of equal opportunity is simultaneously a message of hope and despair and . . . the practice of equal opportunity simultaneously opens and closes doors."[10]

In an expanding economy, opening the door to those who have been shut out may stir the apprehensions of the in-group, but so long as they are not themselves at risk, their discomfort is tolerable. When the economy contracts and jobs become scarce, it's another matter. Then, each time the door swings open for those who were formerly left out—a woman, an African-American, a Native American, and so on—it slams shut on a white man who until then had assumed the privilege of both whiteness and maleness without even knowing it.

Whatever other stereotypes and prejudices whites may hold, however, when they speak about affirmative action, it's blacks who come to the fore most often and most consistently. No matter how the discussion is framed, both men and women nearly always slip from the general to the specific, from talk about minorities to a focus on blacks. Even when I worded a question about preferential treatment in the most general terms, most people responded by talking about blacks. So pronounced is this tendency that, for whites, the very words *affirmative action* or *preferential treatment* conjure up a black face.

Nowhere do we see this more clearly than in the whites' response to the following story:

A company has one hundred employees, ninety-nine of them white. Now there's a job opening, and the employer has to make a decision between two equally qualified applicants—one a minority person, the other one white. Who should get the job?

"It's not fair to give it to him just because he's black," grumbles Steve Patchett, a twenty-five-year-old white welder.

My anecdote referred to a minority person; Steve translated that to mean black. So I commented, "You assume the other person is black, but I said only that it's a minority person."

"Yeah, well, that's what we're really talking about, isn't it? Everybody dances around that all the time, but they're the ones always making all the noise and demanding everything. If it wasn't for them, we wouldn't be sitting here talking about all this crap, would we? They're the ones that are in your face all the time, so that's who I'm talking about."

Undoubtedly, there are regional differences that would contradict this nearly universal perception. It's likely that conversations about these issues with whites in New Mexico would evoke images of Mexican-Americans. Or of Aleuts and Eskimos in Alaska. But except for those sections of the country where a single minority group dominates, it's blacks who come most readily to white minds when they think about affirmative action.

Although gender discrimination also has been targeted by affirmative action policies, few of the women and men in this study thought about gender when asked for an opinion about preferential hiring, a finding that surprised me at first. Why, I wondered, didn't they think about gender issues? The answer, I soon came to realize, is to be found in their class position.

In the professional middle class, a white woman is more likely than a black, Latino, or Asian man to be a serious competitor for a job. Nothing documents this more clearly than student enrollments in law, medicine, psychology, and sociology, to name just a few. Women make up half the students in the elite law schools of the nation, and they're not far behind in the medical schools. And although most professors are still men, women now dominate the graduate programs in both psychology and sociology. Therefore, affirmative action is at least as closely linked to gender as it is to race in the minds of men and women of that class. But in the white working-class world, it's men of color, not women, who are most often the contenders for the jobs traditionally held by white men. Consequently, they tend to focus first on race.

Among white women not only class but the work experience itself makes a difference in how they frame the issue and what they think of when asked about affirmative action. The few women in this study who now work in occupations that formerly were exclusively male are more likely to address themselves to gender issues and significantly more inclined to see value in these programs than women in traditional jobs. "I'm for it all the way," Louise Fairchild, a thirty-five-year-old white UPS driver, says enthusiastically. "No way would I have this job if it weren't for affirmative action. Without it, I wouldn't even have gotten my foot in the door."

For women of color, however, it's race that rises instantly to mind in any discussion of affirmative action. Partly that's because they live in a world where race-based discrimination in the work force, whether against women or men, is a part of daily life. "All my life I've been tracked into the lower-paying jobs just because I'm black," says Angela Worthy, a thirty-four-year-old word processor. "It doesn't matter how good my skills are. There's this woman in my office right now. We both applied for a secretary's job, and she got it. We talked about it, and even she knows my skills are better than hers. I'm a better typist; I don't make so many mistakes, and I'm faster, too. But she's white," she concludes, her words quiet but her eyes blazing with resentment.

Obviously, gender discrimination also has haunted the lives of black, Latino, and Asian women. But for them, this means only that they have two strikes against them—race *and* gender—instead of one. "If you're white, you only have to worry about being a woman, but if you're Hispanic, you get it both ways: You're a 'spic' *and* a woman," Donna Morales, a twenty-nine-year-old Latina office worker, says acidly.

The interaction between race and gender, then, creates a special set of circumstances for women of color. In the world of work, gender has kept all women in their place. But for women of color, race has been primary in determining what that place would be. Together, racial and gender discrimination have consigned them to the lowest-paid menial jobs this society has to offer.[11]

Gender also makes a difference in the response to affirmative action, with the women exhibiting a more complex, differentiated, and subtle view than the men—especially among whites. The same story that revealed how closely blacks are linked to affirmative action in the minds of whites laid bare the gender differences as well.

A company has one hundred employees, ninety-nine of them white. Now there's a job opening, and the employer has to make a decision between two equally qualified applicants—one a minority person, the other one white. Who should get the job?

Whether female or male, Latinos, Asians, and blacks were quick to say fairness dictates that the job should go to the minority person. But white men simply couldn't get past the fact that there was only one job and that the person of color probably would get it because of affirmative action policies. "I know what you want me to say, but I'll be damned if I'm going to say it," says Joe Helsen, a forty-four-year-old white maintenance man. "Why the hell should I? If there's one job, let the best man win."

"But I've said that both are the 'best man.' So now what does the boss do?" I ask.

"You know damn well what he'd do. He'd have to give it to the other guy because that's what they think they have to do now. And it's not fair that a colored guy should take a job away from a white guy just because he's colored," he replies, his face set stubbornly, his eyes meeting mine as if daring me to keep the challenge up.

The white women, however, respond quite differently. Although they're no more sympathetic to affirmative action in the abstract than the men, when faced with the human dilemma that's embedded in the story they're usually brought up short.[12] More often than not, therefore, women tend to think in a more nuanced way about the whole picture.

They worry about what's equitable. "Gee, I don't know," says Lorraine Helsen, Joe's forty-year-old wife. "I guess if there's only one black person, it doesn't seem fair, does it? Maybe if they're *really, really* equal the black person should get the job. But then I guess you have to worry about the white family. What's going to happen to them?"

They wonder about whose need is greatest. "I don't know. It's a hard choice if we both really need the job, isn't it? I mean, if it was me, I'd want the job. But then I think maybe if the other woman doesn't have a husband like me, and she has to support her children, maybe she should have the job," says thirty-one-year-old Maureen McCauley. "But that's only if she wants to work hard and do her job right. The problem is lots of times those black people don't want to."

They remember their own lives and the times when someone gave them a break. "When I first came here, I didn't have the qualifications and somebody gave me a chance," recalls fifty-one-year-old Regina Simovic, who emigrated to this country over a quarter of a century ago. "And then when I went to work again a few years ago after twenty years at home with the children, I also didn't have the qualifications. But I could work and learn. So I don't think it's only qualifications. If that woman could work hard and learn like I did, then sure, she should have the job. But if she's going to be like those people who think they should have a job just because they're black, then I say no because this country doesn't owe her anything. She has to work for it like the rest of us."

By "the rest of us," of course, she means white people. For even women like these, women who struggle to see the larger picture, remain mired in the stereotypes and hostility about African-Americans. "Maybe if they're *really, really* equal," says Lorraine Helsen, as if she can't quite believe it would be possible. "But that's only if she wants to work hard and do her job right," warns Maureen McCauley, whose words assume that a woman of color might not want to do that. "If that woman could work hard and learn like I did, then sure, she should have the job," says Regina Simovic. But the doubt is there, so she qualifies her words immediately: "But if she's going to be like those people who think they should have a job just because they're black, then I say no because this country doesn't owe her anything."

"This country don't owe nobody nothing"—defensive, angry words. But it's the anger born of fear. The flood of immigrants who threaten their jobs and burden their schools, the racial and cultural diversity that has changed the face of America and left them frightened about the shape of things to come, the fear that white privilege is under siege—all these have moved whites to gather their wagons in a circle, a circle of self-protection, to be sure, but also one designed to keep the threatening presence of the alien other on the outside. But such responses cannot be dismissed by name calling or by exhortations to greater charity or nobility. They are the price we pay for a society that rests on the notion of scarcity and a class structure that pits those at or close to the bottom against each other in a struggle for survival.

11

FAMILIES ON THE FAULT LINE

The Bardolinos

It has been more than three years since I first met the Bardolino family, three years in which to grow accustomed to words like *downsizing, restructuring,* or the most recent one, *reengineering*; three years in which to learn to integrate them into the language so that they now fall easily from our lips. But these are no ordinary words, at least not for Marianne and Tony Bardolino.

The last time we talked, Tony had been unemployed for about three months and Marianne was working nights at the telephone company and dreaming about the day they could afford a new kitchen. They seemed like a stable couple then—a house, two children doing well in school, Marianne working without complaint, Tony taking on a reasonable share of the family work. Tony, who had been laid off from the chemical plant where he had worked for ten years, was still hoping he'd be called back and trying to convince himself their lives were on a short hold, not on a catastrophic downhill slide. But instead of calling workers back, the company kept cutting its work force. Shortly after our first meeting, it became clear: There would be no recall. Now, as I sit in the little cottage Marianne shares with her seventeen-year-old daughter, she tells the story of these last three years.

"When we got the word that they wouldn't be calling Tony back, that's when we really panicked; I mean *really* panicked. We didn't know what to do. Where was Tony going to find another job, with the recession and all that? It was like the bottom really dropped out. Before that, we really hoped he'd be called back any day. It wasn't just crazy; they told the guys when they laid them off, you know, that it would be three, four months at most. So we hoped. I mean, sure we worried; in these times, you'd be crazy not to worry. But he'd been laid off for a couple of months before and called back, so we thought maybe it's the same thing. Besides, Tony's boss was so sure the guys would be coming back in a couple of months; so you tried to believe it was true."

She stops speaking, takes a few sips of coffee from the mug she holds in her hand, then says with a sigh, "I don't really know where to start. So much happened, and sometimes you can't even keep track. Mostly what I remember is how scared we were. Tony started to look for a job, but there was nowhere to look. The union couldn't help; there were no jobs in the industry. So he looked in the papers, and he made the rounds of all the places around here. He even went all the way to San Francisco and some of the places down near the airport there. But there was nothing.

"At first, I kept thinking, *Don't panic; he'll find something.* But after his unemployment ran out, we couldn't pay the bills, so then you can't help getting panicked, can you?"

She stops again, this time staring directly at me, as if wanting something. But I'm not sure what, so I sit quietly and wait for her to continue. Finally, she demands, "Well, can you?"

I understand now; she wants reassurance that her anxiety wasn't out of line, that it's not she who's responsible for the rupture in the family. So I say, "It sounds as if you feel guilty because you were anxious about how the family would manage."

"Yeah, that's right," she replies as she fights her tears. "I keep thinking maybe if I hadn't been so awful, I wouldn't have driven Tony away." But as soon as the words are spoken, she wants to take them back. "I mean, I don't know, maybe I wasn't that bad. We were both so depressed and scared, maybe there's nothing I could have done. But I think about it a lot, and I didn't have to blame him so much and keep nagging at him about how worried I was. It wasn't his fault; he was trying.

"It was just that we looked at it so different. I kept thinking he should take anything, but he only wanted a job like the one he had. We fought about that a lot. I mean, what difference does it make what kind of job it is? No, I don't mean that; I know it makes a difference. But when you have to support a family, that should come first, shouldn't it?"

As I listen, I recall my meeting with Tony a few days earlier and how guiltily he, too, spoke about his behavior during that time. "I wasn't thinking about her at all," he explained. "I was just so mad about what happened; it was like the world came crashing down on me. I did a little too much drinking, and then I'd just crawl into a hole, wouldn't even know whether Marianne or the kids were there or not. She kept saying it was like I wasn't there. I guess she was right, because I sure didn't want to be there, not if I couldn't support them."

"Is that the only thing you were good for in the family?" I asked him.

"Good point," he replied laughing. "Maybe not, but it's hard to know what else you're good for when you can't do that."

I push these thoughts aside and turn my attention back to Marianne. "Tony told me that he did get a job after about a year," I remark.

"Yeah, did he tell you what kind of job it was?"

"Not exactly, only that it didn't work out."

"Sure, he didn't tell you because he's still so ashamed about it. He was out of work so long that even he finally got it that he didn't have a choice. So he took this job as a dishwasher in this restaurant. It's one of those new kind of places with an open kitchen, so there he was, standing there washing dishes in front of everybody. I mean, we used to go there to eat sometimes, and now he's washing the dishes and the whole town sees him doing it. He felt so ashamed, like it was such a comedown, that he'd come home even worse than when he wasn't working.

"That's when the drinking really started heavy. Before that he'd drink, but it wasn't so bad. After he went to work there, he'd come home and drink himself into a coma. I was working days by then, and I'd try to wait up until he came home. But it didn't matter; all he wanted to do was go for that bottle. He drank a lot during the day, too, so sometimes I'd come home and find him passed out on the couch and he never got to work that day. That's when I was maddest of all. I mean, I felt sorry for him having to do that work. But I was afraid he'd get fired."

"Did he?"

"No, he quit after a couple of months. He heard there was a chemical plant down near L.A. where he might get a job. So he left. I mean, we didn't exactly separate, but we didn't exactly not. He didn't ask me and the kids to go with him; he just went. It didn't make any difference. I didn't trust him by then, so why would I leave my job and pick up the kids and move when we didn't even know if he'd find work down there?

"I think he went because he had to get away. Anyway, he never found any decent work there either. I know he had some jobs, but I never knew exactly what he was doing. He'd call once in awhile, but we didn't have much to say to each other then. I always figured he wasn't making out so well because he didn't send much money the whole time he was gone."

As Tony tells it, he was in Los Angeles for nearly a year, every day an agony of guilt and shame. "I lived like a bum when I was down there. I had a room in a place that wasn't much better than a flop house, but it was like I couldn't get it together to go find something else. I wasn't making much money, but I had enough to live decent. I felt like what difference did it make how I lived?"

He sighs—a deep, sad sound—then continues, "I couldn't believe what I did, I mean that I really walked out on my family. My folks were mad as hell at me. When I told them what I was going to do, my father went nuts, said I shouldn't come back to his house until I got some sense again. But I couldn't stay around with Marianne blaming me all the time."

He stops abruptly, withdraws to someplace inside himself for a few moments, then turns back to me. "That's not fair. She wasn't the only one doing the blaming. I kept beating myself up, too, you know, blaming myself, like I did something wrong.

"Anyhow, I hated to see what it was doing to the kids; they were like caught in the middle with us fighting and hollering, or else I was passed out drunk. I didn't want them to have to see me like that, and I couldn't help it. So I got out."

For Marianne, Tony's departure was both a relief and a source of anguish. "At first I was glad he left; at least there was some peace in the house. But then I got so scared; I didn't know if I could make it alone with the kids. That's when I sold the house. We were behind in our payments, and I knew we'd never catch up. The bank was okay; they said they'd give us a little more time. But there was no point.

"That was really hard. It was our home; we worked so hard to get it. God, I hated to give it up. We were lucky, though. We found this place here. It's near where we used to live, so the kids didn't have to change schools, or anything like that. It's small, but at least it's a separate little house, not one of those grungy apartments." She interrupts herself with a laugh, "Well, 'house' makes it sound a lot more than it is, doesn't it?"

"How did your children manage all this?"

"It was real hard on them. My son had just turned thirteen when it all happened, and he was really attached to his father. He couldn't understand why Tony left us, and he was real angry for a long time. At first, I thought he'd be okay, you know, that he'd get over it. But then he got into some bad company. I think he was doing some drugs, although he still won't admit that. Anyway, one night he and some of his friends stole a car. I think they just wanted to go for a joyride; they didn't mean to really steal it forever. But they got caught, and he got sent to juvenile hall.

"I called Tony down in L.A. and told him what happened. It really shocked him; he started to cry on the phone. I never saw him cry before, not with all our trouble. But he just cried and cried. When he got off the phone, he took the first plane he could get, and he's been back up here ever since.

"Jimmy's trouble really changed everything around. When Tony came back, he didn't want to do anything to get Jimmy out of juvy right away. He thought he ought to stay there for a while; you know, like to teach him a lesson. I was mad at first because Jimmy wanted to come home so bad; he was so scared. But now I see Tony was right.

"Anyhow, we let Jimmy stay there for five whole days, then Tony's parents lent us the money to bail him out and get him a lawyer. He made a deal so that if Jimmy pleaded guilty, he'd get a suspended sentence. And that's what happened. But the judge laid down the law, told him if he got in one little bit of trouble again, he'd go to jail. It put the fear of God into the boy."

For Tony, his son's brush with the law was like a shot in the arm. "It was like I had something really important to do, to get that kid back on track. We talked it over and Marianne agreed it would be better if Jimmy came to live with me. She's too soft with the kids; I've got better control. And I wanted to make it up to him, too, to show him he could count on me again. I figured the whole trouble came because I left them, and I wanted to set it right.

"So when he got out of juvy, he went with me to my folks' house where I was staying. We lived there for awhile until I got this job. It's no great shakes, a kind of general handyman. But it's a job, and right from the start I made enough so we could move into this here apartment. So things are going pretty good right now."

"Pretty good" means that Jimmy, now sixteen, has settled down and is doing well enough in school to talk about going to college. For Tony, too, things have turned around. He set up his own business as an independent handyman several months ago and, although the work isn't yet regular enough to allow him to quit his job, his reputation as a man who can fix just about anything is growing. Last month the business actually made enough money to pay his bills. "I'll hang onto the job for a while, even if the business gets going real good, because we've got a lot of catching up to do. I don't mind working hard; I like it. And being my own boss, boy, that's really great," he concludes exultantly.

"Do you think you and Marianne will get together again?"

"I sure hope so; it's what I'm working for right now. She says she's not sure, but she's never made a move to get a divorce. That's a good sign, isn't it?"

When I ask Marianne the same question, she says, "Tony wants to, but I still feel a little scared. You know, I never thought I could manage without him, but then when I was forced to, I did. Now, I don't know what would happen if we got together again. It wouldn't be like it was before. I just got promoted to supervisor, so I have a lot of responsibility on my job. I'm a different person, and

I don't know how Tony would like that. He says he likes it fine, but I figure we should wait a while and see what happens. I mean, what if things get tough again for him? I don't ever want to live through anything like these last few years."

"Yet you've never considered divorce."

She laughs, "You sound like Tony." Then more seriously, "I don't want a divorce if I can help it. Right now, I figure if we got through these last few years and still kind of like each other, maybe we've got a chance."

*   *   *

In the opening pages of this book, I wrote that when the economy falters, families tremble. The Bardolinos not only trembled, they cracked. Whether they can patch up the cracks and put the family back together again remains an open question. But the experience of families like those on the pages of this book provides undeniable evidence of the fundamental link between the public and private arenas of modern life.

No one has to tell the Bardolinos or their children about the many ways the structural changes in the economy affect family life. In the past, a worker like Tony Bardolino didn't need a high level of skill or literacy to hold down a well-paying semiskilled job in a steel mill or an automobile plant. A high school education, often even less, was enough. But an economy that relies most heavily on its service sector needs highly skilled and educated workers to fill its better-paying jobs, leaving people like Tony scrambling for jobs at the bottom of the economic order.

The shift from the manufacturing to the service sector, the restructuring of the corporate world, the competition from low-wage workers in underdeveloped countries that entices American corporations to produce their goods abroad, all have been going on for decades; all are expected to accelerate through the 1990s. The manufacturing sector, which employed just over 26 percent of American workers in 1970, already had fallen to nearly 18 percent by 1991.[1] And experts predict a further drop to 12.5 percent by the year 2000.[2] "This is the end of the post–World War boom era. We are never going back to what we knew," says employment analyst Dan Lacey, publisher of the newsletter *Workplace Trends*.[3]

Yet the federal government has not only failed to offer the help working-class families need, but as a sponsor of a program to nurture capitalism elsewhere in the world it has become party to the exodus of American factories to foreign lands. Under the auspices of the U.S. Agency for International Development (AID), for example, Decaturville Sportswear, a company that used to be based in Tennessee, has moved to El Salvador.[4] AID not only gave grants to trade organizations in El Salvador to recruit Decaturville but also subsidized the move by picking up the $5 million tab for the construction of a new plant, footing the bill for over $1 million worth of insurance, and providing low-interest loans for other expenses involved in the move.

It's a sweetheart deal for Decaturville Sportswear and the other companies that have been lured to move south of the border under this program. They build new factories at minimal cost to themselves, while their operating expenses drop dramatically. In El Salvador, Decaturville is exempted from corporate taxes and shipping duties. And best of all, the hourly wage for factory workers there is forty-five cents an hour; in the United States the minimum starting wage for workers doing the same job is $4.25.

True, like Tony Bardolino, many of the workers displaced by downsizing, restructuring, and corporate moves like these will eventually find other work. But like him also, they'll probably have to give up what little security they knew in the past. For the forty-hour-a-week steady job that pays a decent wage and provides good benefits is quickly becoming a thing of the past. Instead, as part of the new lean, clean, mean look of corporate America, we now have what the federal government and employment agencies call "contingent" workers—a more benign name for what some labor economists refer to as "disposable" or "throwaway" workers.

It's a labor strategy that comes in several forms. Generally, disposable workers are hired in part-time or temporary jobs to fill an organizational need and are released as soon as the work load lightens. But when union contracts call for employees to join the union after thirty days on the job, some unscrupulous employers fire contingent workers on the twenty-ninth day and bring in a new crew.

However it's done, disposable workers earn less than those on the regular payroll and their jobs rarely come with benefits of any kind. Worse yet, they set off to work each morning fearful and uncertain, not knowing how the day will end, worrying that by nightfall they'll be out of a job.

The government's statistics on these workers are sketchy, but Labor Secretary Robert Reich estimates that they now make up nearly one-third of the existing work force.[5] This means that about thirty-four million men and women, most of whom want steady, full-time work, start each day as contingent and/or part-time workers. Indeed, so widespread is this practice now that in some places temporary employment agencies are displacing the old ones that sought permanent placements for their clients.[6]

Here again, class makes a difference. For while it's true that managers and professionals now also are finding themselves disposable, most of the workers who have become so easily expendable are in the lower reaches of the work order. And it's they who are likely to have the fewest options. These are the workers, the unskilled and the semiskilled—the welders, the forklift operators, the assemblers, the clerical workers, and the like—who are most likely to seem to management to be interchangeable. Their skills are limited; their job tasks are relatively simple and require little training. Therefore, they're able to move in and perform with reasonable efficiency soon after they come on the job. Whatever lost time or productivity a company may suffer by not having a steady crew of workers is compensated by the savings in wages and benefits the employment of throwaway workers permits. A resolution that brings short-term gains for the company at the long-term expense of both the workers and the nation. For when a person can't count on a permanent job, a critical element binding him or her to society is lost.

The Tomalsons

When I last met the Tomalsons, Gwen was working as a clerk in the office of a large Manhattan company and was also a student at a local college where she was studying nursing. George Tomalson, who had worked for three years in a furniture factory, where he laminated plastic to wooden frames, had been thrown out of a job when the company went bankrupt. He seemed a gentle man then, unhappy over the turn his life had taken but still wanting to believe that it would come out all right.

Now, as he sits before me in the still nearly bare apartment, George is angry. "If you're a black man in this country, you don't have a chance, that's all, not a chance. It's like no matter how hard you try, you're nothing but trash. I've been looking for work for over two years now, and there's nothing. White people are complaining all the time that black folks are getting a break. Yeah, well, I don't know who those people are, because it's not me or anybody else I know. People see a black man coming, they run the other way, that's what I know."

"You haven't found any work at all for two years?" I ask.

"Some temporary jobs, a few weeks sometimes, a couple of months once, mostly doing shit work for peanuts. Nothing I could count on."

"If you could do any kind of work you want, what would you do?"

He smiles, "That's easy; I'd be a carpenter. I'm good with my hands, and I know a lot about it," he says, holding his hands out, palms up, and looking at them proudly. But his mood shifts quickly; the smile disappears; his voice turns harsh. "But that's not going to happen. I tried to get into the union, but there's no room there for a black guy. And in this city, without being in the union, you don't have a chance at a construction job. They've got it all locked up, and they're making sure they keep it for themselves."

When I talk with Gwen later, she worries about the intensity of her husband's resentment. "It's not like George; he's always been a real even guy. But he's moody now, and he's so angry, I sometimes wonder what he might do. This place is a hell hole," she says, referring to the housing project they live in. "It's getting worse all the time; kids with guns, all the drugs, grown men out of work all around. I'll bet there's hardly a man in this whole place who's got a job, leave alone a good one."

"Just what is it you worry about?"

She hesitates, clearly wondering whether to speak, how much to tell me about her fears, then says with a shrug, "I don't know, everything, I guess. There's so much crime and drugs and stuff out there. You can't help wondering whether he'll get tempted." She stops herself, looks at me intently, and says, "Look, don't get me wrong; I know it's crazy to think like that. He's not that kind of person. But when you live in times like these, you can't help worrying about everything.

"We both worry a lot about the kids at school. Every time I hear about another kid shot while they're at school, I get like a raving lunatic. What's going on in this world that kids are killing kids? Doesn't anybody care that so many black kids are dying like that? It's like a black child's life doesn't count for anything. How do they expect our kids to grow up to be good citizens when nobody cares about them?

"It's one of the things that drives George crazy, worrying about the kids. There's no way you can keep them safe around here. Sometimes I wonder why we send them to school. They're not getting much of an education there. Michelle just started, but Julia's in the fifth grade, and believe me, she's not learning much.

"We sit over her every night to make sure she does her homework and gets it right. But what good is it if the people at school aren't doing their job. Most of the teachers there don't give a damn. They just want the paycheck and the hell with the kids. Everybody knows it's not like that in the white schools; white people wouldn't stand for it.

"I keep thinking we've got to get out of here for the sake of the kids. I'd love to move someplace, anyplace out of the city where the schools aren't such a cesspool. But," she says dejectedly, "we'll never get out if George can't find a decent job. I'm just beginning my nursing career, and I know I've got a future now. But still, no matter what I do or how long I work at it, I can't make enough for that by myself."

George, too, has dreams of moving away, somewhere far from the city streets, away from the grime and the crime. "Look at this place," he says, his sweeping gesture taking in the whole landscape. "Is this any place to raise kids? Do you know what my little girls see every day they walk out the door? Filth, drugs, guys hanging on the corner waiting for trouble.

"If I could get any kind of a decent job, anything, we'd be out of here, far away, someplace outside the city where the kids could breathe clean and see a different life. It's so bad here, I take them over to my mother's a lot after school; it's a better neighborhood. Then we stay over there and eat sometimes. Mom likes it; she's lonely, and it helps us out. Not that she's got that much, but there's a little pension my father left."

"What about Gwen's family? Do they help out, too?"

"Her mother doesn't have anything to help with since her father died. He's long gone; he was killed by the cops when Gwen was a teenager," he says as calmly as if reporting the time of day.

"Killed by the cops!" The words leap out at me and jangle my brain. But why do they startle me so? Surely with all the discussion of police violence in the black community in recent years, I can't be surprised to hear that a black man was "killed by the cops."

It's the calmness with which the news is relayed that gets to me. And it's the realization once again of the distance between the lives and experiences of blacks and others, even poor others. Not one white person in this study reported a violent death in the family. Nor did any of the Latino and Asian families, although the Latinos spoke of a difficult and often antagonistic relationship with Anglo authorities, especially the police. But four black families (13 percent) told of relatives who had been murdered, one of the families with two victims—a teenage son and a twenty-two-year-old daughter, both killed in violent street crimes.

But I'm also struck by the fact that Gwen never told me how her father died. True, I didn't ask. But I wonder now why she didn't offer the information. "Gwen didn't tell me," I say, as if trying to explain my surprise.

"She doesn't like to talk about it. Would you?" he replies somewhat curtly.

It's a moment or two before I can collect myself to speak again. Then I comment, "You talk about all this so calmly."

He leans forward, looks directly at me, and shakes his head. When he finally speaks, his voice is tight with the effort to control his rage. "What do you want? Should I rant and rave? You want me to say I want to go out and kill those mothers? Well, yeah, I do. They killed a good man just because he was black. He wasn't a criminal; he was a hard-working guy who just happened to be in the wrong place when the cops were looking for someone to shoot," he says, then sits back and stares stonily at the wall in front of him.

We both sit locked in silence until finally I break it. "How did it happen?"

He rouses himself at the sound of my voice. "They were after some dude who robbed a liquor store, and when they saw Gwen's dad, they didn't ask questions; they shot. The bastards. Then they said it was self-defense, that they saw a gun in his hand. That man never held a gun in his life, and nobody ever found one either. But nothing happens to them; it's no big deal, just another dead nigger," he concludes, his eyes blazing.

It's quiet again for a few moments, then, with a sardonic half smile, he says, "What would a nice, white middle-class lady like you know about any of that? You got all those degrees, writing books and all that. How are you going to write about people like us?"

"I was poor like you once, very poor," I say somewhat defensively.

He looks surprised, then retorts, "Poor and white; it's a big difference."

* * *

Thirty years before the beginning of the Civil War, Alexis de Tocqueville wrote: "If ever America undergoes great revolutions, they will be brought about by the presence of the black race on the soil of the United States; that is to say they will owe their origin, not to the equality, but to the inequality of condition."[7] One hundred and sixty years later, relations between blacks and whites remain one of the great unresolved issues in American life, and "the inequality of condition" that de Tocqueville observed is still a primary part of the experience of black Americans.

I thought about de Tocqueville's words as I listened to George Tomalson and about how the years of unemployment had changed him from, as Gwen said, "a real even guy" to an angry and embittered one. And I was reminded, too, of de Tocqueville's observation that "the danger of conflict between the white and black inhabitants perpetually haunts the imagination of the [white] Americans, like a painful dream."[8] Fifteen generations later we're still paying the cost of those years when Americans held slaves—whites still living in fear, blacks in rage. "People see a black man coming, they run the other way," says George Tomalson.

Yet however deep the cancer our racial history has left on the body of the nation, most Americans, including many blacks, believe that things are better today than they were a few decades ago—a belief that's both true and not true.[9] There's no doubt that in ending the legal basis for discrimination and segregation, the nation took an important step toward fulfilling the promise of equality for all Americans. As more people meet as equals in the workplace, stereotypes begin to fall away and caricatures are transformed into real people. But it's also true that the economic problems of recent decades have raised the level of anxiety in American life to a new high. So although virtually all whites today give verbal assent to the need for racial justice and equality, they also find ways to resist the implementation of the belief when it seems to threaten their own status or economic well-being.

Our schizophrenia about race, our capacity to believe one thing and do another, is not new. Indeed, it is perhaps epitomized by Thomas Jefferson, the great liberator. For surely, as Gordon Wood writes in an essay in the *New York Review of Books*, "there is no greater irony in American history than the fact that America's supreme spokesman for liberty and equality was a lifelong aristocratic owner of slaves."[10]

Jefferson spoke compellingly about the evils of slavery, but he bought, sold, bred, and flogged slaves. He wrote eloquently about equality but he was convinced that blacks were an inferior race and endorsed the racial stereotypes that have characterized African-Americans since their earliest days on this continent. He believed passionately in individual liberty, but he couldn't imagine free blacks living in America, maintaining instead that if the nation considered emancipating the slaves, it must also prepare for their expulsion.

No one talks seriously about expulsion anymore. Nor do many use the kind of language to describe African-Americans that was so common in Jefferson's day. But the duality he embodied—his belief in justice, liberty, and equality alongside his conviction of black inferiority—still lives.

The Riveras

Once again Ana Rivera and I sit at the table in her bright and cheerful kitchen. She's sipping coffee; I'm drinking some bubbly water while we make small talk and get reacquainted. After a while, we begin to talk about the years since we last met. "I'm a grandmother now," she says, her face wreathed in a smile. "My daughter Karen got married and had a baby, and he's the sweetest little boy, smart, too. He's only two and a half, but you should hear him. He sounds like five."

"When I talked to her the last time I was here, Karen was planning to go to college. What happened?" I ask.

She flushes uncomfortably. "She got pregnant, so she had to get married. I was heartbroken at first. She was only nineteen, and I wanted her to get an education so bad. It was awful; she had been working for a whole year to save money for college, then she got pregnant and couldn't go."

"You say she had to get married. Did she ever consider an abortion?"

"I don't know; we never talked about it. We're Catholic," she says by way of explanation. "I mean, I don't believe in abortion." She hesitates, seeming uncertain about what more she wants to say, then adds, "I have to admit, at a time like that, you have to ask yourself what you really believe. I don't think anybody's got the right to take a child's life. But when I thought about what having that baby would do to Karen's life, I couldn't help thinking, *What if* . . . ?" She stops, unable to bring herself to finish the sentence.

"Did you ever say that to Karen?"

"No, I would *never* do that. I didn't even tell my husband I thought such things. But, you know," she adds, her voice dropping to nearly a whisper, "if she had done it, I don't think I would have said a word."

"What about the rest of the kids?"

"Paul's going to be nineteen soon; he's a problem," she sighs. "I mean, he's got a good head, but he won't use it. I don't know what's the matter with kids these days; it's like they want everything but they're not willing to work for anything. He hardly finished high school, so you can't talk to him about going to college. But what's he going to do? These days if you don't have a good education, you don't have a chance. No matter what we say, he doesn't listen, just goes on his smart-alecky way, hanging around the neighborhood with a bunch of no-good kids looking for trouble.

"Rick's so mad, he wants to throw him out of the house. But I say no, we can't do that because then what'll become of him? So we fight about that a lot, and I don't know what's going to happen."

"Does Paul work at all?"

"Sometimes, but mostly not. I'm afraid to think about where he gets money from. His father won't give him a dime. He borrows from me sometimes, but I don't have much to give him. And anyway, Rick would kill me if he knew."

I remember Paul as a gangly, shy sixteen-year-old, no macho posturing, none of the rage that shook his older brother, not a boy I would have thought would be heading for trouble. But then, Karen, too, had seemed so determined to grasp at a life that was different from the one her parents were living. What happens to these kids?

When I talk with Rick about these years, he, too, asks in bewilderment: What happened? "I don't know; we tried so hard to give the kids everything they needed. I mean, sure, we're not rich, and there's a lot of things we couldn't give them. But we were always here for them; we listened; we talked. What happened? First my daughter gets pregnant and has to get married; now my son is becoming a bum."

"Roberto—that's what we have to call him now," explains Rick, "he says it's what happens when people don't feel they've got respect. He says we'll keep losing our kids until they really believe they really have an equal chance. I don't know; I knew I had to *make* the Anglos respect me, and I had to make my chance. Why don't my kids see it like that?" he asks wearily, his shoulders seeming to sag lower with each sentence he speaks.

"I guess it's really different today, isn't it?" he sighs. "When I was coming up, you could still make your chance. I mean, I only went to high school, but I got a job and worked myself up. You can't do that anymore. Now you need to have some kind of special skills just to get a job that pays more than the minimum wage.

"And the schools, they don't teach kids anything anymore. I

went to the same public schools my kids went to, but what a difference. It's like nobody cares anymore."

"How is Roberto doing?" I ask, remembering the hostile eighteen-year-old I interviewed several years earlier.

"He's still mad; he's always talking about injustice and things like that. But he's different than Paul. Roberto always had some goals. I used to worry about him because he's so angry all the time. But I see now that his anger helps him. He wants to fight for his people, to make things better for everybody. Paul, he's like the wind; nothing matters to him.

"Right now, Roberto has a job as an electrician's helper, learning the trade. He's been working there for a couple of years; he's pretty good at it. But I think—I hope—he's going to go to college. He heard that they're trying to get Chicano students to go to the university, so he applied. If he gets some aid, I think he'll go," Rick says, his face radiant at the thought that at least one of his children will fulfill his dream. "Ana and me, we tell him even if he doesn't get aid, he should go. We can't do a lot because we have to help Ana's parents and that takes a big hunk every month. But we'll help him, and he could work to make up the rest. I know it's hard to work and go to school, but people do it all the time, and he's smart; he could do it."

His gaze turns inward; then, as if talking to himself, he says, "I never thought I'd say this but I think Roberto's right. We've got something to learn from some of these kids. I told that to Roberto just the other day. He says Ana and me have been trying to pretend we're one of them all of our lives. I told him, 'I think you're right.' I kept thinking if I did everything right, I wouldn't be a 'greaser.' But after all these years, I'm still a 'greaser' in their eyes. It took my son to make me see it. Now I know. If I weren't I'd be head of the shipping department by now, not just one of the supervisors, and maybe Paul wouldn't be wasting his life on the corner."

*   *   *

We keep saying that family matters, that with a stable family and two caring parents children will grow to a satisfactory adulthood. But I've rarely met a family that's more constant or more concerned than the Riveras. Or one where both parents are so involved with their children. Ana was a full-time homemaker until Paul, their youngest, was twelve. Rick has been with the same company for more than twenty-five years, having worked his way up from clerk to shift supervisor in its shipping department. Whatever the conflicts in their marriage, theirs is clearly a warm, respectful, and caring relationship. Yet their daughter got pregnant and gave up her plans for college, and a son is idling his youth away on a street corner.

Obviously, then, something more than family matters. Growing up in a world where opportunities are available makes a difference. As does being able to afford to take advantage of an opportunity when it comes by. Getting an education that broadens horizons and prepares a child for a productive adulthood makes a difference. As does being able to find work that nourishes self-respect and pays a living wage. Living in a world that doesn't judge you by the color of your skin makes a difference. As does feeling the respect of the people around you.

This is not to suggest that there aren't also real problems inside American families that deserve our serious and sustained attention. But the constant focus on the failure of family life as the locus of both our personal and social difficulties has become a mindless litany, a dangerous diversion from the economic and social realities that make family life so difficult today and that so often destroy it.

The Kwans

It's a rare sunny day in Seattle, so Andy Kwan and I are in his back-yard, a lovely showcase for his talents as a landscape gardener. Although it has been only a few years since we first met, most of the people to whom I've returned in this round of interviews seem older, grayer, more careworn. Andy Kwan is no exception. The brilliant afternoon sunshine is cruel as it searches out every line of worry and age in his angular face. Since I interviewed his wife the day before, I already know that the recession has hurt his business. So I begin by saying, "Carol says that your business has been slow for the last couple of years."

"Yes," he sighs. "At first when the recession came, it didn't hurt me. I think Seattle didn't really get hit at the beginning. But the summer of 1991, that's when I began to feel it. It's as if everybody zipped up their wallets when it came to landscaping.

"A lot of my business has always been when people buy a new house. You know, they want to fix up the outside just like they like it. But nobody's been buying houses lately, and even if they do, they're not putting any money into landscaping. So it's been tight, real tight."

"How have you managed financially?"

"We get by, but it's hard. We have to cut back on a lot of stuff we used to take for granted, like going out to eat once in a while, or going to the movies, things like that. Clothes, nobody gets any new clothes anymore.

"I do a lot of regular gardening now—you know, the maintenance stuff. It helps; it takes up some of the slack, but it's not enough because it doesn't pay much. And the competition's pretty stiff, so you've got to keep your prices down. I mean, everybody knows that it's one of the things people can cut out when things get tough, so the gardeners around here try to hold on by cutting their prices. It gets pretty hairy, real cutthroat."

He gets up, walks over to a flower bed, and stands looking at it. Then, after a few quiet moments, he turns back to me and says, "It's a damned shame. I built my business like you build a house, brick by brick, and it was going real good. I finally got to the point where I wasn't doing much regular gardening anymore. I could concentrate on landscaping, and I was making a pretty good living. With Carol working, too, we were doing all right. I even hired two people and was keeping them busy most of the time. Then all of a sudden, it all came tumbling down.

"I felt real bad when I had to lay off my workers. They have families to feed, too. But what could I do? Now it's like I'm back where I started, an ordinary gardener again and even worrying about how long that'll last," he says disconsolately.

He walks back to his seat, sits down, and continues somewhat more philosophically, "Carol says I shouldn't complain because, with all the problems, we're lucky. She still has her job, and I'm making out. I mean, it's not great, but it could be a lot worse." He pauses, looks around blankly for a moment, sighs, and says, "I guess she's right. Her sister worked at Boeing for seven years and she got laid off a couple of months ago. No notice, nothing; just the pink slip. I mean, everybody knew there'd be layoffs there, but you know how it is. You don't think it's really going to happen to you.

"I try not to let it get me down. But it's hard to be thankful for not having bigger trouble than you've already got," he says ruefully. Then, a smile brightening his face for the first time, he adds, "But there's one thing I can be thankful for, and that's the kids; they're doing fine. I worry a little bit about what's going to happen, though. I guess you can't help it if you're a parent. Eric's the oldest; he's fifteen now, and you never know. Kids get into all kinds of trouble these days. But so far, he's okay. The girls, they're good kids. Carol worries about what'll happen when they get to those teenage years. But I think they'll be okay. We teach them decent values; they go to church every week. I have to believe that makes a difference."

"You say that you worry about Eric but that the girls will be fine because of the values of your family. Hasn't he been taught the same values?"

He thinks a moment, then says, "Did I say that? Yeah, I guess I did. I think maybe there's more ways for a boy to get in trouble than a girl." He laughs and says again, "Did I say *that?*" Then, more thoughtfully, "I don't know. I guess I worry about them all, but if you don't tell yourself that things'll work out okay, you go nuts. I mean, so much can go wrong with kids today.

"It used to be the Chinese family could really control the kids. When I was a kid, the family was law. My father was Chinese-born; he came here as a kid. My mother was born right here in this city. But the grandparents were all immigrants; everybody spoke Chinese at home; and we never lived more than a couple of blocks from both sides of the family. My parents were pretty Americanized everywhere but at home, at least while their parents were alive. My mother would go clean her mother's house for her because that's what a Chinese daughter did."

"Was that because your grandmother was old or sick?"

"No," he replies, shaking his head at the memory. "It's because that's what her mother expected her to do; that's the way Chinese families were then. We talk about that, Carol and me, and how things have changed. It's hard to imagine it, but that's the kind of control families had then.

"It's all changed now. Not that I'd want it that way. I want my kids to know respect for the family, but they shouldn't be servants. That's what my mother was, a servant for her mother.

"By the time my generation came along, things were already different. I couldn't wait to get away from all that family stuff. I mean, it was nice in some ways; there was always this big, noisy bunch of people around, and you knew you were part of something. That felt good. But Chinese families, boy, they don't let go. You felt like they were choking you.

"Now it's *really* different; it's like the kids aren't hardly Chinese any more. I mean, my kids are just like any other American kids. They never lived in a Chinese neighborhood like the one I grew up in, you know, the kind where the only Americans you see are the people who come to buy Chinese food or eat at the restaurants."

"You say they're ordinary American kids. What about the Chinese side? What kind of connection do they have to that?"

"It's funny," he muses. "We sent them to Chinese school because we wanted them to know about their history, and we thought they should know the language, at least a little bit. But they weren't really interested; they wanted to be like everybody else and eat peanut butter and jelly sandwiches. Lately it's a little different, but that's because they feel like they're picked on because they're Chinese. I mean, everybody's worrying about the Chinese kids being so smart and winning all the prizes at school, and the kids are angry about that, especially Eric. He says there's a lot of bad feelings about Chinese kids at school and that everybody's picking on them—the white kids and the black kids, all of them.

"So all of a sudden, he's becoming Chinese. It's like they're making him think about it because there's all this resentment about Asian kids all around. Until a couple of years ago, he had lots of white friends. Now he hangs out mostly with other Asian kids. I guess that's because they feel safer when they're together."

"How do you feel about this?"

The color rises in his face; his voice takes on an edge of agitation. "It's too bad. It's not the way I wanted it to be. I wanted my kids to know they're Chinese and be proud of it, but that's not what's going on now. It's more like . . . ," he stops, trying to find the words, then starts again. "It's like they have to defend themselves *because* they're Chinese. Know what I mean?" he asks. Then without waiting for an answer, he explains, "There's all this prejudice now, so then you can't forget you're Chinese.

"It makes me damn mad. You grow up here and they tell you everybody's equal and that any boy can grow up to be president. Not that I ever thought a Chinese kid could ever be president; any Chinese kid knows that's a fairy tale. But I did believe the rest of it, you know, that if you're smart and work hard and do well, people will respect you and you'll be successful. Now, it looks like the smarter Chinese kids are, the more trouble they get."

"Do you think that prejudice against Chinese is different now than when you were growing up?"

"Yeah, I do. When I was a kid like Eric, nobody paid much attention to the Chinese. They left us alone, and we left them alone. But now all these Chinese kids are getting in the way of the white kids because there's so many of them, and they're getting better grades, and things like that. So then everybody gets mad because they think our kids are taking something from them."

He stops, weighs his last words, then says, "I guess they're right, too. When I was growing up, Chinese kids were lucky to graduate from high school, and we didn't get in anybody's way. Now so many Chinese kids are going to college that they're taking over places white kids used to have. I can understand that they don't like that. But that's not our problem; it's theirs. Why don't they work hard like Chinese kids do?

"It's not fair that they've got quotas for Asian kids because the people who run the colleges decided there's too many of them and not enough room for white kids. Nobody ever worried that there were too many white kids, did they?"

*   *   *

"It's not fair"—a cry from the heart, one I heard from nearly everyone in this study. For indeed, life has not been fair to the working-class people of America, no matter what their color or ethnic background. And it's precisely this sense that it's not fair, that there isn't enough to go around, that has stirred the racial and ethnic tensions that are so prevalent today.

In the face of such clear class disparities, how is it that our national discourse continues to focus on the middle class, denying the existence of a working class and rendering them invisible?

Whether a family or a nation, we all have myths that play tag with reality—myths that frame our thoughts, structure our beliefs, and organize our systems of denial. A myth encircles reality, encapsulates it, controls it. It allows us to know some things and to avoid knowing others, even when somewhere deep inside we really know what we don't want to know. Every parent has experienced this clash between myth and reality. We see signals that tell us a child is lying and explain them away. It isn't that we can't know; it's that we won't, that knowing is too difficult or painful, too discordant with the myth that defines the relationship, the one that says: *My child wouldn't lie to me.*

The same is true about a nation and its citizens. Myths are part of our national heritage, giving definition to the national character, offering guidance for both public and private behavior, comforting us in our moments of doubt. Not infrequently our myths trip over each other, providing a window into our often contradictory and ambivalently held beliefs. The myth that we are a nation of equals lives side-by-side in these United States with the belief in white supremacy. And, unlikely as it seems, it's quite possible to believe both at the same time. Sometimes we manage the conflict by shifting from one side to the other. More often, we simply redefine reality.[11] The inequality of condition between whites and blacks isn't born in prejudice and discrimination, we insist; it's black inferiority that's the problem. Class distinctions have nothing to do with privilege, we say; it's merit that makes the difference.

It's not the outcome that counts, we maintain; it's the rules of the game. And since the rules say that everyone comes to the starting line equal, the different results are merely products of individual will and wit. The fact that working-class children usually grow up to be working-class parents doesn't make a dent in the belief system, nor does it lead to questions about why the written rule and the lived reality are at odds. Instead, with perfect circularity, the outcome reinforces the reasoning that says they're deficient, leaving those so labeled doubly wounded—first by the real problems in living they face, second by internalizing the blame for their estate.

Two decades ago, when I began the research for *Worlds of Pain*, we were living in the immediate aftermath of the civil rights revolution that had convulsed the nation since the mid-1950s. Significant gains had been won. And despite the tenacity with which this headway had been resisted by some, most white Americans were feeling good about themselves. No one expected the nation's racial problems and conflicts to dissolve easily or quickly. But there was also a sense that we were moving in the right direction, that there was a national commitment to redressing at least some of the worst aspects of black–white inequality.

In the intervening years, however, the national economy buckled under the weight of three recessions, while the nation's industrial base was undergoing a massive restructuring. At the same time, government policies requiring preferential treatment were enabling African-Americans and other minorities to make small but visible inroads into what had been, until then, largely white terrain. The sense of scarcity, always a part of American life but intensified sharply by the history of these economic upheavals, made minority gains seem particularly threatening to white working-class families.

It isn't, of course, just working-class whites who feel threatened by minority progress. Wherever racial minorities make inroads into formerly all-white territory, tensions increase. But it's working-class families who feel the fluctuations in the economy most quickly and most keenly. For them, these last decades have been like a bumpy roller coaster ride. "Every time we think we might be able to get ahead, it seems like we get knocked down again," declares Tom Ahmundsen, a forty-two-year-old white construction worker. "Things look a little better; there's a little more work; then all of a sudden, boom, the economy falls apart and it's gone. You can't count on anything; it really gets you down."

This is the story I heard repeatedly: Each small climb was followed by a fall, each glimmer of hope replaced by despair. As the economic vise tightened, despair turned to anger. But partly because we have so little concept of class resentment and conflict in America, this anger isn't directed so much at those above as at those below. And when whites at or near the bottom of the ladder look down in this nation, they generally see blacks and other minorities.

True, during all of the 1980s and into the 1990s, white ire was fostered by national administrations that fanned racial discord as a way of fending off white discontent—of diverting anger about the state of the economy and the declining quality of urban life to the foreigners and racial others in our midst. But our history of racial animosity coupled with our lack of class consciousness made this easier to accomplish than it might otherwise have been.

The difficult realities of white working-class life not withstanding, however, their whiteness has accorded them significant advantages—both materially and psychologically—over people of color. Racial discrimination and segregation in the workplace have kept competition for the best jobs at a minimum. They do, obviously, have to compete with each other for the resources available. But that's different. It's a competition among equals; they're all white. They don't think such things consciously, of course; they don't have to. It's understood, rooted in the culture and supported by the social contract that says they are the superior ones, the worthy ones. Indeed, this is precisely why, when the courts or the legislatures act in ways that seem to contravene that belief, whites experience themselves as victims.

From the earliest days of the republic, whiteness has been the ideal, and freedom and independence have been linked to being white. "Republicanism," writes labor historian David Roediger, "had long emphasized that the strength, virtue and resolve of a people guarded them from enslavement."[12] And it was whites who had these qualities in abundance, as was evident, in the peculiarly circuitous reasoning of the time, in the fact that they were not slaves.

By this logic, the enslavement of blacks could be seen as stemming from their "slavishness" rather than from the institution of slavery. Slavery is gone now, but the reasoning lingers on in white

America, which still insists that the lowly estate of people of color is due to their deficits, whether personal or cultural, rather than to the prejudice, discrimination, and institutionalized racism that has barred them from full participation in the society.

This is not to say that culture is irrelevant, whether among black Americans or any other group in our society. The lifeways of a people develop out of their experiences—out of the daily events, large and small, that define their lives; out of the resources that are available to them to meet both individual and group needs; out of the place in the social, cultural, and political systems within which group life is embedded. In the case of a significant proportion of blacks in America's inner cities, centuries of racism and economic discrimination have produced a subculture that is both personally and socially destructive. But to fault culture or the failure of individual responsibility without understanding the larger context within which such behaviors occur is to miss a vital piece of the picture. Nor does acknowledging the existence of certain destructive subcultural forms among some African-Americans disavow or diminish the causal connections between the structural inequalities at the social, political, and economic levels and the serious social problems at the community level.

In his study of "working-class lads" in Birmingham, England, for example, Paul Willis observes that their very acts of resistance to middle-class norms—the defiance with which these young men express their anger at class inequalities—help to reinforce the class structure by further entrenching them in their working-class status.[13] The same can be said for some of the young men in the African-American community, whose active rejection of white norms and "in your face" behavior consigns them to the bottom of the American economic order.

To understand this doesn't make such behavior, whether in England or the United States, any more palatable. But it helps to explain the structural sources of cultural forms and to apprehend the social processes that undergird them. Like Willis's white "working-class lads," the hip-hoppers and rappers in the black community who are so determinedly "not white" are not just making a statement about black culture. They're also expressing their rage at white society for offering a promise of equality, then refusing to fulfill it. In the process, they're finding their own way to some accommodation and to a place in the world they can call their own, albeit one that ultimately reinforces their outsider status.

But, some might argue, white immigrants also suffered prejudice and discrimination in the years after they first arrived, but they found more socially acceptable ways to accommodate. It's true—and so do most of today's people of color, both immigrant and native born. Nevertheless, there's another truth as well. For wrenching as their early experiences were for white ethnics, they had an out. Writing about the Irish, for example, Roediger shows how they were able to insist upon their whiteness and to prove it by adopting the racist attitudes and behaviors of other whites, in the process often becoming leaders in the assault against blacks. With time and their growing political power, they won the prize they sought—recognition as whites. "The imperative to define themselves as white," writes Roediger, "came from the particular 'public and psychological wages' whiteness offered to a desperate rural and often preindustrial Irish population coming to labor in industrializing American cities."[14]

Thus does whiteness bestow its psychological as well as material blessings on even the most demeaned. For no matter how far down the socioeconomic ladder whites may fall, the one thing they can't lose is their whiteness. No small matter because, as W. E. B. DuBois observed decades ago, the compensation of white workers includes a psychological wage, a bonus that enables them to believe in their inherent superiority over nonwhites.[15]

It's also true, however, that this same psychological bonus that white workers prize so highly has cost them dearly. For along with the importation of an immigrant population, the separation of black and white workers has given American capital a reserve labor force to call upon whenever white workers seemed to them to get too "uppity." Thus, while racist ideology enables white workers to maintain the belief in their superiority, they have paid for that conviction by becoming far more vulnerable in the struggle for decent wages and working conditions than they might otherwise have been.

Politically and economically, the ideology of white supremacy disables white workers from making the kind of interracial alliances that would benefit all of the working class. Psychologically, it leaves them exposed to the double-edged sword of which I spoke earlier. On one side, their belief in the superiority of whiteness helps to reassure them that they're not at the bottom of the social hierarchy. But their insistence that their achievements are based on their special capacities and virtues, that it's only incompetence that keeps others from grabbing a piece of the American dream, threatens their precarious sense of self-esteem. For if they're the superior ones, the deserving ones, the ones who earned their place solely through hard work and merit, there's nothing left but to blame themselves for their inadequacies when hard times strike.

In the opening sentences of *Worlds of Pain* I wrote that America was choking on its differences. If we were choking then, we're being asphyxiated now. As the economy continues to falter, and local, state, and federal governments keep cutting services, there are more and more acrimonious debates about who will share in the shrinking pie. Racial and ethnic groups, each in their own corners, square off as they ready themselves for what seems to be the fight of their lives. Meanwhile, the quality of life for all but the wealthiest Americans is spiraling downward—a plunge that's felt most deeply by those at the lower end of the class spectrum, regardless of color.[16]

As, more and more mothers of young children work full-time outside the home, the question of who will raise the children comes center stage. Decent, affordable child care is scandalously scarce, with no government intervention in sight for this crucial need. In poor and working-class families, therefore, child care often is uncertain and inadequate, leaving parents apprehensive and children at risk. To deal with their fears, substantial numbers of couples now work different shifts, a solution to the child-care problem that puts its own particular strains on family life.

In families with two working parents, time has become their most precious commodity—time to attend to the necessary tasks of family life; time to nurture the relationships between wife and husband, between parents and children; time for oneself, time for others; time for solitude, time for a social life.[17] Today more than ever before, family life has become impoverished for want of time, adding another threat to the already fragile bonds that hold families together.

While women's presence in the labor force has given them a measure of independence unknown before, most also are stuck with doing two days' work in one—one on the job, the other when they get home at night. Unlike their counterparts in the earlier era, today's women are openly resentful about the burdens they carry, which makes for another dimension of conflict between wives and husbands.

Although the men generally say they've never heard of Robert Bly or any of the other modern-day gurus of manhood, the idea of men as victims has captured their imagination.[18] Given the enormous amount of publicity these men's advocates have garnered in the last few years, it's likely that some of their ideas have filtered into the awareness of the men in this study, even if they don't know how they got there. But their belief in their victimization is also a response to the politics of our time, when so many different groups—women, gays, racial minorities, the handicapped—have demanded special privileges and entitlements on the basis of past victimization. And once the language of victimization enters the political discourse, it becomes a useful tool for anyone wanting to resist the claims of others or to stake one of their own.

As the men see it, then, if their wives are victims because of the special burdens of women, the husbands, who bear their own particular hardships, can make the claim as well. If African-American men are victims because of past discrimination, then the effort to redress their grievances turns white men into victims of present discrimination.

To those who have been victimized by centuries of racism, sexism, homophobia, and the like, the idea that straight white men are victims, too, seems ludicrous. Yet it's not wholly unreal, at least not for the men in this study who have so little control over their fate and who so often feel unheard and invisible, like little more than shadows shouting into the wind.

Whether inside the family or in the larger world outside, white men keep hearing that they're the privileged ones, words that seem to them like a bad joke. How can they be advantaged when their inner experience is that they're perched precariously on the edge of a chasm that seems to have opened up in the earth around them? It's this sense of vulnerability, coupled with the conviction that their hardships go unseen and their pain unattended, that nourishes their claim to victimhood.

Some analysts of family and social life undoubtedly will argue that the picture I've presented here is too grim, that it gives insufficient weight to both the positive changes in family life and the gains in race relations over these past decades. It's true that the social and cultural changes we've witnessed have created families that, in some ways at least, are more responsive to the needs of their members, more democratic than any we have known before.[19] But it's also true that without the economic stability they need, even the most positive changes will not be enough to hold families together.

Certainly, too, alongside the racial and ethnic divisions that are so prominent a part of American life today is the reality that many more members of these warring groups than ever before are living peaceably together in our schools, our factories, our shops, our corporations, and our neighborhoods. And, except for black–white marriages, many more are marrying and raising children together than would have seemed possible a few decades ago.

At the same time, there's reason to fear. The rise of ethnicity and the growing racial separation also means an escalating level of conflict that sometimes seems to threaten to fragment the nation. In this situation, ethnic entrepreneurs like Al Sharpton in New York and David Duke in Louisiana rise to power and prominence by fanning ethnic and racial discord. A tactic that works so well precisely because the economic pressures are felt so keenly on all sides of the racial fissures, because both whites and people of color now feel so deeply that "it's not fair."

As I reflect on the differences in family and social life in the last two decades, it seems to me that we were living then in a more innocent age—a time, difficult though it was for the working-class families of our nation, when we could believe anything was possible. Whether about the economy, race relations, or life inside the family, most Americans believed that the future promised progress, that the solution to the social problems and inequities of the age were within our grasp, that sacrifice today would pay off tomorrow.

This is perhaps the biggest change in the last twenty years: The innocence is gone.

But is this a cause for mourning? Perhaps only when innocence is gone and our eyes unveiled will we be able to grasp fully the depth of our conflicts and the sources from which they spring.

We live in difficult and dangerous times, in a country deeply divided by class, race, and social philosophy. The pain with which so many American families are living today, and the anger they feel, won't be alleviated by a retreat to false optimism and easy assurances. Only when we are willing to see and reckon with the magnitude of our nation's problems and our people's suffering, only when we take in the full measure of that reality, will we be able to find the path to change. Until then, all our attempts at solutions will fail. And this, ultimately, will be the real cause for mourning. For without substantial change in both our public and our private worlds, it is not just the future of the family that is imperiled but the very life of the nation itself.

NOTES

Prologue

1. Robert Hughes, *Culture of Complaint* (New York: Oxford University Press, 1993), p. 28.

2. Although all the people in this book are real, their names have been changed to protect their privacy.

Chapter 1: Introduction

1. Lillian B. Rubin, *Worlds of Pain: Life in the Working-Class Family* (New York: Basic Books, 1976).

2. For in-depth studies of the school busing controversy in two different communities—one in the west, the other in the east—, see Lillian B. Rubin, *Busing & Backlash: White Against White in an Urban School District* (Berkeley: University of California Press, 1972), and Anthony J. Lukas, *Common Ground* (New York: Alfred Knopf, 1986).

3. *New York Times*, February 6, 1992.

4. For a discussion and analysis of this "ethnic fever," see Stephen Steinberg, *The Ethnic Myth* (Boston: Beacon Press, 1989).

5. The thrust toward assimilation was not given to whites only. African-Americans, Latinos, Chinese, Japanese, and other peoples of color were similarly motivated, but prejudice and discrimination made assimilation difficult, if not impossible, for them.

6. Roger Daniels, *Coming to America: A History of Immigration and Ethnicity in American Life* (New York: HarperCollins, 1990), cites (p. 152) what he calls "an extreme example" in Missouri where, as late as 1888, some school districts had to fight local boards to stop them from using German as the language of instruction.

7. Some recent white immigrants—the Iranians, for example—do maintain some

structural bases for ethnic identification. But as in the past, it's likely that these will wane as successive generations assimilate into the American mainstream.

8. Steinberg, *The Ethnic Myth.*

9. Robert Blauner, "Talking Past Each Other," *The American Prospect* (Summer 1992): 55–64, argues also that ethnicity is defined by a common ancestral past and "customs, culture, and outlook [that] are distinctive" (p. 61). Using this definition, he suggests that these ethnic realities "get lost under the racial umbrella" when it is blacks who are "being ethnic"—that is, finding comfort in association with others like themselves. If we could change the language of race and ethnicity, he suggests, whites would come to understand that black students who prefer to associate with each other are simply expressing the same "ethnic affinities" that motivate Jewish students to participate in activities at the campus Hillel Foundation. While I believe that Blauner is right about the wish of African-Americans to express their ethnic affinity and solidarity, his argument doesn't sufficiently come to grips with the depth of America's racial anxieties, which no amount of tinkering with the language will change easily.

Indeed, in a new introduction to *Worlds of Pain* (1992), I have argued that the recent effort by some blacks to define themselves in ethnic terms by calling themselves "African-American" instead of "black" has unwittingly made it easier for whites to sustain the denial of their racial consciousness and the fear and hostility it generates. If African-Americans are just another ethnic group, white reasoning goes, no different from Italian-Americans or Irish-Americans or German-Americans, then it's their problem if they can't make it in America.

10. A snowball sample is one in which each respondent refers the researcher on to the next, so that the sample grows like a snowball rolling downhill. In deciding whom to interview from the long list of names I eventually accumulated this way, I always chose the family that was socially and geographically most distant from the referring family. That way, I avoided falling into networks of friends, family, or neighbors. Although such a sample obviously can't be random, these precautions make it possible to collect a sample that's fairly representative of the larger population.

11. Nationally, just under 17 percent of families are headed by a woman (*Statistical Abstract of the United States* [U.S. Bureau of the Census, 1992, Table 56, p. 46]).

12. Reported in the *Wall Street Journal*, January 4, 1993.

13. *Statistical Abstract*, U.S. Bureau of the Census, 1992, Table 80, p. 64.

14. The phrase "divorce-extended" is taken from Judith Stacey, *Brave New Families* (New York: Basic Books, 1990), who offers a finely textured description and analysis of what she calls "postmodern families" who live in divorce-extended kin networks.

15. "Greater Seattle Area Demographic Profile," Seattle Chamber of Commerce, 1992.

16. Rubin, *Worlds of Pain*, p. 8.

Chapter 2: The Invisible Americans

1. Reported in the *New York Times*, January 11, 1992. Even Katherine Newman, in her otherwise exemplary study of the declining fortunes of the middle class, cites $18,000–55,000 as the income range for middle-class families (see Katherine S. Newman, *Declining Fortunes* [New York: Basic Books, 1993]), p. 44.

2. *New York Times,* January 11, 1992.

3. *Statistical Abstract,* U.S. Bureau of the Census (1992), Table 709, p. 452. Median income for families in which the wife was *not* in the paid labor force was only $30,265 (*Statistical Abstract* [U.S. Bureau of the Census, 1992, Table 708, p. 452]).

4. It's true, of course, that some professionals destined for the upper middle class earn little more than $35,000 a year at the beginning of their careers. But there's a crucial difference between them and a working-class woman or man. The professional person is at the beginning of a long career ladder that promises vastly increased earnings, while the working-class person in this income bracket can look forward to little more than cost-of-living increases.

5. The spectacular success, for example, of Ross Perot, America's allegedly quintessential self-made man, was built on more than brains, boldness, grit, and determination. It all started with the help of large and lucrative government contracts, awards whose legitimacy came under investigation by a congressional subcommittee a few years later.

6. *New York Times,* December 16, 1990.

7. *Statistical Abstract,* U.S. Bureau of the Census (1992), Table 703, p. 449. This does not contradict the $46,777 for two-earner families cited earlier (see n. 3). The $35,353 figure cited here includes both one- and two-earner families, which brings the median down substantially from the income figure cited there.

8. *Statistical Abstract,* U.S. Bureau of the Census (1992), Table 703, p. 449. At the end of 1992, median weekly earnings for whites working at full-time jobs were $462 compared to $357 for blacks and $324 for Hispanics (*U.S. Department of Labor News,* February 1, 1993). When broken down by race, median annual income for the families in this study is $33,000 for whites, $28,500 for Asians, $21,000 for Latinos, and $19,500 for blacks.

9. *Wall Street Journal,* August 10, 1992. David Hale, the author of the article, reports that these same companies cut 3.5 million jobs during the 1980s and another 600,000 in the eighteen months between the beginning of 1991 and July 1992. And the cuts keep coming.

10. For an excellent account of how the Reagan policies favored the rich and penalized the poor, see Kevin Phillips, *The Politics of Rich and Poor* (New York: Random House, 1990). See also Paul R. Krugman, "The Right, the Rich, and The Facts," *The American Prospect* (Fall 1992): 19–31, for an analysis of the rising income inequality in the United States.

11. The proportion of Americans with middle incomes fell from 71.2 percent in 1969 to 63.3 percent in 1989 (*New York Times,* February 22, 1992).

12. *New York Times,* May 11, 1992.

13. *New York Times,* December 16, 1990.

14. *San Francisco Chronicle,* December 29, 1991. Recent changes in the law, which have made it easier to file for personal bankruptcy, may account for part of this increase. But there's little doubt that most of these bankruptcies are attributable to the swollen ranks of the unemployed and underemployed. Moreover, it's not only personal bankruptcies that have climbed so sharply. In the twelve months between July 1991 and June 1992, bankruptcy filings among small businesses increased by 38 percent

over the same twelve-month period three years earlier (*Wall Street Journal*, November 4, 1992).

15. While their workers were going broke, life in the executive suite remained as plush as ever. In the same years that joblessness was rising and profits falling, the lower-paid chief executives of some of our largest companies typically earned over $3 million; those in the higher brackets counted their annual earnings in the tens of millions. These income figures are especially striking when compared with those of the chief executives of major corporations in other industrial nations, who take home a fraction of the earnings of American CEOs.

When salary and stock options are included, the co-chief executives of Time Warner earned $99.6 million; the head of Reebok International took home $33.3 million; U.S. Surgical paid its top man $15 million; ITT's CEO earned $11.5 million; and the chairman of Walt Disney pocketed $11.2 million. Compare these with the salaries at big firms in Great Britain, Germany, and Japan, where average earnings for chief executives were $1.1 million, $800,000, and $250,000, respectively (*New York Times*, January 20, 1992).

16. See Rubin, *Worlds of Pain*, for a discussion and analysis of the ways in which the institutions of our society and the processes of socialization all work to ensure that working-class families reproduce themselves. There I argue that the working-class subculture is a response to the difficulties of their class position, past and present—difficulties that not only define the ways families approach their problems but that limit the solutions available to them.

17. See, for example, Jonathan Kozol, *Savage Inequalities* (New York: Crown Publishers, 1991).

18. Ibid., p. 157.

19. James S. Coleman et al., *Equality of Educational Opportunity* (Washington, D.C.: U.S. Government Printing Office, 1966); Christopher Jencks et al., *Inequality: A Reassessment of the Effect of Family and Schooling in America* (New York: Basic Books, 1972); and Christopher Jencks, *Rethinking Social Policy* (Cambridge: Harvard University Press, 1992).

20. Reported in the *San Francisco Chronicle*, February 22, 1993.

21. *Statistical Abstract*, U.S. Bureau of the Census (1992), Table 672, p. 422.

22. This is a play on the words of William Julius Wilson, whose well-known and controversial work argued for the declining significance of race (*The Declining Significance of Race* [Chicago: University of Chicago Press, 1978]).

23. Cf. David R. Roediger, *The Wages of Whiteness* (New York: Verso, 1991).

24. See Ibid., for an excellent discussion of the artisan in American labor history. Earlier in our history, the artists and craftsmen who worked with both head and hands were viewed as the pillars of the community and revered by all. Then, to be a free worker engaged in a craft was to have achieved all this fledgling nation had to offer. These were the Americans who could believe they were among the elect, who saw themselves—and were seen by others—as the very foundation on which this society rested.

The Industrial Revolution changed all that. As work became mechanized and was brought into factories, the collaboration of head and hand was no longer necessary.

The head could be left at the factory door, while hands came to be seen as little more than appendages of the machine. By the time the twentieth century came into view, the split was complete. The greatest rewards—whether in status, prestige, or money—were reserved for those who worked with their heads, not with their hands; those who wore a white collar, not a blue one.

25. Richard Sennett and Jonathan Cobb, *The Hidden Injuries of Class* (New York: Vintage Books, 1973).

26. The GED is the General Equivalency Diploma, which certifies that a person has the equivalent of a high-school education.

Chapter 3: "People Don't Know Right from Wrong Anymore!"

1. In a reversal of this generational conflict, some children are angry at their parents for abandoning the more traditional norms and values of family life—parents who divorce, who live a "single" life-style, and so on. But their complaints are as much about the dislocation of their own lives as they are about parental behavior. And when these same children become teenagers, they adopt the norms, values, and behavior of modern teenage life, often much to their parents' dismay.

2. For an extended discussion and analysis of the sexual revolution and its consequences, see Lillian B. Rubin, *Erotic Wars: What Happened to the Sexual Revolution* (New York: Harper Perennial Library, 1991). There, I argue that the two words that describe the sexual sensibility of today's youth are *tolerance* and *entitlement*—ideas that were wholly absent from the sexual culture in which their parents came of age.

3. Class, race, and education make a difference in when people marry and have children. In the upper middle-class professional families I interviewed twenty years ago, only two of the women married before their twentieth birthday, one because she was pregnant. The rest, having waited until they had completed college and/or professional training, were, on average, twenty-two, while the men were nearly twenty-five.

4. U.S.Bureau of the Census, *Monthly Vital Statistics Report* 40, no. 4(S), August 26, 1991, Table 11. These changes in the age at first marriage also undoubtedly reflect the increasing number of young people in college. But the fact that so many more women are choosing college over early marriage today is itself indicative of the shift I'm speaking of here.

5. U.S. Bureau of the Census, *Marital Status and Living Arrangements*, P-20, no. 468, Table C (1993).

6. *Statistical Abstract*, U.S. Bureau of the Census (1992), Table 103, p. 76. Although the life span for blacks is substantially lower than for whites—74.5 for black women and 66.0 for black men, compared with 79.3 for white women and 72.6 for white men—the difference is not enough to affect my argument.

7. The extension of adolescence well into the twenties and beyond is related to the increased need for advanced training and to the diminishing number of self-supporting occupations, both of which leave young adults dependent on parents much longer than in earlier generations.

8. *Statistical Abstract*, U.S. Bureau of the Census (1992), Table 49, p. 44.

9. U.S.Bureau of the Census, *Current Population Reports, Marital Status and Living Arrangements*, March 1990.

10. *U.S. Department of Labor News,* July 2, 1992, Table A-2. During the same period (June 1992), the official unemployment rate for black males between sixteen and nineteen was 46.8 percent. The comparable rate for white males of the same age was 22.1 percent.

11. Cited in Andrew Hacker, *Two Nations* (New York: Charles Scribner's Sons, 1992), p. 184.

12. Patrick W. O'Carroll, "Homicides Among Black Males 15–24 Years of Age, 1970–1984," *Morbidity and Mortality Weekly Report (CDC), Statistical Supplement* 37 (1988): 52–59; Michael R. Rand, "Handgun Crime Victims," *U.S. Bureau of Justice Statistics, Special Report* (Washington, D.C.: U.S. Justice Statistics Clearinghouse/NCJRS, 1990); and Lois A. Fingerhut and Joel C. Kleinman, "International and Interstate Comparisons of Homicide Among Young Males," *Journal of the American Medical Association* 263 (1990): 3292–3295.

Jewelle T. Gibbs, ed., *Young, Black, and Male in America* (Dover, Mass.: Auburn House, 1988), p. 261, says that "a young black male has a 1 in 21 lifetime chance of being killed, most likely by one of his contemporaries." Most other statistics range from one in seventy to one in eighty. Despite some disagreements about the actual figures, researchers agree that homicide is now the leading cause of death among African-American males. Dr. Antonia Novello, the former U.S. surgeon general, estimates that the homicide rate among black men between the ages of fifteen and twenty-four is seven to eight times higher than among white men of the same age.

13. *Statistical Abstract,* U.S. Bureau of the Census (1992), Table 330, p. 197.

14. William Julius Wilson, *The Truly Disadvantaged* (Chicago: University of Chicago Press, 1987), pp. 83–92, uses statistics showing the high proportion of black men who are unemployed, in jail, in the armed services, or murdered to develop a "male marriageable pool index" that documents the scarcity of marriageable men in the African-American community.

15. See Terry McMillan, *Waiting to Exhale* (New York: Viking Press, 1992), a novel about the trials of black professional women in search of marriageable men.

16. Cited in Katherine S. Newman, *Declining Fortunes* (New York: Basic Books, 1993), p. 54. She also notes that the most impressive shifts over time are among young men: "In 1970, less than 10 percent of single *and* married men in the twenty-five to thirty-four age group lived with their parents. By 1990, the figure had grown to 15 percent. . . . The rates for women increased only half as fast." Partly this could be because, even during an economic slump, women are more able than men to marry out of the parental household. But I also believe that women are less likely to make the choice to live at home precisely because they would be subject to far more constraints than are imposed on their brothers. Indeed, it's worth noting that parental concern about their grown children's moral behavior virtually always focuses on daughters, not sons, largely because it's still a woman's virtue that's at issue.

17. Ibid., p. 53.

18. Tales from the abortion battlefront suggest that this is not uncommon, even among people who are antiabortion activists. During the 1992 presidential election, Vice President Dan Quayle, an ardent and outspoken foe of abortion, was asked what he'd do if his teenage daughter became pregnant. The politician retreated; the father

stepped forward. "I hope that I never have to deal with it," he replied. "But obviously I would counsel her and talk to her and support her on whatever decision she made." Incredulous, the interviewer pressed on: "If the decision was abortion you'd support her?" The vice president stood firm: "I'd support my daughter."

A few days later, President Bush, also a staunch opponent of abortion, was asked what he'd do if one of his granddaughters told him she was considering an abortion. He'd try to talk her out of it, he said, but would support her decision. "So in the end the decision would be hers?" the interviewer asked. "Well, who else's—who else's could it be?" said this president, who has spoken out frequently and forcefully against allowing other women to make that choice.

Even more interesting than what these politicians-turned-father and -grandfather said is what they didn't say. Neither ruled out the question as absurd, a product of some wild fantasy, of the fevered imagination of the media in an election year. Neither said: My teenage daughter sexually active? Impossible! My granddaughter pregnant and unmarried? Never! Nor did anyone else, not even Marilyn Quayle, who disagreed with her husband and insisted that she'd force her daughter to carry the child to term.

For an early study of the politics of the pro-life activists, see Kristin Luker, *Abortion & the Politics of Motherhood* (Berkeley: University of California Press, 1984).

19. For a detailed discussion of women's responses to their own behavior in the early days of the sexual revolution, see Rubin, *Erotic Wars*.

20. See Phillipe Ariès, *Centuries of Childhood* (New York: Alfred A. Knopf, 1962); Stephanie Coontz, *The Way We Never Were* (New York: Basic Books, 1992); Carl Degler, *At Odds: Women and the Family in America from the Revolution to the Present* (New York: Oxford University Press, 1980); John Demos, "Myths and Realities of American Family Life," in Henry Grunebaum and Jacob Christ, eds., *Contemporary Marriage: Structure, Dynamics, and Therapy* (Boston: Little, Brown, 1976), pp. 9–31; Tamara K. Hareven, "The Dynamics of Kin in an Industrial Community," in John Demos and Sarane Spence Boocock, eds., *Turning Points* (Chicago: University of Chicago Press, 1978); Tamara K. Hareven, "American Families in Transition: Historical Perspectives on Change," in Froma Walsh, ed., *Normal Family Process* (New York: Guilford Press, 1982); Peter Laslett, *The World We Have Lost* (New York: Scribner's, 1965); Edward Shorter, *The Making of the Modern Family* (New York: Basic Books, 1975); Arlene Skolnick, *Embattled Paradise: The American Family in an Age of Uncertainty* (New York: Basic Books, 1991); and Lawrence Stone, *The Family, Sex, and Marriage in England, 1500–1800* (New York: Harper & Row, 1977).

21. The phrase "haven in a heartless world" is taken from the title of Christopher Lasch's 1977 book (New York: Basic Books).

22. Skolnick, *Embattled Paradise*.

Chapter 4: Mother Goes to Work

1. *Statistical Abstract*, U.S. Bureau of the Census (1992), Table 620, p. 388.

2. Ibid.

3. The depressed housewife was a staple of the psychiatrist's couch and of what were called "the women's pages" in newspapers and magazines of that period.

4. The women I interviewed twenty years ago resisted the feminist emphasis on

work as liberating partly because, for them, work was an economic necessity, not a choice. For women who found themselves working at menial, dead-end jobs and also coming home to a second shift of housework and child care, it was hard to think of going to work as emancipating.

5. For an extended discussion of the backlash against feminism, see Susan Faludi, *Backlash* (New York: Crown Publishers, 1991).

6. The complaint among women of color—that is, that feminism is essentially a white movement that fails to attend to their concerns—cuts across class and racial groups.

7. Angela P. Harris, "Race and Essentialism in Feminist Legal Theory," *Stanford Law Review* 42 (1990): 592.

8. Ibid., pp. 598, 599.

9. Obviously, it's not in working-class families alone that resigned acceptance holds sway. But it's equally obvious that middle-class women have more resources to help soften the worst effects of the second shift. For a fuller discussion of the second shift and its impact on family life, see Arlie Hochschild, *The Second Shift: Working Parents and The Revolution at Home* (New York: Viking Press 1989).

10. For an interesting and provocative analysis of what happens when men and women actually parent together, see Diane Ehrensaft, *Parenting Together* (New York: Free Press, 1987).

11. *Statistical Abstract*, U.S. Bureau of the Census (1992), Table 710, p. 452.

12. *San Francisco Examiner*, March 28, 1993, from a report issued by California's Census Data Center.

13. *Statistical Abstract*, U.S. Bureau of the Census (1992), Table 654, p. 412.

Chapter 5: The Transformation of Family Life

1. James Sweet, Larry Bumpass, and Vaugn Call, *National Survey of Families and Households* (Madison, Wisc.: Center for Demography and Ecology, University of Wisconsin, 1988). This study featured a probability sample of 5,518 households and included couples with and without children. See also Joseph Pleck, *Working Wives/Working Husbands* (Beverly Hills: Sage Publications, 1985), who summarizes time-budget studies; and Iona Mara-Drita, "The Effects of Power, Ideology, and Experience on Men's Participation in Housework," unpublished paper (1993), whose analysis of Sweet, Bumpass, and Call's data shows that when housework and employment hours are added together, a woman's work week totals 69 hours, compared to 52 hours for a man.

2. Rubin, *Worlds of Pain*, p. 93.

3. See Daniel Stern, *The Interpersonal World of the Infant* (New York: Basic Books, 1985), who argues that a child's capacity for self-reflection coincides with the development of language.

4. For an excellent analysis of the increasing amount of time Americans spend at work and the consequences to family and social life, see Juliet B. Schor, *The Overworked American* (New York: Basic Books, 1992). See also Carmen Sirianni and Andrea Walsh, "Through the Prism of Time: Temporal Structures in Postindustrial America," in Alan Wolfe, ed., *America at Century's End* (Berkeley: University of California Press, 1991), for their discussion of the "time famine."

5. For the origin of the term "his and her marriage," see Jessie Bernard, *The Future of Marriage* (New York: Bantam Books, 1973).

6. David Elkind, *The Hurried Child* (New York: Addison-Wesley, 1981).

Chapter 6: "When You Get Laid Off, It's Like You Lose a Part of Yourself"

1. It's not possible to compare the rate of unemployment in these families with those I interviewed two decades ago because the previous sample was made up of men who were employed. But comparing the unemployment rates in 1970 and 1991 is instructive. Among white men with less than four years in high school, 4.5 percent were unemployed in 1970, 10.3 percent in 1991. The figures for high-school graduates are 2.7 percent and 5.4 percent, respectively. For blacks with less than four years in high school, the 1970 unemployment rate stood at 5.2 percent, compared to 14.7 percent in 1991. For black high-school graduates, the rates are 5.2 and 9.9, respectively (*Statistical Abstract*, [U.S. Bureau of the Census, 1992, Table 637, p. 400]). The number of food stamp recipients, which typically rises as the unemployment rate climbs, jumped to an all-time high in 1993, when one in ten Americans were in the food stamp program.

2. Barbara Ehrenreich, *Fear of Falling* (New York: Pantheon Books, 1989), and Katherine S. Newman, *Falling from Grace* (New York: Free Press, 1988), write compellingly about middle-class fears of what Newman calls "falling from grace." But these fears probably are more prevalent among working-class families, and with good reason, since job security is still so much more tenuous there than in the middle class.

3. Cf. Rubin, *Worlds of Pain*, and Lillian B. Rubin, *Women of a Certain Age: The Midlife Search for Self* (New York: Harper Perennial, 1986).

4. John Hill, "The Psychological Impact of Unemployment," *New Society* 43 (1978): 118–120; and Linford W. Rees, "Medical Aspects of Unemployment," *British Medical Journal* 6307 (1981): 1630–1631.

5. See Newman, *Falling from Grace*, pp. 174–201, for an excellent analysis of what happened when the Singer Sewing Machine plant in Elizabeth, New Jersey, closed and downward mobility inundated a whole community.

6. Hill, "The Psychological Impact of Unemployment"; and Rees, "Medical Aspects of Unemployment."

7. Barry Glassner, *Career Crash* (New York: Simon & Schuster, 1994) studied career crashes among baby boomer managers and professionals and provides an interesting counterpoint to the people I'm writing about here. Unlike the men and women of the working class, Glassner found that the people he studied have a range of options and a variety of resources to help cushion the blow of unemployment.

8. Women's friendships on and off the job are very different from those men form. Especially among working-class men, friendships on the job are likely to be compartmentalized and segregated from the rest of their lives. For women, however, these friendships tend to become an integral part of their social lives, therefore usually are sustained by both face-to-face and telephone interactions after they leave the job. See Lillian B. Rubin, *Just Friends: The Role of Friendship in Our Lives* (New York: Harper Perennial, 1986).

9. Rubin, *Just Friends*, p. 73. For similar findings about the fragility of male friendships, see Robert Brain, *Friends and Lovers* (New York: Basic Books, 1976); Sarah A. Haley, "Some of My Best Friends Are Dead," in William E. Kelley, ed., *Post-Traumatic Stress Disorder and the War Veteran Patient* (New York: Brunner/Mazel, 1986); Stuart Miller, *Men and Friendship* (Boston: Houghton Mifflin, 1983); and John M. Reisman, *Anatomy of Friendship* (New York: Irvington Publishers, 1979).

10. Rubin, *Just Friends*, p. 73.

11. A few researchers argue that, since the majority of men who batter their wives are gainfully employed, unemployment is of little value in explaining battering (H. Saville et al., "Sex Roles, Inequality and Spouse Abuse," *Australian and New Zealand Journal of Sociology* 17 [1981]: 83–88; and Martin D. Schwartz, "Work Status, Resource Equality, Injury and Wife Battery," *Creative Sociology* 18 [1990]: 57–61). But the evidence is much stronger in the direction of a relationship between unemployment and family violence; see Frances J. Fitch and Andre Papantonio, "Men Who Batter," *Journal of Nervous and Mental Disease* 171 (1983): 190–191; Richard J. Gelles and Murray A. Straus, "Violence in the American Family," *Journal of Social Issues* 35 (1979): 15–39; New York State Task Force on Domestic Violence, *Domestic Violence: Report to the Governor and Legislature: Families and Change* (New York: Praeger Publishers, 1984); and Suzanne K. Steinmetz, "Violence-prone Families," *Annals of the New York Academy of Sciences* 347 (1980): 251–265.

12. John A. Byles, "Violence, Alcohol Problems and Other Problems in Disintegrating Families," *Journal of Studies on Alcohol* 39 (1978): 551–553; Ronald W. Fagan, Ola W. Barnett, and John B. Patton, "Reasons for Alcohol Use in Maritally Violent Men," *Journal of Drug and Alcohol Abuse* 14 (1988): 371–392; Fitch and Papantonio, "Men Who Batter"; Kenneth E. Leonard et al., "Patterns of Alcohol Use and Physically Aggressive Behavior in Men," *Journal of Studies on Alcohol* 46 (1985): 279–282; Larry R. Livingston, "Measuring Domestic Violence in an Alcoholic Population," *Journal of Sociology and Social Welfare* 13 (1986): 934–951; Albert R. Roberts, "Substance Abuse Among Men Who Batter Their Mates," *Journal of Substance Abuse Treatment* 5 (1988): 83–87; J. M. Schuerger and N. Reigle, "Personality and Biographic Data That Characterize Men Who Abuse Their Wives," *Journal of Clinical Psychology* 44 (1988): 75–81; and Steinmetz, "Violence-prone Families."

13. Reported in the *San Francisco Chronicle*, February 14, 1992. The study found that in the same year that unemployment rose from 6.5 to 9.2 percent, there was a 30 percent increase in the number of couples seeking advice from marriage counselors about their waning sex lives.

14. Ethel Spector Person, "Sexuality as the Mainstay of Identity," *Signs* 5 (1980): 605–630.

15. An article in the *San Francisco Chronicle*, October 19, 1992, surveyed several recent studies of divorce, one of which found that when income drops 25 percent, divorce rises by more than 10 percent; another predicted ten thousand divorces for every 1 percent rise in unemployment.

16. Cited in the *San Francisco Chronicle*, October 19, 1992.

17. Unemployment benefits vary from state to state. In California, a state where benefits are among the most generous, the range is $40–230 a week for a maximum of

twenty-six weeks. How much a person actually collects depends upon how long she worked and how much she earned. Even at the highest benefit level, available only to workers who have worked steadily at one of the relatively well-paid blue-collar jobs, the income loss is staggering. For workers in the lower-level jobs, for those who worked intermittently through no fault of their own, or for those who depended on the underground economy to supplement their meager wages, benefits can be so small as to be relatively meaningless.

Chapter 7: Shattered Dreams

1. By the time the 1990s came into view, the $286 billion annual interest on the $3.1 trillion national debt was the third largest expense in the federal budget. Between 1980 and 1990, U.S. industry increased its debt from $1.4 trillion to $3.5 trillion, while consumer debt rose from $1.4 trillion to $3.7 trillion (*Time*, January 13, 1992).

2. After a steep round of cutbacks in the middle of the 1990–1992 recession, for example, the CEO of Eastman Kodak explained: "If it were just the recession, we would be hiring these people back again. And we aren't going to do that." At about the same time, when Xerox announced a 20 percent cut in its work force, the chairman of the company said that the economic slump was only speeding up cost-cutting plans that were already in place (quoted in the *New York Times*, December 16, 1991).

3. The end of the cold war and the defense cuts that are sure to follow mean that at least a million more defense industry jobs probably will be slashed over the next several years.

4. Quoted in *Time*, July 20, 1992.

5. *Statistical Abstract*, U.S. Bureau of the Census (1992), Table 713, p. 454.

6. Rubin, *Worlds of Pain*, p. 209.

7. Bennett Harrison and Barry Bluestone, *The Great U-Turn: Corporate Restructuring and the Polarizing of America* (New York: Basic Books, 1988), p. 127.

8. *Wall Street Journal*, May 14, 1992.

9. *San Francisco Examiner*, March 1, 1992.

10. The most recent statistics from the U.S. Census Bureau show that 27 percent of adults under thirty-five live with their parents. Separating out those between the ages of eighteen and twenty-four, the bureau estimates that the figure has risen from just over 40 percent three decades ago to more than 50 percent today (*New York Times*, February 12, 1993). But all these figures can be no more than estimates, since these young people are transients, tending to move in and out as both their economic fortunes and their tolerance for family living rise and fall.

11. *Wall Street Journal*, March 18, 1992.

12. *Wall Street Journal*, October 13, 1992.

13. Ibid.

14. Until the most recent decline, the inflationary spiral of the last two decades sent the median price of a starter home up 21 percent at the same time that real income of young working-class families *declined* by anywhere from 12 to 20 percent. From 1979 to 1989, workers with a high-school diploma saw their wages decline by

9.8 percent, while the wages of high-school dropouts fell by 17.3 percent. Over the next three years, the decline continued, falling another 2.2 percent and 3.9 percent, respectively (*Wall Street Journal*, May 14, 1992).

15. *New York Times*, October 20, 1991. In southern California, the land of sunshine and single-family dwellings, home ownership has declined to 54 percent of all households, a rate well below the 64 percent in the nation at large (*Wall Street Journal*, October 12, 1992). Focusing on the generation that came of age in the Reagan era, Newman, *Declining Fortunes*, p. 32, reports that only 15 percent of families in this age group owned their own homes in 1990, compared to 23 percent in 1973.

16. *San Francisco Chronicle*, November 29, 1991. Newman, *Declining Fortunes*, p. 38, notes that "only 9 percent of the nation's renters are able to afford a home"—a figure that includes all races. The figures for African-American and Latino families are even more bleak: 98 percent of both these groups can't afford a median-priced starter home.

17. See "Waiting for the Windfall," *Time*, January 18, 1993, for an examination of the effects of inheritance on the baby boom generation. According to this article, the share of total household net worth derived from inheritances and family gifts rose from 47 percent in 1962 to 71 percent in 1989.

18. Newman, *Declining Fortunes*, p. 123.

19. "Employment and Earnings," U.S. Department of Labor (December 1991), Table C-2, pp. 90–91. This figure assumes an inflation factor of 4 percent in 1991.

Chapter 8: Past History/Present Reality

1. See especially Mary C. Waters, *Ethnic Options* (Berkeley: University of California Press, 1990), who compared ethnic identification among white upper middle-class Catholics in two suburbs—one outside of San Jose, California, the other near Philadelphia, Pennsylvania—and found no differences. But I wonder what Waters would have found if she had compared her upper middle-class ethnics with an equivalent working-class sample. See also Howard F. Stein and Robert F. Hill, *The Ethnic Imperative* (University Park, Penn.: Pennsylvania State University Press, 1977); and Herbert Gans, "Symbolic Ethnicity: The Future of Ethnic Groups and Cultures in America," *Ethnic and Racial Studies* 2 (January 1979): 1–18.

2. In California, as in other border states in the West and Southwest, it's in the Mexican-American community that a continuing stream of immigrants has consistently revitalized ethnic life. In recent years, a vastly increased Chinese immigration has done the same for that community.

3. Richard Rodriguez, *Hunger of Memory* (New York: Bantam Books, 1983).

4. Ibid., p. 183.

5. Several studies of African-American children show that they absorb negative images about blackness very early in their lives. See, for example, Kenneth and Mamie Clark, "Racial Identification and Preference in Negro Children," in Eleanore Maccoby, Theodore Newcomb, and Shirley Hartley, eds., *Readings in Social Psychology* (New York: Holt Rinehart, 1958), for their famous experiment in which black children more often than not chose a white doll to play with and tended to see the black doll as "bad." In the aftermath of the civil rights movement, several researchers replicated

and/or modified the Clarks' experiment, which, although published in 1958, was actually done in 1941 (Philip Friedman,"Racial Preferences and Identifications of White Elementary School Children," *Contemporary Educational Psychology* 5 [1980]: 256–265; Juneau Mahan, "Black and White Children's Racial Identification and Preference," *Journal of Black Psychology* 3 [1976]: 47–58; Albert Roberts, Kathleen Y. Moseley, and Maureen W. Chamberlain, "Age Differences in Racial Self-Identity of Young Black Girls," *Psychological Reports* 37 [1976]: 1263–1266). While their results all show some decrease in the preference for white dolls—a response, they suggest, that was due to the civil rights movement with its "black is beautiful" theme—there remains a majority of both black and white children whose negative attitudes about being black are reflected in their choice of dolls and the qualities they attribute to dolls of different color.

6. Michael Rogin, who is presently working on the history of blackface in America, reminds me that "blacking up" is an American tradition, part of the way whites historically have gained access to their shadow, or instinctual, side. Nevertheless, it's unlikely that any white child ever told her parents that she wanted to be black or thought some movie star or model was "too white" to be pretty.

7. An article in *Time* (May 27, 1993) entitled "Growing Up in Black and White" cited more recent research, which found that 65 percent of black children preferred white dolls, some of them explaining that "black is dirty." The author of the article, an African-American father, wrote from the anguished personal experience of hearing his three-year-old daughter say, "Mommy, I want to be white."

8. Toni Morrison, *Playing in the Dark* (Cambridge: Harvard University Press, 1992), p. 38. See also Roediger, *The Wages of Whiteness*, for an astute historical analysis of how the whole idea of whiteness and its value was highlighted by the presence of black slavery.

9. Roediger, *Wages of Whiteness*, offers a detailed analysis of how the white working-class came to define itself in opposition to blacks.

10. Morrison, *Playing in the Dark*, p. 12.

11. It's no accident that most bias crimes are committed against blacks. According to an FBI study, blacks are the target of 36 percent of all reported bias attacks, followed by Jews at 17 percent. These numbers represent only the tip of the hate crimes iceberg, since only three thousand of the sixteen thousand law enforcement agencies whose cooperation was requested elected to participate in the survey (*Time*, January 18, 1993).

12. Harris, "Race and Essentialism in Feminist Legal Theory, " p. 588. In a powerful critique of essentialism in feminist theory, Harris insists that women's experience cannot "be described independent of other facets of experience like race, class, and sexual orientation."

13. Ibid., p. 604.

14. Cited in Roger Sanjek, "Intermarriage and the Future of the Races in the United States," paper presented at the American Anthropological Association meetings, Chicago, August 1991.

15. *Statistical Abstract*, U.S. Bureau of the Census (1992), Table 53, p. 45.

16. Sanjek, "Intermarriage."

Chapter 9: "Is This a White Country, or What?"

1. Roediger, *The Wages of Whiteness*, p. 133.

2. I'm aware, that many Americans who have none of the characteristic features associated with their African heritage are still defined as black. This is one reason why I characterize race as an idea, not a fact. Nevertheless, the main point I am making here still holds—that is, the visible racial character of a people makes a difference in whether white Americans see them as assimilable or not.

3. See, for example, Richard D. Alba, *Ethnic Identity* (New Haven, Conn.: Yale University Press, 1990); Gans, "Symbolic Ethnicity; Mark Leeds, *Ethnic New York* (New York: Passport Books, 1991); Stanley Leiberson and Mary C. Waters, *From Many Strands* (New York: Russell Sage, 1990); Alejandro Portes and Rubén G. Rumbaut, *Immigrant America* (Berkeley: University of California Press, 1990); Werner Sollors, ed., *The Invention of Ethnicity* (New York: Oxford University Press, 1989); Steinberg, *The Ethnic Myth*; and Waters, *Ethnic Options*.

4. As I have already indicated, Jews and African-Americans are notable exceptions.

5. Waters, *Ethnic Options*.

6. *New York Times*, April 30, 1993.

7. For an excellent historical portrayal of the formation of ethnic communities among the east central European immigrants in Pennsylvania, the development of ethnic identity, and the process of Americanization, see Ewa Morawska, *For Bread with Butter* (New York: Cambridge University Press, 1985).

8. Ibid.

9. Portes and Rumbaut, *Immigrant America*.

10. One need only walk the streets of New York to see the concentration of Koreans in the corner markets and the nail care salons that dot the city's landscape.

In San Francisco the Cambodians now own most of the donut shops in the city. It all started when, after working in such a shop, an enterprising young Cambodian combined the family resources and opened his own store and bakery. He now has twenty shops and has been instrumental in helping his countrymen open more, all of them buying their donuts from his bakery.

11. Gans, "Symbolic Ethnicity."

12. Despite nativist protests, immigration had proceeded unchecked by government regulation until the end of the nineteenth century. The first serious attempt to restrict immigration came in 1882 when, responding to the clamor about the growing immigration of Chinese laborers to California and other western states, Congress passed the Chinese Exclusion Act. But European immigration remained unimpeded. In the years between 1880 and 1924, twenty-four million newcomers arrived on these shores, most of them eastern and southern Europeans, all bringing their own language and culture, and all the target of pervasive bigotry and exploitation by native-born Americans. By the early part of the twentieth century, anti-immigration sentiments grew strong enough to gain congressional attention once again. The result was the National Origins Act of 1924, which established the quota system that sharply limited immigration, especially from the countries of southern and eastern Europe.

13. Daniels, *Coming to America*, pp. 338–344.

14. Daniels, *Coming to America*, p. 341, writes further, "In his Liberty Island speech Lyndon Johnson stressed the fact that he was redressing the wrong done [by the McCarran-Walter Act] to those 'from southern or eastern Europe,' and although he did mention 'developing continents,' there was no other reference to Asian or Third World immigration."

15. For a further review of the Immigration Act of 1965, see chapter 13 (pp. 328–349) of *Coming to America*.

16. *Statistical Abstract*, U.S. Bureau of the Census (1992), Table 8, p. 11.

17. *Statistical Abstract*, U.S. Bureau of the Census (1992), Table 45, p. 42.

18. *Statistical Abstract*, U.S. Bureau of the Census (1992), Table 18, p. 18, and Table 26, p. 24.

19. U. S. Bureau of the Census, *Population Reports*, 1970 and 1990. Cited in Mike Davis, "The Body Count," *Crossroads* (June 1993). The difference in the racial composition of New York and San Francisco explains, at least in part, why black–white tensions are so much higher in New York City than they are in San Francisco. In New York, 38 percent of the population is now white, 30 percent black, 25 percent Hispanic, and 7 percent Asian. In San Francisco, whites make up 47 percent of the residents, blacks 11 percent, Hispanic 14 percent, and Asians 29 percent. Thus, blacks in New York reflect the kind of critical mass that generally sparks racial prejudices, fears, and conflicts. True, San Francisco's Asian population—three in ten of the city's residents—also form that kind of critical and noticeable mass. But whatever the American prejudice against Asians, and however much it has been acted out in the past, Asians do not stir the same kind of fear and hatred in white hearts as do blacks.

20. Zoë Baird, the first woman ever to be nominated to be attorney general of the United States, was forced to withdraw when it became known that she and her husband had hired an illegal immigrant as a nanny for their three-year-old child. The public indignation that followed the revelation came largely from people who were furious that, in a time of high unemployment, American workers were bypassed in favor of cheaper foreign labor.

21. This is now beginning to happen in more skilled jobs as well. In California's Silicon Valley, for example, software programmers and others are being displaced by Indian workers, people who are trained in India and recruited to work here because they are willing to do so for lower wages than similarly skilled Americans (*San Francisco Examiner*, February 14, 1993).

22. From Emma Lazarus's "The New Colossus," inscribed at the base of the Statue of Liberty in New York's harbor, the gateway through which most of the immigrants from Europe passed as they came in search of a new life.

23. These were, and often still are, the commonly held stereotypes about Jews. Indeed, the Asian immigrants are often referred to as "the new Jews."

24. In the fall 1992 freshman class at the University of California at Berkeley, Asians accounted for 37 percent of the students, the largest single group admitted; at the university's Los Angeles campus, they were nearly 40 percent of incoming freshmen; and at Irvine, Asian students made up just under half the first-year class.

Final admission figures for the 1993–94 academic year are not available at this writing, but it's already clear that the proportion of Asians will increase substantially.

25. Soon Ja Du, the Korean grocer who killed fifteen-year-old Latasha Harlins, was found guilty of voluntary manslaughter, for which she was sentenced to four hundred hours of community service, a $500 fine, reimbursement of funeral costs to the Harlins family, and five years' probation.

26. The incident in Berkeley didn't happen in the black ghetto, as most of the others did. There, the Korean grocery store is near the University of California campus, and the woman involved in the incident is an African-American university student who was Maced by the grocer after an argument over a penny.

27. Jack Miles, "Blacks vs. Browns," *Atlantic Monthly* (October 1992), pp. 41–68.

28. For an interesting analysis of what he calls "the transformation of ethnicity," see Alba, *Ethnic Identity*.

29. On college campuses the idea of whites as an ethnic group is not so unformed. A recent publication of the University of California at Berkeley detailing the racial breakdown in undergraduate admissions conflates race and ethnicity and refers to whites who were admitted to advanced standing as "the single largest ethnic group" (Office of Student Research, University of California, Berkeley, December 16, 1992).

30. While such an organization is still in an embryonic state, if the 1992 presidential election can be taken as a measure, the idea itself seems to have had some effect. Race, a central issue in earlier campaigns, dropped from view, as the candidates of both parties focused their political energy on winning the votes of the white working-class ethnics who are coming to be known as European-Americans.

31. For a detailed account of this struggle, see Jonathan Rieder, *Canarsie* (Cambridge: Harvard University Press, 1985).

32. "The Diversity Project: Final Report," a publication of the Institute for the Study of Social Change, University of California, Berkeley (November 1991).

33. In the past, many of those who agitated for a halt to immigration were immigrants or native-born children of immigrants. The same often is true today. As anti-immigrant sentiment grows, at least some of those joining the fray are relatively recent arrivals. One man in this study, for example—a fifty-two-year-old immigrant from Hungary—is one of the leaders of an anti-immigration group in the city where he lives.

Chapter 10: "This Country Don't Owe Nobody Nothing!"

1. See the *New York Times* (July 25, 1993) for a front-page story about the reluctance of some new immigrants to become American citizens. "Immigrants who find it harder to return home for visits—political refugees and those who come from farther away—are likeliest to become citizens," the author writes. "Vietnamese refugees are eight times more likely to naturalize than economic immigrants from Canada, for instance."

2. *San Francisco Chronicle*, February 28, 1992. One of the problems school districts faced was how to meet the state's requirement for classroom diversity. In San

Francisco the report created a sensation when it was revealed that native English-speaking children were assigned to classes conducted entirely in a foreign language. These children, usually black and poor—the very children our schools are most likely to fail even when they're taught in English—were then doubly disadvantaged by having to sit in classrooms where they were unable to understand what the teacher was saying. When the children became restless and bored, as they sometimes did, teachers and school administrators labeled them as behavior problems and blamed their families for not instilling in them proper respect for education.

3. For a ringing defense of bilingualism, see Portes and Rumbaut, *Immigrant America*; for an astringent critique of existing bilingual programs, see Rosalie Pedalino Porter, *Forked Tongue* (New York: Basic Books, 1990).

4. In the 1993 session of the California legislature, Republican assemblyman Richard Mountjoy introduced a bill designed to deprive children of illegal immigrants of an education by blocking their admission to all levels of the state's educational system, from kindergarten through college. In addition to the Mountjoy bill, two other Republican assemblymen submitted legislation that would (1) prohibit undocumented youths from enrolling in college or other postsecondary public education classes and (2) require educators to inquire about the legal status of pupils when they enroll in public schools.

5. Cf. Rubén G. Rumbaut, "Passages to America: Perspectives on the New Immigration," in Alan Wolfe, ed., *America at Century's End* (Berkeley: University of California Press, 1991). Rumbaut, an advocate of bilingual programs, writes that "without exception, the children [of all ethnic groups] consistently prefer English to their mother tongue (p. 243)."

6. Henry Louis Gates, Jr., "The Weaning of America" (*New Yorker*, April 19, 1993).

7. See Jennifer L. Hochschild, "The Double-Edged Sword of Equal Opportunity," in Ian Shapiro and Grant Reeher, eds., *Power, Inequality, and Democratic Politics: Essays in Honor of Robert A. Dahl* (Boulder and London: Westview Press, 1988).

8. It has become fashionable lately for some people of color in public life—Supreme Court Justice Clarence Thomas, for example—to decry affirmative action policies. See, for example, Stephen L. Carter, *Reflections of an Affirmative Action Baby* (New York: Basic Books, 1991); Shelby Steele, *The Content of Our Character* (New York: St. Martin's Press, 1990); and Richard Rodriguez, *Hunger of Memory* (New York: Bantam Books, 1983). While some of the arguments of these writers may make some sense, the bottom line, it seems to me, is their resentment about being seen as an "affirmative action hire" with all that implies, and their pain at having their accomplishments derogated and diminished with that phrase.

9. Unfortunately, many of the African-American families who actually make it into the middle class can't hold on there. It has become a cliché to say that blacks are the last hired and first fired. But it's also true. Without seniority on the job, they are, in fact, the most vulnerable to the shifting economic needs of America's corporate and industrial world. So much so that it's not uncommon for black families to find themselves falling out of the middle class before they really have a chance to become accustomed to being there. For unlike those who have long tenure in the

middle class, people who are new to it rarely have the capital or other resources to cushion job losses and to sustain a middle-class life-style without the weekly paycheck.

10. Hochschild, "The Double-Edged Sword of Equal Opportunity," p. 169.

11. Historically, it has been easier for black women to find work than it has been for black men. But that doesn't negate the point I'm making here, which is simply that their demeaned status in the work force is a function of the interaction of race and gender.

12. See Carol Gilligan, *In a Different Voice* (Cambridge: Harvard University Press, 1982), who argues that men and women have "a different voice" when dealing with moral issues, with men being more focused on a solution and women being more concerned with relational issues. For a more elaborated discussion of what the authors call "women's way of knowing," see Mary Field Belenky et al., *Women's Ways of Knowing* (New York: Basic Books, 1986).

Chapter 11: Families on the Fault Line

1. *Statistical Abstract*, U.S. Bureau of the Census (1992), Table 632, p. 396.

2. Ibid., Table 633, p. 397.

3. Quoted in *Time*, July 20, 1992.

4. For a full account of the Decaturville story, see the *New York Times*, October 19, 1992.

5. According to an article in *Time* (March 29, 1993), temporary employment agencies like Manpower, Inc., and Kelly Services dispatch 1.5 million workers to an assortment of temporary jobs every day—about three times as many as ten years ago. In the same issue, Labor Secretary Robert Reich noted that about half the new hires in 1992 were part-time or temporary workers, up from less than a quarter a decade earlier. Of the 1.2 million new jobs created in the first six months of 1993, 60 percent were part-time. Most of the rest were at the low end of the service sector, often temporary and all offering few or no benefits.

6. For more detail, see "New Jobs Lack the Old Security in Time of 'Disposable Workers,'" *New York Times*, March 15, 1993. One Cornell University study suggests that by the year 2000, contingent workers will make up 43 percent of support staff and 7 percent of management in the service sector (*San Francisco Chronicle*, October 28, 1992).

7. Alexis de Tocqueville, *Democracy in America*, George Lawrence, trans., J. P. Mayer, ed. (New York: Anchor Books, 1969), p. 639.

8. Ibid.

9. For a longitudinal study of racial attitudes among both African-Americans and whites, see Robert Blauner, *Black Lives, White Lives* (Berkeley: University of California Press, 1989).

10. *New York Review of Books*, May 13, 1993.

11. The acquittal, in the first trial, of four white Los Angeles policemen accused of using excessive force when they beat Rodney King, a black man, into near unconsciousness is a good example. "Race had nothing to do with it," explained one of the white jurors in response to media questions about what influenced the verdict. She

wasn't dissembling; she believed what she said. In a society that was forged on the notion that "all men are created equal," a society that says proudly that every citizen is entitled to "equal justice under the law," that insists that "justice is blind," how could that juror allow herself to know that race had something to do with it?

12. Roediger, *Wages of Whiteness*, p. 35.

13. Paul Willis, *Learning to Labour* (New York: Columbia University Press, 1977).

14. Roediger, *Wages of Whiteness*, p. 137. For a full discussion of this issue, see chapter 7, pp. 133–163, "Irish-American Workers and White Racial Formation in the Antebellum United States."

15. W. E. B. DuBois, *Black Reconstruction in the United States, 1860–1880* (New York: Harcourt Brace, 1935).

16. When adjusted for inflation, the average after-tax income of the one hundred million Americans who make up the bottom two-fifths of the income spectrum has fallen sharply since 1977. The average of the middle fifth of households has edged up 2–4 percent. But the average after-tax income of upper middle-income households has climbed more than 10 percent. And among the wealthiest 5 percent of taxpayers— those with incomes of $91,750 and more—after-tax income rose more than 60 percent during this period (Robert Greenstein, "The Kindest Cut," *The American Prospect* [Fall 1991]: 49–57.

17. Schor, *The Overworked American*, shows that Americans now work 140 hours a year more than they did twenty years ago. Partly at least this is because most people need every dollar they can earn, so they're reluctant to give up any part of their income for leisure. In fact, large numbers of working-class people forego taking their vacation time off and take the money instead while continuing to work, thereby earning double wages for the vacation period.

18. Robert Bly, *Iron John* (Reading, Mass.: Addison-Wesley, 1990). See also Sam Keen, *Fire in the Belly* (New York: Bantam Books, 1991).

19. See, for example, Judith Stacey, *Brave New Families* (New York: Basic Books, 1990); Stephanie Coontz, *The Way We Never Were*; and Arlene Skolnick, *Embattled Paradise*.

BIBLIOGRAPHY

Alba, Richard D. *Ethnic Identity*. New Haven: Yale University Press, 1990.

Anderson, Elijah. *Street Wise*. Chicago: University of Chicago Press, 1990.

Ariès, Phillipe. *Centuries of Childhood*. New York: Alfred A. Knopf, 1962.

Barber, Benjamin R. "The Reconstruction of Rights." *The American Prospect* (Spring 1991): 36–46.

Belenky, Mary Field, Blythe McVicker Clinchy, Nancy Rule Goldberger, and Jill Mattuck Tarule. *Women's Ways of Knowing*. New York: Basic Books, 1986.

Bell, Derrick. *Faces at the Bottom of the Well*. New York: Basic Books, 1992.

Berman, Paul, ed. *Debating P.C.* New York: Laurel, 1992.

Bernard, Jessie. *The Future of Marriage*. New York: Bantam Books, 1973.

Blankenhorn, David. "Ozzie and Harriet: Have Reports of Their Death Been Greatly Exaggerated?" *Family Affairs* 2 (Summer/Fall 1989): 10.

Blauner, Robert. *Black Lives, White Lives*. Berkeley: University of California Press, 1989.

———. "Racism, Race, and Ethnicity: Some Reflections on the Language of Race." Paper presented at the meetings of the American Sociological Association, Cincinnati, August 23, 1991.

———. "Talking Past Each Other." *The American Prospect* (Summer 1992: 55–64.

Bly, Robert. *Iron John*. Reading, Mass.: Addison-Wesley, 1990.

Bodnar, John. *The Transplanted*. Bloomington, Ind.: Indiana University Press, 1985.

Brain, Robert. *Friends and Lovers*. New York: Basic Books, 1976.

Byles, John A. "Violence, Alcohol Problems and Other Problems in Disintegrating Families." *Journal of Studies on Alcohol* 39 (1978): 551–553.

Carter, Stephen L. *Reflections of an Affirmative Action Baby*. New York: Basic Books, 1991.

Clark, Kenneth, and Mamie Clark. "Racial Identification and Preference in Negro Children." In Eleanore Maccoby, Theodore Newcomb, and Shirley Hartley, eds., *Readings in Social Psychology*. New York: Holt Rinehart, 1958.

Cohen, Lizbeth. *Making a New Deal*. New York: Cambridge University Press, 1990.

Coleman, James S., et al. *Equality of Educational Opportunity*. Washington, D.C.: U.S. Government Printing Office, 1966.

Coontz, Stephanie. *The Way We Never Were*. New York: Basic Books, 1992.

Daniels, Roger. *Coming to America: A History of Immigration and Ethnicity in American Life*. New York: HarperCollins, 1990.

Degler, Carl. *At Odds: Women and the Family in America from the Revolution to the Present*. New York: Oxford University Press, 1980.

D'Emilio, John, and Estelle B. Freedman. *Intimate Matters: A History of Sexuality in America*. New York: Harper & Row, 1988.

Demos, John. "Myths and Realities in the History of American Family Life." In Henry Grunebaum and Jacob Christ, eds., *Contemporary Marriage: Structure, Dynamics and Therapy*. Boston: Little, Brown, 1976: 9–31.

DeMott, Benjamin. *The Imperial Middle*. New Haven, Conn.: Yale University Press, 1992.

de Tocqueville, Alexis. *Democracy in America* (George Lawrence, trans., J. P. Mayer, ed.) New York: Anchor Books, 1969.

Dionne, E. J., Jr. *Why Americans Hate Politics*. New York: Simon & Schuster, 1991.

D'Souza, Dinesh. *Illiberal Education*. New York: Free Press, 1991.

DuBois, W. E. B. *Black Reconstruction in the United States, 1860–1880*. New York: Harcourt Brace, 1935.

Edsall, Thomas Byrne, with Mary D. Edsall. "Race." *Atlantic Magazine* (May 1991): 53–86.

———. *Chain Reaction*. New York: W. W. Norton, 1991.

Ehrenreich, Barbara. *Fear of Falling*. New York: Pantheon Books, 1989.

Ehrensaft, Diane. *Parenting Together*. New York: Free Press, 1987.

Elkind, David. *The Hurried Child*. New York: Addison-Wesley, 1981.

Epstein, Leslie. "Civility and Its Discontents." *The American Prospect* (Summer 1991): 23–29.

Ezorsky, Gertrude. *Racism & Justice*. Ithaca, N.Y.: Cornell University Press, 1991.

Fagan, Ronald W., Ola W. Barnett, and John B. Patton. "Reasons for Alcohol Use in Maritally Violent Men." *Journal of Drug and Alcohol Abuse* 14 (1988): 371–392.

Faludi, Susan. *Backlash*. New York: Crown Publishers, 1991.

Fessler, Loren W., ed. *Chinese in America*. New York: Vantage Press, 1983.

Fingerhut, Lois A., and Joel C. Kleinman. "International and Interstate Comparisons of Homicide Among Young Males." *Journal of the American Medical Association* 263 (1990): 3292–3295.

Fitch, Frances J., and Andre Papantonio. "Men Who Batter." *Journal of Nervous and Mental Disease* 171 (1983): 190–191.

Foucault, Michel. *The History of Sexuality*. New York: Vintage Books, 1980.

Franklin, Raymond S. *Shadows of Race and Class*. Minneapolis: University of Minnesota Press, 1991.

Freedman, Samuel G. *Small Victories*. New York: HarperCollins, 1990.

Friedman, Philip. "Racial Preferences and Identifications of White Elementary School Children." *Contemporary Educational Psychology* 5 (1980): 256–265.

Gans, Herbert. "Symbolic Ethnicity: The Future of Ethnic Groups and Cultures in America." *Ethnic and Racial Studies* 2 (January 1979): 1–18.

Gelles, Richard J., and Murray A. Straus. "Violence in the American Family." *Journal of Social Issues* 35 (1979): 15–39.

Gibbs, Jewelle T., ed. *Young, Black, and Male in America*. Dover, Mass.: Auburn House, 1988.

Gilligan, Carol. *In a Different Voice*. Cambridge: Harvard University Press, 1982.

Glassner, Barry. *Career Crash*. New York: Simon & Schuster, 1994.

Goldfield, Michael. "Class, Race, and Politics in the United States: White Supremacy as the Main Explanation for the Peculiarities of American Politics from Colonial Times to the Present." *Research in Political Economy* 12 (1990): 83–127.

Goode, William J. *World Revolution and Family Patterns*. New York: Free Press, 1963.

Gould, Stephen Jay. *The Mismeasure of Man*. New York: W. W. Norton, 1981.

Greenstein, Robert. "The Kindest Cut." *The American Prospect* (Fall 1991): 49–57.

Hacker, Andrew. *Two Nations*. New York: Charles Scribner's Sons, 1992.

Haiman, Franklyn S. "The Remedy Is More Speech." *The American Prospect* (Summer 1991): 30–35.

Haley, Sarah A. "Some of My Best Friends Are Dead." In William E. Kelley, ed., *Post-Traumatic Stress Disorder and the War Veteran Patient*. New York: Brunner/Mazel, 1986.

Halle, David. *America's Working Man*. Chicago: University of Chicago Press, 1984.

Halle, David, and Frank Romo. "The Blue-Collar Working Class: Continuity and Change." In Alan Wolfe, ed., *America at Century's End*. Berkeley: University of California Press, 1991.

Handel, Gerald. "Abandoned Ambitions: Transition to Adulthood in the Life Course of Working-Class Boys." *Sociological Studies of Child Development* 4 (1991): 225–245.

Haraven, Tamara K. "The Dynamics of Kin in an Industrial Community." In John Demos and Sarane Spence Boocock, eds., *Turning Points*. Chicago: University of Chicago Press, 1978.

———."American Families in Transition: Historical perspectives on Change. In Froma Walsh, ed., *Normal Family Process*. New York: Guilford Press, 1982.

Harris, Angela P. "Race and Essentialism in Feminist Legal Theory." *Stanford Law Review* 42 (1990): 581–616.

Harrison, Bennett, and Barry Bluestone. *The Great U-Turn: Corporate Restructuring and the Polarizing of America*. New York: Basic Books, 1988.

Hill, John. "The Psychological Impact of Unemployment." *New Society* 43 (1978): 118–120.

Hochschild, Arlie. *The Second Shift: Working Parents and the Revolution at Home*. New York: Viking Press, 1989.

Hochschild, Jennifer L. "The Double-Edged Sword of Equal Opportunity." In Ian Shapiro and Grant Reeher, eds., *Power, Inequality, and Democratic Politics: Essays in Honor of Robert A. Dahl*. Boulder and London: Westview Press, 1988.

———. "Equal Opportunity and the Estranged Poor." *Annals, AAPSS* 501 (1989): 143–155.

———. "Middle Class Blacks and the Complexities of Success." In Paul Sniderman and Philip Tetlock, eds., *Prejudice, Politics, and Race*. Palo Alto, Calif.: Stanford University Press, 1991.

———. "The Politics of the Estranged Poor." *Ethics* 101 (1991): 560–578.

Hochschild, Jennifer L., and Monica Herk. "'Yes, But . . . : Principles and Caveats in American Racial Attitudes." In John W. Chapman and Alan Wertheimer, eds., *Majorities and Minorities*. New York: New York University Press, 1990.

Hughes, Robert. *Culture of Complaint*. New York: Oxford University Press, 1993.

Jencks, Christopher. *Rethinking Social Policy*. Cambridge: Harvard University Press, 1992.

Jencks, Christopher, Marshall Smith, Henry Acland, Mary Jo Bane, David Cohen, Herbert Gintis, Barbara Heyns, amd Stephan Michelson. *Inequality: A Reassessment of the Effect of Family and Schooling in America*. New York: Basic Books, 1972.

Jones, Jacqueline. *The Dispossessed*. New York: Basic Books, 1992.

Kaestle, Carl F., Helen Damon-Moore, Lawrence C. Stedman, Katherine Tinsley, and William Vance Trollinger, Jr. *Literacy in the United States*. New Haven, Conn.: Yale University Press, 1991.

Katz, Donald. *Homefires*. New York: HarperCollins, 1992.

Keen, Sam. *Fire in the Belly*. New York: Bantam Books, 1991.

Kidder, Tracy. *Among Schoolchildren*. New York: Avon Books, 1990.

Kilson, Martin, and Clement Cottingham. "Thinking About Race Relations." *Dissent* (Fall 1991): 520–530.

Kimball, Roger. *Tenured Radicals*. New York: Harper & Row, 1990.

Kinkead, Gwen. *Chinatown*. New York: HarperCollins, 1992.

Komarovsky, Mirra. *Blue-Collar Marriage*. New York: Vintage Books, 1962.

Kornblum, William. "Who Is the Underclass?" *Dissent* (Spring 1991): 202–211.

Kotlowitz, Alex. *There Are No Children Here*. New York: Doubleday, 1991.

Kozol, Jonathan. *Savage Inequalities*. New York: Crown Publishers, 1991.

Krugman, Paul R. "The Right, the Rich, and the Facts." *The American Prospect* (Fall 1992): 19–31.

Kuttner, Robert. "Notes from Underground." *Dissent* (Spring 1991): 212–217.

———. "Is There a Democratic Economics?" *The American Prospect* (Winter 1992): 25–37.

Landry, Bart. "The Enduring Dilemma of Race in America." In Alan Wolfe, ed., *America at Century's End*. Berkeley: University of California Press, 1991.

Lasch, Christopher. *Haven in a Heartless World*. New York: Basic Books, 1977.

Laslett, Peter. *The World We Have Lost*. New York: Charles Scribner's Sons, 1965.

Leeds, Mark. *Ethnic New York*. New York: Passport Books, 1991.

Leiberson, Stanley, and Mary C. Waters. *From Many Strands*. New York: Russell Sage, 1990.

Lemann, Nicholas. *The Promised Land*. New York: Alfred A. Knopf, 1991.

Leonard, Kenneth E., et al. "Patterns of Alcohol Use and Physically Aggressive Behavior in Men." *Journal of Studies on Alcohol* 46 (1985): 279–282.

Livingston, Larry R. "Measuring Domestic Violence in an Alcoholic Population." *Journal of Sociology and Social Welfare* 13 (1986): 934–951.

Lukas, J. Anthony. *Common Ground*. New York: Alfred A. Knopf, 1986.

Luker, Kristin. *Abortion & the Politics of Motherhood*. Berkeley: University of California Press, 1984.

Mahan, Juneau. "Black and White Children's Racial Identification and Preference." *Journal of Black Psychology* 3 (1976): 47–58.

Mainardi, Pat. "The Politics of Housework." In Shulamith Firestone, ed., *Notes from the Second Year: Women's Liberation.* New York: Radical Feminism, 1970.

Mara-Drita, Iona. "The Effects of Power, Ideology, and Experience on Men's Participation in Housework." Unpublished paper, 1993.

McLaughlin, Neil. "Beyond 'Race vs. Class.'" *Dissent* (Winter 1993): 1–6.

McMillan, Terry. *Waiting to Exhale.* New York: Viking Press, 1992.

Miller, Stuart. *Men and Friendship.* Boston: Houghton Mifflin, 1983.

Mintz, Steven, and Susan Kellogg. *Domestic Revolutions: A Social History of American Family Life.* New York: Free Press, 1988.

Mishel, Lawrence, and Ruy A. Teixeira. "The Myth of the Coming Labor Shortage." *The American Prospect* (Fall 1991): 98–103.

Morawska, Ewa. *For Bread with Butter.* New York: Cambridge University Press, 1985.

Morrison, Toni. *Playing in the Dark.* Cambridge: Harvard University Press, 1992.

———. *Jazz.* New York: Alfred A. Knopf, 1992.

Moynihan, Daniel Patrick. *Pandaemonium: Ethnicity in International Politics.* New York: Oxford University Press, 1993.

Newman, Katherine S. *Falling from Grace.* New York: Free Press, 1988.

———. "Uncertain Seas: Cultural Turmoil and the Domestic Economy." In Alan Wolfe, ed., *America at Century's End.* Berkeley: University of California Press, 1991.

———. *Declining Fortunes.* New York: Basic Books, 1993.

New York State Task Force on Domestic Violence. *Domestic Violence: Report to the Governor and Legislature: Families and Change.* New York: Praeger Publishers, 1984.

O'Carroll, Patrick W. "Homicides Among Black Males 15–24 Years of Age, 1970–1984. *Morbidity and Mortality Weekly Report (CDC), Statistical Supplement* 37 (1988): 52–59.

Person, Ethel Spector. "Sexuality as the Mainstay of Identity." *Signs* 5 (1980): 605–630.

Phillips, Kevin. *The Politics of Rich and Poor.* New York: Random House, 1990.

Pleck, Joseph. *Working Wives/Working Husbands.* Beverly Hills: Sage Publications, 1985.

Porter, Rosalie Pedalino. *Forked Tongue.* New York: Basic Books, 1990.

Portes, Alejandro, and Rubén G. Rumbaut. *Immigrant America.* Berkeley: University of California Press, 1990.

Rand, Michael R. "Handgun Crime Victims." In *U.S. Bureau of Justice Statistics, Special Report.* Washington, D.C.: U.S. Justice Statistics Clearing house/NCJRS, 1990.

Rees, Linford W. "Medical Aspects of Unemployment." *British Medical Journal* 6307 (1981): 1630–1631.

Reisman, John M. *Anatomy of Friendship*. New York: Irvington Publishers, 1979.

Reynolds, Gretchen. "The Rising Significance of Race." *Chicago* (December 1992): 81–85, 126–130.

Rieder, Jonathan. *Canarsie*. Cambridge: Harvard University Press, 1985.

Roberts, Albert R. "Substance Abuse Among Men Who Batter Their Mates." *Journal of Substance Abuse Treatment* 5 (1988): 83–87.

Roberts, Albert, Kathleen Y. Mosley, and Maureen W. Chamberlain. "Age Differences in Racial Self-Identity of Young Black Girls." *Psychological Reports* 37 (1976): 1263–1266.

Robertson, Nan. *The Girls in the Balcony*. New York: Random House, 1992.

Rodriguez, Richard. *Hunger of Memory*. New York: Bantam Books, 1983.

Roediger, David R. *The Wages of Whiteness*. New York: Verso, 1991.

Rose, Stephen J. *Social Stratification in the United States*. New York: New Press, 1992.

Rubin, Lillian B. *Busing & Backlash: White Against White in an Urban School District*. Berkeley: University of California Press, 1972.

———.*Worlds of Pain: Life in the Working-Class Family*. New York: Basic Books, 1976. New paperback edition with new introduction, 1992.

———. *Women of a Certain Age: The Midlife Search for Self*. New York: Harper Perennial, 1981.

———. *Intimate Strangers: Men & Women Together*. New York: Harper Perennial, 1984.

. *Just Friends: The Role of Friendship in Our Lives*. New York: Harper Perennial, 1986.

———. *Erotic Wars: What Happened to the Sexual Revolution*. New York: Harper Perennial, 1991.

Rumbaut, Rubén G. "Passages to America: Perspectives on the New Immigration." In Alan Wolfe, ed., *America at Century's End*. Berkeley: University of California Press, 1991.

Sanjek, Roger. "Intermarriage and the Future of the Races in the United States." Paper presented at the American Anthropological Association meetings, Chicago, August 1991.

Saville, H., et al. "Sex Roles, Inequality and Spouse Abuse." *Australian and New Zealand Journal of Sociology* 17 (1981): 83–88.

Schlesinger, Arthur M., Jr. *The Disuniting of America*. New York: W. W. Norton, 1992.

Schor, Juliet B. *The Overworked American*. New York: Basic Books, 1992.

Schuerger, J. M., and N. Reigle. "Personality and Biographic Data That Characterize Men Who Abuse Their Wives." *Journal of Clinical Psychology* 44 (1988): 75–81.

Schwartz, Martin D. "Work Status, Resource Equality, Injury and Wife Battery." *Creative Sociology* 18 (1990): 57–61.

Sennett, Richard, and Jonathan Cobb. *The Hidden Injuries of Class*. New York: Vintage Books, 1973.

Shorter, Edward. *The Making of the Modern Family*. New York: Basic Books, 1975.

Sirianni, Carmen, and Andrea Walsh. "Through the Prism of Time: Temporal Structures in Postindustrial America." In Alan Wolfe, ed., *America at Century's End*. Berkeley: University of California Press, 1991.

Skolnick, Arlene. *Embattled Paradise: The American Family in an Age of Uncertainty*. New York: Basic Books, 1991.

Sleeper, Jim. *The Closest of Strangers*. New York: W. W. Norton, 1990.

Snitow, Ann, Christine Stansell, and Sharon Thompson, eds. *Powers of Desire*. New York: Monthly Review Press, 1983.

Sollors, Werner, ed. *The Invention of Ethnicity*. New York: Oxford University Press, 1989.

Stacey, Judith. *Brave New Families*. New York: Basic Books, 1990.

———. "Backward Toward the Postmodern Family: Reflections on Gender, Kinship, and Class in the Silicon Valley." In Alan Wolfe, ed., *America at Century's End*. Berkeley: University of California Press, 1991.

Starr, Paul. "Civil Reconstruction: What to Do Without Affirmative Action." *The American Prospect* (Winter 1992): 7–16.

Steele, Shelby. *The Content of Our Character*. New York: St. Martin's Press, 1990.

Stein, Howard F., and Robert F. Hill. *The Ethnic Imperative*. University Park, Penn.: Pennsylvania State University Press, 1977.

Steinberg, Stephen. *The Ethnic Myth*. Boston: Beacon Press, 1989.

Steinmetz, Suzanne K. "Violence-prone Families." *Annals of the New York Academy of Sciences* 347 (1980): 251–265.

Stern, Daniel. *The Interpersonal World of the Infant*. New York: Basic Books, 1985.

Stone, Deborah A. "Race, Gender, and the Supreme Court." *The American Prospect* (Winter 1992): 63–73.

Stone, Lawrence. *The Family, Sex, and Marriage in England, 1500–1800*. New York: Harper & Row, 1977.

Sunstein, Cass R. "Ideas, Yes; Assaults, No." *The American Prospect* (Summer 1991): 35–39.

Sweet, James, Larry Bumpass, and Vaugn Call. "National Survey of Families and Households." Madison, Wisc.: University of Wisconsin, Center for Demography and Ecology, 1988.

Talese, Gay. *Unto the Sons*. New York: Alfred A. Knopf, 1992.

Tate, Katherine. "Invisible Woman." *The American Prospect* (Winter 1992): 74–81.

Trimberger, Ellen Kay. "Feminism, Men, and Modern Love: Greenwich Village, 1900–1925." In Ann Snitow, Christine Stansell, and Sharon Thompson, eds., *Powers of Desire*. New York: Monthly Review Press, 1983.

Turner, Margery Austin, Michael Fix, and Raymond J. Struyk. *Opportunities Denied, Opportunities Diminished.* Urban Institute Report 91-9. Washington, D.C.: Urban Institute Press, 1991.

U.S. Bureau of the Census. *Statistical Abstract of the United States: 1992* (112th ed.). Washington, D.C.: U.S. Government Printing Office, 1992.

Waters, Mary C. *Ethnic Options.* Berkeley: University of California Press, 1990.

Weitzman, Lenore J. *The Divorce Revolution.* New York: Free Press, 1985.

West, Cornel. "Nihilism in Black America." *Dissent* (Spring 1991): 221–226.

Wilkinson, Rupert. *The Pursuit of American Character.* New York: Harper & Row, 1988.

Williams, Patricia J. *The Alchemy of Race and Rights.* Cambridge: Harvard University Press, 1991.

Willis, Paul. *Learning to Labour.* New York: Columbia University Press, 1977.

Wilson, William Julius. *The Declining Significance of Race.* Chicago: University of Chicago Press, 1978.

———. *The Truly Disadvantaged.* Chicago: University of Chicago Press, 1987.

Wolfe, Alan. "The Return of the Melting Pot." *The New Republic* (December 31, 1990): 27–34.

———, ed. *America at Century's End.* Berkeley: University of California Press, 1991.

Zandy, Janet, ed. *Calling Home.* New Brunswick: Rutgers University Press, 1990.

INDEX